John Doe vs Evil

Zsolt Zsemba

Edited by Janet Graham

Copyright © 2021 Zsolt Zsemba

All rights reserved.

ISBN: **979-8454341428**

DEDICATION

This book is dedicated to my mother Ann, may she rest in peace, my father, George and my brother Gabor.

We have worked hard from childhood to bring our business to heights that were unimaginable to an immigrant family that landed in Canada on December 2nd, 1978. Together we built a very successful business that grew from a tiny company to an incredible size and achieved great success. A betting man may have bet against us, but as a family we never gave up. From day one we sacrificed so much, mostly our childhood. Sometimes all we wanted to be was kids. Working long hours and two jobs for years on end never mattered to our parents. Providing for our family was always the goal. The driving force behind every day and every hour of hard work was to make sure the family could live a better life and never be a burden to Aunt Livia and Uncle Joe.

Life goes on, and in the end, everyone talks about the good old days. The good old days came faster than we had hoped. However, we have enough time to set new goals and achieve them. There are many lessons to be learned. Some can only be learned by making mistakes or making decisions that go against the grain. Stepping out of one's comfort zone and marching full speed ahead is the only thing we ever knew how to do. Thus, we were able to achieve the goals we set out for ourselves. We as a family wanted more and we worked hard for it.

This book is also dedicated to every single person that was hurt by this family's business demise. Those that know the family know very well the dedication we had and the effort that went into keeping everyone employed. That is why this book had to be written and the story made public. We would like to thank everyone for their support; and hope that over the years we have been forgiven for a situation that was out of our control.

Wishing you all, nothing but the best…

CONTENTS

	Acknowledgments	i
Chapter 1	JD and you	Pg 3
Chapter 2	Eastern Europe to Canada	Pg 14
Chapter 3	The bits and pieces	Pg 27
Chapter 4	The new world	Pg 38
Chapter 5	The massive surprise	Pg 48
Chapter 6	The hamster wheel	Pg 57
Chapter 7	Get up, stand up, start again	Pg 67
Chapter 8	Kids being kids	Pg 76
Chapter 9	The growth	Pg 85
Chapter 10	The move	Pg 96
Chapter 11	The move to?	Pg 105
Chapter 12	The move to Caledon	Pg 114
Chapter 13	Partnership	Pg 124
Chapter 14	Say no to partners	Pg 133
Chapter 15	Together again	Pg 144
Chapter 16	Change is constant	Pg 155
Chapter 17	Problems and more	Pg 164
Chapter 18	Next	Pg 174
Chapter 19	The shit hits the fan	Pg 182
Chapter 20	The witch hunt	Pg 194
Chapter 21	The dirty truth	Pg 204
Chapter 22	The lawsuit	Pg 212
Chapter 23	The cookie crumbles	Pg 222

John Doe vs Evil

ACKNOWLEDGMENTS

There were far too many factors in writing this book. The circumstances and the unfairness of the situation is unexplainable. However, there were a few exceptional people that we can always count on in life and they know who they are. Even when facing evil, they will always come through for us.

This book was written to answer the many questions of how a thriving family business closed under very dire circumstances. It's a story that had to be told and understood from a family point of view. A large company running wild and rampant, overreaching and bullying the companies that supply them, to lower costs while they rake in billions. This is just one of many stories, one of many examples and it's not just the YB company but this is the story I know.

"250 employees lost their jobs, a family business was ruined and rather than working with the company to ramp down the business, they chose to screw this business over."

This is the story of what happened to us. Admittedly there were many tears shed over parts of this book. Some were tears of happiness and some were from the pain of the ups and downs of 35 years in business. This is the struggle of one family to overcome the odds only to be shafted in the end. Some emotions can't possibly be explained or written but I hope that some people will learn and other people will understand how and why things happened the way they did. These are explanations that could never be told to each and every person affected by the terrible things that happened. Please enjoy the story. As hard as it was to write, it is the truth. JD's view is a perspective of what can and does happen in life. He is fictional, but the story is real.

Chapter 1. JD and you

The streetlights clicked on at the corner of Yonge and Dundas Streets. The center of Toronto, the Times Square of Canada and home to many. To the few million people that live in and around Toronto, and the millions of visitors every year, the lights and glitter at the corner of Yonge and Dundas provide a great spot for Instagram and Facebook posts. The dancers, the street performers and visitors from many parts of the world can be seen standing, turning and smiling in amazement. The spectacle of people, food and energy surrounds every single person that shares this wonder of lights and sounds.
Cars honk, tires squeal, sirens blare; all mixed in with the occasional helicopter landing at the hospitals to the west. It makes Toronto the city that it is. It brings visitors to this very place and to Yonge Street which is the longest street in the world. There are many fun facts about Toronto and Canada that are not necessarily known by everyone. The Canadian flag stuck on Maple syrup bottles and the beer that everyone from south of the border raves about. Having the largest underground shopping area in the world, not underground as in Mafia or gang run but actual shopping and tunnel area called the Path.
What very few visitors pay attention to are the real people here. The people that live and work in the area and the people coming and going making a living to live their best life. The visitors see the good

and rarely get affected by the bad. While there are always exceptions, people come, people go leaving with memories that put a smile on their faces.

Few people know the people that they pass, or even exchange a word with a person from "Toronto" and that's ok. They visit, they leave, that's what tourists do. We all do it and that's all well and good but next time you visit a place, visit the people. Take in the people as well as the ambiance. Take a look at the girl that came out of the subway tunnel with tears in her eyes.

Pause for a second and look at the little boy who just said bye to his dad because it was mom's turn to have him for the week. Take a look at the bald woman who didn't shave her head on purpose, the old man in a wheelchair with the oxygen bottle attached with the oxygen mask that hangs on one ear in case he needs it. How about the people up the road at Church and Wellesley? The transgender people or the ones holding a small gathering for black lives matter?

This is the city and this is what you notice at the corner of Yonge and Dundas. Now look deeper, look much deeper at what you don't see as visitors to Toronto or visitors to any large city.

Examine your surroundings. See the things you didn't come here to see. Past the lights and past the glitter of shiny objects that grab your attention and make you feel like you have the memory of a goldfish. Look on the ground among the cigarette butts, the gum that turned to little black patches on the concrete and the pieces of garbage. Do you see the men, women and children that live on the street?

The man leaning his head against a large red newspaper box that ironically says "The Toronto Sun" or the next one that says "The Toronto Star". False hope and lies are what The Sun and The Star bring to the people sitting at eye level to those boxes.

A band starts up, the drummer that has played the same street corner for a decade blows your mind away at how good he is and the dancers that spin a mile a minute on their heads grab your attention. The sounds of drums, laughter and people talking fill your senses and takes over. Once again, your mind purposely distracts you. Your brain turned off the awful things it refused to see…

You didn't see the boy and girl holding hands a few meters away from you. You don't see how they look at each other in silence with pure love in their eyes. A joint shared in silence and deep love. Their love is pure because that's all they have. They don't own a car, they don't own a house and they most likely don't know where their next meal will come from. But they have something you may not have... Such is life in the big city. Many headlines captured, so many stories missed. Look there, over there… A man with a beard, piercing blue eyes and disheveled hair clutches a backpack and checks the contents a few times. It's an old black backpack that the Nike name and logo has partly worn off. It is torn and in rough shape, but the man holds on to it tightly, as it's all he has.

He has developed OCD. He takes out a paper bag and checks it. He seems relieved each time he checks it and places it back in the backpack. This man, or a man just like him, you've passed many times… Not just here and not just now but many times before. Never again will you pass this man or the many like him without thinking. You will never pass Romeo and Juliette who share nothing but love and the warmth of their bodies on a cold winter night.

No, you will not pass them because I will not let you pass them without thinking of this. The man that you passed earlier is John Doe, and John was once exactly like you! Just like you! You have passed John a million times. Except before John was wearing a suit. John was a successful man who had a family and kids. For all intents and purposes, anyone can become John Doe.

John lays on the ground, his feet are close together showing off his shoes and the hole he has worn in the left front bottom part of it. John gazes up at the people walking past, and he knows full well how much of a scum of the earth every single person thinks he is. The lowlife that can't get a job, the bum who should go and get a job and take better care of himself. To all the people who look down at John and to every single person who feels that John can and should do better… Shame on you! Shame on you for thinking that John is a useless old man waiting for a handout! Waiting on you for the quarter or the dollar you flip into his hat, hand or tin can placed by his side.

Shame on you for thinking that John is a nameless, faceless man on the street that could and should do better.

One day, long ago terrible things happened; and the downward spiral of John Doe began. No matter how impossible you think it is, it happened. The true story of John must come out because without that you will always think of the John and Jane Doe's the same way.

You, the clear thinking, level-headed, well-adjusted person that you think you are. You must be made to understand. Don't feel offended. Our friend JD thought the same thing you are thinking, and look at him now. He is beneath you as he glares up and past you to the top of the skyscrapers that surround him. He already feels as low as he can. He does not need you to look down at him. To feel pity for him or cry for him. He doesn't need you to do that because he does that for himself every single second of every day.

His piercing blue eyes meet yours. You don't know what to do. Smile? Look away? Keep staring or reach into your pocket? Toss a coin at JD or run before he gets up and robs you? JD is JD and you are you. Today we will change that. Today and from now on you are JD, be JD, feel like JD and act like JD. Trade places with JD and get deep within JD's soul, mind and heart. Feel the tears that JD shed and open your heart a little and let JD in.

JD wasn't always like this. He didn't always reside at the corner of Yonge and Dundas in downtown Toronto. He didn't always occupy a street corner with all his worldly belongings in that Nike backpack. Once... Many years ago, JD had everything he wished for. At the time it was not enough. Like many of us nothing is ever enough until one day you realize you should have been grateful for what you had. It's typical, it's human and it's wrong. We all need to learn but we don't. We all run and run until we can no longer run and die or hopefully retire. In JD's case and I am sure for many, many others, things took a turn for the worse. Maybe taking a turn for the worse is an understatement.

Years ago, JD was well off and while he was not a multi-millionaire, he was well off and had much more than many others. It wasn't greed, it wasn't that JD wanted more. He ran his family business as well as he could and maybe even to a certain point he was comfortable and like we all do with businesses, marriages or relationships we all think it will go on and on forever.

There was a sense of security and a sense of comfort. It was the perfect pair of jeans or one amazing blanket that was worn to shreds, but we still wash them and use them because nothing feels as cozy and comfy as that one item. The comfort zone was so comfortable that JD didn't prepare for the new, very uncomfortable pair of jeans that he would receive. The new, scary uncomfortable feeling of losing the perfect item and watching it burn up before your eyes is what happened to JD. The teddy bear that was with you all your life and shared your deepest secrets. The only pacifier that could quiet you when you were a baby was now up in smoke, torched, vanished into thin air overnight.

This is where JD found himself one day. Imagine your morning when you got up and the roof over your head and the shelter for your family was suddenly whisked away and you had nothing but the clothes on your back. Your short walk to the bathroom, and your longer walk to the kitchen to grab that amazing cup of coffee, poof! Gone… The laughter of your son, daughter, the morning kiss from your better half disappearing. Instead your mind is filled with fear. The uncertainty of what will happen minutes, hours and days later fills your head.

You have been rudely awakened to reality and joined JD in his quest for survival. The familiarity and the routine of each day has been barfed up and there it lays on the floor before you. The little pieces of your life and the mistake you made is there, look at it… Touch it, feel it, smell it, see how meaningless it is, how meaningless it was and how it means nothing to anyone else but you.

The roof over your head is disappearing, the clothes from your closet are blowing in the wind and the money from your bank account is running like the neighbor's hose as he washes his car. Your car is being towed away by the leasing company because… well because… you don't really know. You can't process this information because your balls are freezing, your stomach grumbles and all of a sudden, the coffee you so desperately wanted is irrelevant.

Your fight or flight response kicks in, your mind spins uncontrollably. You feel like throwing up again but you remember that you have nothing left. You feel weak, hurt, and the world is a terrible, unforgiving place. You wonder what you should do. Who can you blame for this very unfortunate and disgusting moment of your life.

It's nobody's fault but your very own. While that is not true, try and convince others that it's not your fault. The only people that will listen and "help" are the super helpful, blood sucking leeches that give you the greatest, most amazing and helpful advice for a few hundred thousand dollars. They promise you the world and give you the confidence back that you have lost. They promise to win, promise that they have things under control; while the only thing they have under control is you and your bank account.

Imagine your money flowing down the subdivision street to the sewers, the roof over your head blown away and your clothes scattered on the street before you. You try to hold onto the roof over your head. Try turning off the tap and all the while desperately trying to grab pieces of clothing that twirl around you in the tornado that life has thrown you in the middle of.

JD sat in the middle of a farmer's field. His wonderful country home torn to pieces. His lifetime work gone in a matter of seconds. His life savings being sucked up in a lawsuit to save what little he had left and all the while getting the wrong advice at every turn. JD felt alone and sad in his puddle of tears beneath him but he was not going to give up. Fight or flight, JD chose to fight because he knew he was right and needed to save his pride more than his money.

The comfort zone turned to burning hell was JD's new reality. To blame for this was JD and the "wonderful" Yellow and Blue mega furniture company whose name we shall not mention.

The YB, they know who they are…

The amazing, wonderful, brilliant, caring, green, behemoth of a company that makes millions and billions of dollars each year chose to fight as well, and the battle was on. While this may make no sense to anyone it made sense to JD. As he sat in the middle of this mess, he wished he had a person with foresight and understanding to make him whole and lead him down a path that would save him and not destroy him. There was no God to speak of, no guiding light or angels sent from heaven. Not a halo to be seen but the burning anger of the devil himself was evident. They were draped in yellow and blue and named bloody Swedish names.

JD was down, not yet out. He decided to go down the road less traveled and be the David in the Goliath story. Goliath was big and finding the weakest point of a giant is the key to bringing them down. JD knew what it was.

Sitting on the sidewalk today JD thinks back often and wonders where it went sideways and how he could fix it. Fixing what is broken is possible. Fixing what you don't know is broken is impossible.

Being in the wrong mindset and working with people who are not working with you but are working for you are two very different things. People working with you are your people on your side.

People working for you are the ones getting paid and they work for money. The people working with you are not experts and the people working for you are, they insist on getting paid and whether they win or lose they don't care.

This is what people miss and this is where you can fall and break your heart. No matter what, eventually your willpower goes the way of the Dodo bird. The breaking point was the point JD was not used to. This is where we go back to the beginning of the story about the man with piercing blue eyes that now sits on the street. JD no longer questions his decision-making abilities. He no longer asks what, why or how. He is over that. His mind is blank and there are only a few things on his mind. Eat, sleep and hold on to the backpack. Cups of coffee are far and few in between. Waking up with a roof over his head are past and while the birds chirp every morning, they too fight for the same scraps of food that he searches for to fill the hunger in his stomach at the crack of dawn.

You know you are down and out when you look at the squirrel and wish that you had the nut in his mouth. Or the raccoon that got to the garbage can before you did and you would chase the little fucker down if you weren't scared of him being hungrier than you and beating you up.

There was no three second rule in JD's world. If the food was not taken away by the garbage man, it was fair game. Yet many days JD knew that Romeo and Juliette needed the food more than he did. So even though his pain and hunger was real, more real than ever, he still hoped that with his miniscule sacrifice, Romeo and Juliette may have a future if he gave them a helping hand that no one gave him when he sat alone is his field of desperation.

You know a person of integrity, honesty and of good heart when he has nothing and still gives to those who have even less. JD didn't care what happened to Romeo and Juliette, in the future. Much like his future, no one has control over the future. In the present and in the now he can help the couple who still believe in rainbows and unicorns and the pot of gold at the end of the rainbow. His belief in angels and fairies were only real on Halloween, and the Pride Parade. At least the fairies and angels were caring and giving to those less fortunate and never discriminated no matter how much he was down and out.

So many times, JD had thought about the past that it hurt his brain to think about anything but the night before or the morning of. He learned to live in the present and while he didn't talk much, when he did he always talked in the present. Do this and do that but do it now. Don't leave it to chance, don't leave it till tomorrow if you can do it today. Tomorrow may change and tomorrow may never come. This is from first-hand experience… Years ago when JD first ended up on the street, he met Peter. Peter was an alcoholic and spent many years fighting his demons. His demons were real, and his reality was fake Peter said. JD had no way of disproving him and therefore he didn't care, nor did he want to argue.

Peter wanted to go home so badly but he was scared of what may or may not happen that when JD agreed to go with him and be his support, he agreed to do it tomorrow. That night Peter crawled into his cardboard box under the bridge and they pulled out his dead body the next afternoon. So much for waiting till tomorrow. Lesson learned, don't wait.

Don't wait.

Woke up to the birds stealing my crumbs.
They were right and I was wrong.
I slept in and they were wide awake.
I couldn't be angry or mad.
I put out my hat and held out my hand.
Today Romeo and Juliette never came.
I wondered if they were dead or alive.
It wasn't my problem, not my fight.
People walked past and looked down.
I wanted food and they gave me stares.
Stares made me think of stakes.
Not the ones you eat but the wooden ones.
I waited for Romeo and Juliette.
Not my fight but I was concerned.
I waited and waited but they never came.
Did they pull a Peter on me?
That thought made me sad.
I waited and waited but no,
Romeo and Juliette never came.
I went to get breakfast.
Don't wait.

In many ways JD was and still is a self-made man. He is an entrepreneur as much as he was from the moment he decided to start his own business and from the moment he chose to move to Canada and take on the "American dream". Is that the "American dream" Or the "North American dream"?

It didn't matter, he is what many think an entrepreneur is. Most people have this so wrong. Having your own business is not about setting your own hours, which JD did. Most people think that when you have your own business it's all about doing what you want. It certainly isn't.

In business you do what you need to do. Your business controls you, not the other way around. Most businesses start off with little money and lots of enthusiasm. The money comes later, if all goes well. The rewards come to the early bird. Hard work and even harder work must happen before you set your own hours and go to the office from 10-3. No, your own business is harder than setting your own hours and telling people what to do.

Having your own business is getting your ass there and back and getting stuff done. Hoping you get some sleep in between, so you can get up early and work hard until late into the night the next day. Right now, JD was the ultimate self-made man. He did what he wanted, when he wanted. He didn't work from dawn to dusk. He didn't need to work, in fact he was as good as a stockbroker because people gave him money to blow. It was up to him to save it or spend it. This was the ultimate revenge… This all came at a cost to his family he had pushed away and hurt. It didn't matter, he had to be selfish and do what he wanted. To never second guess himself like he did before. In the early days, that was JD's strength, never second guessing himself. Throughout the years that was worn away ever so slowly as the business grew.

Reflections:

I love to people watch. Staring in the distance and seeing people walking, driving, cycling, or on a train in any location. A coffee in hand and watching, seeing them go about their everyday life.
None of us knows what each person is dealing with or what they are going through. Not because we don't care, but because we don't know them. We don't know their problems or their lives. The next time a barista hands you a coffee or the next time you meet a someone new, think of how little we know about the person.
Many times, I felt the same with our employees. We saw them every day and we worked with them but I didn't know their hobbies, or their problems.
In the end it didn't matter, but…it may have mattered at the time. It may have given that person a boost the needed that day or that week. Often times I, or we as "bosses" forgot that those people looked up to us. While I or we thought we were the same as them, we were not. We handed these people their paychecks and our responsibility to them was a great one. We knew the meaning of having nothing, many of our employees were new immigrants. They too were newcomers to Canada and we were their source of income. We knew this even if they didn't know we knew. We truly cared about them because we were once them.

Chapter 2. Eastern Europe to Canada

In Hungary, life was difficult. Much like everywhere else the attitude of 'I scratch your back and you scratch mine' was prevalent. However, in Hungary under Communist rule it was more difficult and very few people knew what it was like unless you lived it.
In 1976, JD's sister, who escaped from Hungary during the 1956 revolution invited JD and his wife to come for a visit. JD finally had a chance to come to Canada with his wife. In Hungary at the time, it meant that they would need to leave their two boys behind. Why? Well, there was no way JD would get permission to travel. You had to show the Communist regime that you are a good Communist and will return to Hungary. Of course, you will return, they have your kids. Such was Communism.
If there was one thing JD had, it was determination and fight. This was evident right down to his last penny in his fight against the YB. Back then was very different. JD was young and had all the energy in the world. He decided to take on the Communists.
He fell in love with the freedom and the opportunities in Canada. Seeing Canada and the opportunities here made him desperate to escape from Hungary but not alone. No, it had to involve the family. It was a plan that had to be well laid out because if you didn't you may never see the light of day again. The Communist regime was

tough. If you went against them, they would not give a second thought to having you killed or framed. This was not a joke. Planning and planning very far in advance was needed.

This was much like making a business plan. The only difference was that your life may be at stake. Even worse was that they may separate you from your family and for JD that was worse than being dead. Planning had to be perfect, planning had to be better than any business plan and any forecast your customer gives you. Upon returning from Canada JD didn't call his brother who was the police chief in Budapest and surrounding area. It was late so JD thought he would call tomorrow for the simple reason that he needed to go to the post office because Hungarians didn't have the luxury of having a phone in every house.

Again, don't wait, lesson learned when JD's brother informed him that he will never leave Hungary again because he didn't inform him that he was back in Hungary after his trip. This was senseless but his brother was a police chief and as hard-headed as a Communist could be.

So, the planning began. Though now the birds may steal crumbs from JD on the occasional morning, no one would steal the dream JD had developed to come to the land of freedom.

Back in 1976, driving through Canada in a 2 door Cadillac with power windows, air conditioning and a floaty cushy ride and so big that a couple could lay down in the back was a dream. A dream that had to come true. JD wanted the dream so bad he could taste it. It was the ultimate dream that many Europeans fought hard to make come true. People found different ways to make this happen. This just happens to be the way JD did it. The feeling of freedom and wind in your hair was so tempting and so alluring that it was worth the risk.

JD and the family needed to move from his brother's area of rule so to speak. Being a police chief in Hungary at that time meant you had a lot of power and with that power came a big head and with the big head came power that JD and the average factory worker couldn't even come close to. There was no way his brother would listen to any rational thoughts because Communism had people brainwashed. People didn't like not having the things that were available in North America or in West Germany. But then many didn't know any better and accepted what was and how it was. This was JD's strength, he knew what life was like and even though he told people he seemed like a liar. These things couldn't be true, it's all against Communism. These were not lies. Life was as good as it gets and life was as good or even better than JD described and this dream pushed and encouraged him to live a better life and to plan and escape the claws of Communist Hungary.

JD's wife was not as happy about leaving. She knew she would miss her parents and family but JD knew that as long as he had his wife and kids he would be fine. They would be fine, so the planning continued. The plan was much more complicated than JD's current days of getting up, foraging for food and placing his hat out in hopes of getting enough money for a coffee and some savings.

This called for action; no one could know, no one could even be suspicious. Any hint of this to the wrong person and JD and his family are history. There could be no leaks, no suspicion and no glitches.

Having to move out of JD's brother's jurisdiction was not easy. New city, new job and keeping quiet. It just so happens that JD's father and mother in-law were moving in with their daughter and so their house came available. It was far enough away that it was out of the police jurisdiction of the older brother. This was a lucky break and one that needed to be explored. This was a chance that couldn't be passed up. The drive at the time was about two to two and a half hours away. It was far enough to begin again and take on a new life and continue with the plan.

JD's sister waited anxiously for her brother and family to come to Canada, preparing a plan for the rest of the family to set things in motion. In her case, she and her husband escaped in 1956 and when they escaped, they had border guards shoot at them and they had to cross a river to get to western Germany. While they had their own story to tell, they didn't have kids to worry about like JD did. With two sons, aged 9 and 6 escaping was much more complicated than a couple escaping without kids.

JD and his sister finished up the plan. Since they were good Communists, they would most likely get a passport and visa to visit western Germany. If and when they did they needed a place to stay and because they had relatives in Germany it was going to be easy. People like that were eager to help as they too all escaped once from the Communist regime.

As JD thought this all through in his mind, he was getting anxious. So many things were possible in the past and so many years have passed that it brought tears to his eyes in the present. All that work and all that planning to these days when he is alone on the streets waiting for the kindness and generosity of others to make sure he can live another day and wake up another morning unlike Peter.

Life is a mystery, a pain in the ass, so many days he thought of ending it and thought *don't wait, just do it*. This was not his way, he was determined to live and finish this, no matter what it takes, no matter what; the YB is not gonna take his life. He is stronger and braver even if the YB is bigger and richer than he is. Reliving the memories of the past was painful but manageable. He had been in worse pain and he had been in rougher shape earlier. This was not going to bring him down.

Having his sister on the other side and the support and guidance of people that took these brave steps decades earlier was going to help him through whatever life throws at him. This was JD's attitude throughout life. There was no way of holding back and holding down a man wanting to escape from the prison he was in right now. It wasn't a prison as in being behind bars and handcuffed. Communism was a mental prison, don't think, don't say, don't, don't, don't. Just do as you are told and being under Russian rule, the Hungarians did as they were told.

When JD was in the army he learned that you do not go against the Russians or their Communist ways. Be a good soldier, be a good man and the country will be good to you. Basically, it meant that they would leave you alone and let you be. Just be like everyone else and no harm shall come to you. Be the same because if you are different you will not live a long life.

With these thoughts hanging above his head, JD made plans. Selling a place and moving was not the Hungarian way. In Hungary you live your life in one place. People live in the same place for decades. Aunts and Uncles can be found in the same place for 50 years and if you go and knock on the door it will be one of them opening the door. It's a concept that may be a little strange to the average North American who moves here and there quite often. JD had to move with his family and on top of that he had to sell his car. The current car, a Wartburg, was an East German car and there was no way to sell it in West Germany. JD searched for a Japanese car in Budapest.

The most interesting part was that this little Datsun was one of only three in all of Hungary and because it was expensive, everyone was sure that JD's sister bought the car for him. The real story was much more interesting. Having sold the apartment that JD and the family lived in and moving to the in-law's house gave JD enough money to not only buy the car but the house. The money was used for the car and the house. But the house was never signed over to JD and his wife. Instead it remained in the in-law's name for the sole reason that if JD and the family defected it would be confiscated by the government. If it remained in the in-law's name, they would get to sell the property again.

Most of the planning that went into the escape was related to such things so that the Communists would not be able to prove anything. No one could know and no one could suspect that anyone else knew. This was the Communist way of moving through friends and family members and confiscating things from them, if there was any indication of aiding with the escape.

Having bought the Japanese Datsun also meant that JD and the family drove their savings across the border. Being able to sell the car in Germany gave them the money to live on and stay in Germany until the paperwork was processed and all the medical examinations were taken care of.

Having settled into the new house and new surroundings and new job, JD and the family were much closer to JD's wife's family and this made it even harder to leave. The plan was not going to be delayed or held back, the family decided to leave and it was going to happen. Or so JD thought….

One night when returning home from work JD became very ill and had to go straight to hospital. The hope to leave the Communist regime came screeching to a halt when he and the family found out that he had a very bad ulcer. He needed to be hospitalized immediately. The trip to Germany that no one knew about would have to be delayed. This was devastating and the thought of all this planning and hard work may have been for nothing. JD was very ill. Special medicine had to be flown in from Russia to save his life. In Hungary, kids were not allowed in the hospital. JD was so far gone that no one thought he would make it. They let the kids in to see their dying father.

I heard his words...

It's dark and cold in my room.
Lights from the hallway is all I see.
Echoes of people saying.
He won't make it something is wrong.
In a cold sweat I lay.
I am cold and shivering.
Beads of sweat roll down my face.
The blood they gave me, killing me.
My body rejects it along with my thoughts.
I can't stay calm, somethings wrong.
I have a dream; I have a dream…
I must survive, I must stay alive.
Fever ravages my body and I am dying.
The man beside me prays.
I can't make out the prayer.
I can't hear the words; my teeth are chattering.
Being a priest, I trust whatever he says.
I can't think I don't care.
All I know is, I don't want to die.
I'll believe if that's what it takes.
It's his voice I heard…
It wasn't God or angels by my side.
I listened as hard as I could.
To this day I don't know what was said.
His words calmed me and I hung on.
I don't know whose voice I heard that night.
I never asked.
I heard his words and I survived.

When JD was in the hospital, he met a priest. A priest of all things and while this seems cliché and so movie like it was a priest. The priest had ways of getting money across to Germany and since JD was desperate to get money across the border why not trust the priest that offered him comfort and prayed for his well-being in the bed next to his. This was no coincidence, was it divine intervention? JD was not religious and never took to being a bible thumper but this was something he could look back on and thank God for. The priest prayed for a healthy recovery along with JD's recovery and one day JD took a trip to the priest's home in Hungary and handed him a pile of cash that he hoped to see in Germany after crossing the border safely.

"This was trust on a grand scale… Handing over a ton of cash to a priest that you shared a hospital room with was not normal."

Much like today on the streets, seeing the next morning and fighting for the next day was what gave JD hope. He had to get better and he had to leave his country of birth to get to Canada. It was his dream to have the freedom of the long straight never ending highway and the open country that he and his family will ride down one day.
With the help of drugs, hope and perseverance JD managed to get healthy and even attended a wedding with the family the night before the trip. This was to make all things as normal as possible so no one would suspect that this was planned and that no else in the family was in on it.
The wedding was a perfect distraction and even though it was a late night and the nervousness was playing on both JD and his wife it was better than sitting at home worrying about crossing the border the next day. Even though the paperwork was all good, that didn't mean the border guards would let you cross. This was Communist Hungary after all.
The wedding was a perfect opportunity for JD and his wife to say goodbye to everyone. By goodbye it meant two things. If by chance something happened and they were caught it would be goodbye and never see the light of day except from a jail cell. Or it meant that it was goodbye because the family would be sentenced to prison and not be able to return to Hungary. This was bye and a long bye even if it was not goodbye forever.

Piling things in the car that morning was hard. There was no way to take everything, it was supposed to be a week in Germany; not a relocation to Canada. Toys, clothes and personal things couldn't be taken as they would raise suspicion.

This was hard, looking back at the house that you will never see again or may see but not for many, many years caused JD to have mixed feelings.

Saying goodbye to people was very hard and leaving behind the place where you lived was also very hard. JD paused his reminiscence for a while. Having moved over 15 times in a span of 40 years in Canada was not something that was planned. It was always a business decision. Having a home business meant you moved for a bigger basement and truck accessibility. This was moving to a different country. The way JD related was when he lost everything and had to sell the house to pay the lawyers.

The house that JD lost was a mistake to buy in the first place. When JD's wife passed away, he wanted to move as soon as possible. He knew he couldn't sleep in the same room where she had been ill. This was too hard, so he sold the house and bought a wonderful property where he and his wife would be happy. But the property was only for him and his wife could only join him from the heavens above. The loss of that house was the loss of everything and in one way compared with leaving your country behind. There was an emptiness and a sadness. Both cases were very painful and mere words could not explain the feeling.

If JD could, he would change a few things in his life. Not many but a few... He was past that, now he only looked forward to waking up and breakfast. The rest is a blur of people walking past and the sounds of coins falling in the hat before him.

The sounds of coins falling brought JD back to the very long line at the Hungarian/Austrian border. Strikes were rare but there was something wrong across the Austrian border and the lineup was a few kilometers long. It took nearly 5 hours to cross. Having two kids in the back of the car, combined with the approaching armed guards was extremely stressful.

After hours of waiting, they made it across the border. This was a moment two years in the making. This was a moment of incredible freedom. A moment that was enjoyed so much, that no one in the cars around the family knew why they drove a few kilometers away from the border, got out and jumped for joy.

No one understood what was going on and why this family would be so happy. The stress that was lifted from the shoulders of the family. Now looking forward to either staying in Germany, Austria or heading off to Canada were the only choices that they had to make. Getting across the border from Hungary to Austria was a cause for a celebration in more ways than one. This was a victory, it was a big old screw you to Communism and something that very few people achieved in life.

"Many people thought of leaving, many people dreamt of leaving but very few people make their dreams come true."

JD and the family had left, they did it and they lived the dream. They were the ones that everyone else will want to be in the future. Crossing the border was not a simple line on a map. This was not a dream but JD and the family did the unthinkable and the impossible for Hungarian people. Being on the Austrian side and looking back to their country of birth was a relief. This was much more than moving on and leaving, this was a new beginning and a fresh start. Not many people know, only the ones that experienced this… No matter how hard you work in Communism you will be common. You will not stand out. Whether you work your ass off or if you didn't work as hard as the person next to you. You are both common people wearing the same shoes, similar clothes and watching the same propaganda on television while reading the same crap in the newspaper.

Only when you had a taste of what hard work and blood, sweat and tears can truly deliver are you baited, enticed and seduced by the western ways. This was the bug that bit JD and this was the do or die that he signed up for. With a big smile on his face he knew he didn't need the "die" part of the do or die. He now had to do and prove to his wife and family that his hard work and his dream will come true. He believed in himself wholeheartedly and knew he could and would do this.

Many people didn't believe in the western ways. JD's Brother didn't believe and neither did his father in-law. No, they were hard core Communist. Frank, JD's father in-law was a hard-core Communist. He fought in the war and was a prisoner of war. Despite being a prisoner of war and spending years in a Russian camp he still believed in the Communist dream. JD stealing his daughter and "brainwashing" her to leave was a slap in the face for him and his ways.

Frank was a typical Communist who worked in a factory where they made pots and pans. JD always had the best pots and pans since there were ways of making things happen for others in the Communist regime. Frank was a big man, he was a manager of sorts and tough as nails, or pots and pans in this case. He was a well-respected man. Thank goodness he was retired when the escape took place because an escape of a family member could have severely affected his pension.

This was the common Communist after all. Stepping out of line or having others under you step out of line was not common. The news of the escape had not reached home yet. No, this burden was laid on the most honest and the quietest man, Uncle John. Uncle John was the type of person that could and would sit in the same spot for 8 hours and if you didn't speak to him he wouldn't speak to you.

He loved black coffee, the TV and a newspaper. He always kept up with the latest news and knew a little about everything. He worked with his hands most of his life. He welded and did bodywork on cars and drove a bus at some point in life. The one thing Uncle John was not; a talker. He was quiet, honest and trustworthy, he was the poster boy for the word.

Uncle John knew of the plan and knew what was going down but he didn't have the balls to pull the trigger on such a plan. He was not the type of person that wanted all that and more. He was content and as his personality suggested he was quiet, worked as hard as he needed to and was always doing something on the side to make a little extra cash. This was Uncle John and his family loves him for what he is and how he is. A lovable character who is quiet but quick to smile and crack a joke once you have engaged him.

This is why JD and his wife trusted Uncle John with the truth and told him two things. "We are not coming back" and "if you get a postcard from Germany that reads 'We are in Bamberg and staying a little longer' that was code for we are not returning to Hungary and we are going to Canada".

This may seem simple, but curious why a code was needed. Code was needed because once you defect you are the enemy in the eyes of Communist Hungary. Everything you did in life will be questioned and torn to shreds because you were not a true believer in the Communist ways. Code was necessary because the Communist government could not be given even the slightest hint that anyone was aware of JD's plans of escaping. No letter could be sent back that would read, "Glad we made it out. Thanks for all your help!" No, those bastards at the time would make sure that they tore the rest of the family apart and imprisoned them for taking part in the escape and being an accomplice. The code was set and Uncle John was now an informant. He carried information that he held on to with dear life and often we wondered how he did it but he was a trusted man, he would not let JD down.

It now made sense to Uncle John why it was so important for JD and his wife to say goodbye to each and every person at the wedding the other day. It made sense why the family had to move out of big brother's jurisdiction in the Budapest area. Because JD's brother was physically in charge of signing the passports for every single person, allowing them to leave the country. Moving out of his jurisdiction meant he would not be held personally responsible. Even though in the end he was affected by the escape, JD did his best to lessen the blow by the move. Uncle Z's position in the police force was too high and his fellow officers couldn't let this pass. He did get demoted and offered early retirement. Once more the Communist ways came shining through and while the police chief and others were way above the common Communist, the same rules applied. You brought shame to the regime and you had to be punished whether you agreed with it or not.

Many didn't agree with the ways of the government, but they were the ways of operation. For example, for JD's kids to be able to go to kindergarten, JD had to go back to play soccer for the factory soccer team. This was a favor and strings that could be pulled. This was a small example that Communists had their ways and it was silly for JD to be on the company payroll and not work. He played soccer and he was on the payroll to make sure the company won. Silly but true, so many little things that people who didn't live it wouldn't believe it. You had to know the right person to bring in Puma soccer shoes, or to be treated to something simple as oranges or bananas.

So many little things that JD would be pissed off about. Why was life so hard in a country that closed its borders, its mind and held back the future of the people? Because it was convenient for the Communist elites. Because it was not Communism but opportunistic people who lived in huge homes and had so much more than the average person in Hungary. How can there be rich and poor and very rich and very poor in Communism? There shouldn't be, every man, woman and child should be the same. No one should stand out. Every man, woman and child should dress, act and behave the same way. Be a good little boy and do as the other little boys and girls are doing. Grow up work hard and repeat.

This was not going to be JD. Crossing the border JD shed this elephant on a rope life and he became a new person. A free person and a hard-working person that can now work harder and achieve as much or as little as he wanted. This was what the plan meant and this was what he dreamt of. Rarely do people have their dreams come true. Rarely do people work so hard to make their dreams come true. Rarely do they get to look back and stand on the side of the border of one country and look back at the other and be in the dream. Live the dream and possibly be in the dream yet be in the driver's seat of the dream you had dreamt of.

The mastermind of this plan was JD, the dream, the planning and effort, the tiny little details of not physically purchasing his father in-laws house was planned down to the tiniest detail. Not signing the deed to the house meant it was to remain in Frank's name. Screwing over the Commies was fun. Investing your money in a car and driving it across the border was brilliant. But there was luck, trust and other details that were imperative for this escape to be successful.

Once the dream of the border crossing was reality it was time to pull together the bits and pieces of the plan that would make it possible to complete the dream for JD and stand under the wonderful red and white maple leaf of the Canadian flag.

Reflections:

Today the difference between Canada and Hungary is not nearly as big as it was in 1978. At that time Levi's jeans, Puma soccer shoes, bananas and oranges were for those with connections. Today this would be a petty thing to mention and for those born after the 90's the notion of not having something is quite ridiculous.

But back in 1978 these little differences made the Communist life difficult and most people were poor and barely got by. Having a car was a luxury, having a roof over your head was a priority and you gave up eating meat and vegetables to do so. Bread and butter, jam and cold cuts were common meals. If we were lucky, we had meat once a week and while I do not remember that; I do remember how life was.

School uniforms and getting the strap when my writing was messy was the norm. Teachers checking your ears and nails to make sure they were clean and if they were not, they would make you put your fingers together and whack them with the edge of a ruler. One thing was for sure. The teachers had the respect of the students and no one ever talked back. Maybe that was something of a positive in the Communist era.

Chapter 3. The bits and pieces

So much of the plan was based on simple trust. Two Uncles and a few relatives played vital roles in this very simple but daring escape from Hungary to Austria on to Germany and then to Canada. Keeping a family together, keeping the dream alive during two years of planning. The small carefully planned steps that this man and his family took to make the dream of freedom come true. If not for him but for his kids. JD didn't let the ropes that the Communist government had him tied up in stop him.

Today JD does not have the same fight within him. No, today he pauses and looks back at his life and his achievements and asks himself if it was worth it. To end up broke and to end up in this position; was the dream, the grand spectacle worth it? Was this karma for being able to live the North American dream? Was it worth it? When the end is as bad as having stayed in a country that gave him nothing and end up in a country that gave him everything yet took everything away in the end.

If he could have had a glimpse into the future, where JD knew the outcome, he would most likely have chosen the same path but would have fought to change it. That was JD, having hope that all the bits and pieces fall into place was something he was willing to take a chance on. Believing in the people that said they would help was something not so common today. The world has surely changed and so has JD. Humbled by having lived and lost in both physical and monetary means.

One of the little bits and pieces still to fall into place was JD's sister flying from Canada to Germany. The process to immigrate to Canada couldn't be finalized until the family was across the border. Now that this was done, the immigration process from Canada was in full swing.

Along the way there were other people and places to visit. Driving through Austria was a buffer zone. It was not the final destination, but it was a free country and a chance to visit another Uncle along the route. Vienna was an amazing place. Wonderful architecture and amazing gardens, the locations visited escapes the memory since nearly 40 years have passed.

The buffer zone was needed. It was a time to take a deep breath and let all the tension settle and let this process sink in so that one's brain can stop spinning and understand that there will be no going back, only going forward. Leaving Hungary at the time was like putting on rose colored glasses. No matter what was on the other side it was amazing to see and everything was greener, everything was cleaner, fresher and so much more motivating.

The food tasted better, most likely because it was. The people were happier, most likely because they were. The world seemed better because it was. People were free to think and do as they pleased. They were not in fear nor were they scared to speak out against or in favor of political parties. This was a different world even though the old world was only hours away.

Amazing to think that the slight shift in geographical location could make such a difference. We have no say where we are born. We may have a choice in where we will die but not where we are born. If you don't like your current situation, change it. Sure, not as easy as it sounds but here was JD who knew it was not easy but did it anyway. The harder part was the numerous medical exams in Germany to appease the Canadian government. Since they were not all in one place there were several hours of driving between locations. The timing of all this was up to the professionals and not the people that need the tests done. Some locations were in Hamburg and Bonn or places like Stuttgart. At these places blood tests were done, x-rays were taken, and medicals given. These were necessary and that is why plan B was to remain in Germany if by chance plan A was stopped by some condition that the family was not aware of. These were all part of the plan that was orchestrated by a simple man, a man with a dream to live a better life in a better part of the world. While there were details that had to be ironed out and organized it all took time. Time was something that was allotted for and the more time it took, the more money was needed. It was time to visit the pre-arranged funds that the priest arranged to send to Germany. How and when it was sent was unknown. All JD knew was to show up at a given address in a small town called Ulm.

It was hours away from Stuttgart but nothing is so far in Europe. Unlike the vast expanse of space in Canada where a person can fly 5 hours in any direction from the center of the country and never leave Canada. In Europe, several countries can be crossed in a short time. This was a good thing, crossing into Austria from Hungary and through to Germany was not a long drive. Coming and going between countries was wonderful and easy.

The trip to Ulm was fascinating… A few priests working for the people and with people in different countries to help smuggle cold hard cash between borders. Now this was doing God's work. Not that it mattered, there was no reason to question anyone's motives here. All that was important was the fact that the money was there and now it was in JD's hand. This was amazing, JD had escaped death with a priest for a buddy in the next bed who happened to be able smuggle money between borders. Truly a miracle or was it God's work to help out JD? We will never know…

The sound of a siren woke JD and brought him back to reality. No, he didn't believe in God. He never did and never will. This mess, this life was the devils work. Having nothing, having everything and then all was slowly being plucked away from JD. One by one the shit hit the fan. Getting up JD dusted himself off and looked across the road where he could see the top of St. Michael's Church and wondered if maybe he should go and make peace with himself. There was no point, his wife was no longer here, she couldn't be brought back. The house and the business had been ripped out of his hands and there was no way to get it back.

Picking up his backpack JD checked his paper bag three times and wandered down the street. Looking across the street, he noticed that Romeo and Juliette were back. Smiling a little, although it was hard to see under his bushy beard; JD was happy that they were back. It would probably be better if the two were gone and settled into jobs that pay the bills and working hard to establish a permanent roof over their heads like he and his wife did.

He shook his head, not these days of social media influencers and YouTube stars. These kids don't have the patience that he had. They don't have the willpower, the true grit and strength to fight and the patience to see all this through. There was a long pause after that… "Look who's talking" JD said out loud. He was not about to give advice to anyone. He was so far past opening his mouth or giving advice that it didn't matter… Not like it did years and years ago. The stroll on Dundas St. was not long, but it was enough to make JD drift back to his past.

Once a base had been established at JD's wife's Uncle's house, there was a feeling that things were moving in the right direction. The family was welcomed with open arms. It was a warm feeling, living in a large fully finished attic, about the same size as the apartment the family had lived in. It didn't matter where they were as long as things were moving forward.

Time was not a factor either as long as things were getting done and the process was moving forward and not stalled. This was hard, it was costing money, it was costing time and testing everyone's patience. If plan A fell through it would be almost too close to home. Knowing you could see the relatives and parents hours away but they may not be able to come and see you is tough. Being hours and hours away by plane made it a bit more understandable.

JD's wife was often homesick and questioned herself so many times that she had lost count. She was close to her parents while JD had lost both of his. He had nothing to stay for but she did. Her sister, Mother, Father and other relatives were missed. Knowing that you cannot come back and the likelihood of them being able to visit would slim to none was sad.

This feeling took some getting used to. It was a bit of a trap but knowing you simply couldn't, made it so much easier. It was full stop and made you focus on no other direction but forward.

Being with relatives helped, they were a wonderful family and they had one son who was a few years older around 12. He had a go cart a bicycle, and they had a spacious backyard. This was a blessing, the kids were happy, they had space, very much like they will have in Canada. Watching the kids enjoy themselves was making all this worth it. Even if Germany was the final destination it was already worth the effort. But this wasn't the final destination and nothing was indicating that it would be. The only thing that was testing everyone in the family was time and the patience to wait for all those little things to fall into place.

JD was never one to sit still, he had to figure out how to make money. Sometimes with persistence and hard work one gets lucky. Such was the case and having a relative that was a fashion designer and pretty well-known was helpful.

There was nothing that JD wouldn't do. When he was asked to do deliveries of patterns and samples hours away, he of course volunteered. On top of that he got to drive a 5 series BMW. This may seem silly and superficial; but being in a 5 series BMW was beyond amazing. There was no way a regular Hungarian could afford such a car. Even if you worked like a horse all your life there was no way he would ever hope to drive such a car.

Being on the autobahn in Germany was freedom in itself. The open, vast road felt a bit like Canada. The Cadillac was a BMW, the roads were open, the signs were in German but it was close. Holding the steering wheel of this awesome machine made JD feel as if he made it. No matter what he made it because he was free. Work was work, the pay was in cash and having cash handed to you in Germany was already a huge step forward.

Cash, not a check. It was enough and it was good enough to buy food and the daily things needed by the family. The second or actually the first job that JD had was working in a metal working shop. JD had always been good with his hands. He was a welder and a blacksmith. Not a professional blacksmith but he did work a few summers in a blacksmith shop in Hungary. Bending and forging metal was something he loved. When his relative introduced him to the shopkeeper he didn't quite know what he was in for but he was led to a machine where he had to rivet a hook onto a cone shaped 15 cm tall metal object with sharp edges.

Never having seen such a thing JD kind of chuckled and asked what this was. The funny looking object was a pig scraper. A tool made to scrape the hair off of pigs after slaughter. This was amazing… being in Germany, delivering designer patterns and making pig scrapers for far more money per hour than he would ever dream of making in Hungary. What other doors would open up if he and the family would seek asylum here and stay in Germany? The job was boring, it was a machine putting rivets into two pieces of metal and clamping them together.

This was nothing compared to being a foreman in a bus and truck manufacturing plant with 1500 workers in Hungary. JD being in charge of 150 people and making sure production of nuts and bolts and other parts were being manufactured and made on time. This job was all him and just him. It gave JD lots of time to think, 8 hours a day, a few days a week was enough. The other days he would do deliveries or stay at home in the attic with the family.

Time passed at an alarming rate. It was summer and then fall came so fast that it felt like someone was turning the clock forward at twice the speed. The documents were taking a long time. Communication between immigration and the governments was slow. The weather started getting cold and the kids needed warm clothes. The Datsun had to go. It was amazing to everyone that this little Trojan horse was a cash cow and had been driven out of the country. No one ever asked, no one ever suspected a thing. Sometimes the most obvious thing, that's right before your eyes is the thing that every single person misses. So caught up are we in the magic that we miss seeing the trick. This was the little Datsun that was to be sold. It was bought to be sold, it was not brought to keep. This was not a sad moment, it was a planned moment.

Kids needed warm clothes and the car had to go. It did what it was meant to do. It was bought to be driven across a border without suspicion and without a bag full of cash in the trunk. Giving the keys to the new owner was a moment knowing that the plan went according to plan and things were right on track as they were supposed to be.

Some of the tests were now coming back and this was all positive and giving much needed positivity to the family and JD's sister in Canada who flew back and forth a few times and each time taking a few Deutsche Marks to Canada. Not having to pay rent and making a little bit of money on the side sure went a long way. While they did not have all their life savings with them, JD worked hard to recoup as much as possible to start off on the right foot in Canada.

Bit by bit the money trickled from one town to another in Hungary, rolled through Austria and Germany and now it was making its way to Canada a few thousand dollars at a time. Back in 1978 smuggling money around the world was much easier than it is today but this was not illegal. This was a smart way and a lucky way to be able to move funds between countries. Having people in all the right places

and for them to be able to move freely around the world was also a big plus. Something a regular Hungarian would have no use for.
As winter rolled into Europe, it was unsure whether the family would celebrate Christmas in Canada or Germany. While either was acceptable it became a target to be in Canada by Christmas. It was the goal, the hope and the ultimate gift for the holidays.
Unlike the holidays now, Christmas is a downer, there is no wonderful cheerful family get together, there is no reason to. Much like Thanksgiving, what is there to give thanks for?
What is there to celebrate? Being alive? There is no celebration in life, not now, not today and not for the past few years. After JD's wife passed away the celebrations went quiet. It was a time of "Oh if Mom was here." The Mother, the wife that made the celebrations special was not here. The holidays, the special moments, the feeling of each was lost. The miracle of Christmas, the thanks in the giving and the love at Valentine's day and even Halloween felt hollow without that special person that you fought through thick and thin with over the many years.
JD's wife was always a bit weary, very conservative and to this day it is beyond belief that she agreed to go on this wild and crazy journey from Hungary to Canada. In Germany, there were many days and nights of arguing, convincing and motivation to keep things moving forward. The winter nights were long and cold, the days were filled with keeping two kids entertained and thinking of JD and the family pushing through those days of little hope and great distances was unbelievable.
Primitive man was free to roam, sure there were tribes and wars and killing amongst them but they were free to go wherever they wanted. Amazingly as we grew as a civilization we put up borders and invisible lines to keep others out and today we can't stop thinking of how to be more inclusive. How to be fair and stop racism and give people freedom all the while invisible forces are working against the common "man" keeping them down and out from moving forward. Sounds like Communism, sounds like the old days where a few had a lot and the many had much less. We have not moved forward as a society…
As the fall slowly slipped into winter there was little hope to be in Canada by the Christmas deadline. All the medical and physical tests were done, all were in line with the requirements. Now it was the paperwork that had to be pushed through. There was no way of

rushing this. There was no way of paying off someone or expediting the process. There were hundreds of phone calls, no fax machines and things depended on the postal service. Oh, the good old days of running to the mailbox and checking your watch because the mailman was late by five minutes. Nowadays, JD uses those mailboxes to lean his head against and once in a while says hello to the mailman if he is not asleep.

JD's wife was homesick, the holidays coming and not being able to bake all the Christmas cookies for the family and the kids waiting to eat the raw dough. This was not normal, this was stressful and the routine of cooking and baking weeks before Christmas could not be followed. While there was a kitchen it was not made to cook, and bake like at home. This was not home, not yet, this was temporary and this was a pain in the ass to be stuck here like refugees.

Nights were filled with tears and arguments. Days were filled with stress and worrying about the next day and the next night and hoping that things fall into place before everyone goes nuts in the limbo they were stuck in. Each moment was stressful and the only thing that made the time pass was the smile of the children and the occasional goofiness that was sure to arise in times of desperation such as this. When things get so bad that you have no choice but laugh, it is as close acceptance as it gets.

That's why JD is furious, he has yet to have acceptance. He has yet to accept what the world has dealt him. He is still filled with and fueled by anger, fear and the people that put him here, the big YB. He has yet to accept it and each time he thinks even a little he boils with anger at the assholes that dealt him this card. A lifetime of work flushed away and down the drain and no one cares. No one gives a shit, they pretend to but they walk away saying, "Damn, I am glad that wasn't me" "I feel sorry for him but he should have protected himself"

A long time ago JD would have gotten up and gotten ready for the next round. But the fuel that would be ignited by that spark was missing. The spark of anger was there, however the fuel to drive all that forward was missing. He was a car ready to go on that long country drive that brought him here, but the tank was bone dry without a gas station for a million miles. The road was empty and even if it wasn't, no one would pull over and give this old man a hand. This is what was missing today… This is what was available decades ago.

The goofiness came out through the kids and the only thing goofy now are the idiots who walk down the street bumping into telephone poles while looking down at their phones, that somehow never gets old. Unlike JD, somethings never get old…

He never thought he would get old either. Back then full of energy and full of ambition but now, it's just the rage against the YB. Back then the YB was unknown, yes it existed and its founder who claimed to be poor and fly coach and drive an old Volvo didn't give a rat's ass about the suppliers and never did.

The goofiness was plenty and there was happiness to be had especially when a phone call came that the application for immigration to Canada had been approved. The family was ready to fly! JD, and the family were elated. The planning and slightly extended stay in Germany paid off. Flying out and arriving in Canada on December second 1978! This was a well-executed plan with amazing results.

Looking back and packing up for the first flight was a big deal. Getting on a plane and flying across the ocean seemed so much easier than the wait they have been subjected to for the past 6 months. Nevertheless, this was an exercise in patience, judgement and survival skills. Not speaking a word of German and learning English from a dictionary. Not knowing the correct pronunciation from the dictionary made communication fun to say the least. But now there was only one language to focus on and that was English. It was crunch time and a crash course was needed so extra dictionary time was booked before the flight date.

Being in someone's house for nearly six months was not easy. Having them put up with virtual strangers for 6 months is also hard. But again, these people were the old kind, the good kind, the trustworthy kind. They didn't expect anything in return, they didn't want anything. What these people wanted was nothing but the best for all in the future. They were good people with good hearts and full of positivity as well as honesty and goodness. While they were relatives they were not close relatives to begin with but they did become close relatives over the time that was spent with them.

Packing up and leaving the attic apartment was wonderful. Until that very moment, no one had given a thought as to where the new home would be. All JD and his wife knew that they were going to the same place in Canada that they had been to before. It was a large 100-acre farm in a place called Caledon Ontario Canada. Oh, how JD wished he could visit that farm and go back to the day that he arrived there with the family.

Reflections:

I admire people who have a dream, be it a crazy, silly dream about anything, it doesn't matter. As long as you can dream there is a fire inside you that still burns bright. That dream can lead you down the path you want to go or like us, have a small business fall in your lap. That is what helped us achieve the dream of many.
It took guts, courage and hard work to leave Hungary. It took planning, and the willingness to risk it all. This was not an easy dream to fulfill with 2 kids, driving into not one but two unknown countries and making a go of it only because you, you alone thought you could and would make it. There could be no if's or maybe's, failure was not an option. I admire my dad for this and regardless of what happened in the end, he made his dream come true. He was able to do what many people are unable to do and for that he deserves great acknowledgement. Having the nerve to sit through all the waiting, then the hard work. Seeing the fruit of his labor is something not many people can say they have accomplished. For those that have, they know it was the harder road to travel but they also know the meaning of a dream come true.

Chapter 4. The new world

The day of the flight was a day of reckoning. Going back home was still an option, going back now would mean no jail time and no one would have been aware of the plan.

But this family was not going back.

No, this family was going to the airport and on the way to the airport there was a postcard that had to be mailed. The code that was established had to be sent. By now the Hungarian government has been opening any and all mail coming to JD and his family. The police and the Communist hard heads were all over the family back home since this family had not returned to Hungary, everyone was under investigation. Every document had to be turned over to the government and they took whatever they could legally take. Because of the well thought out plan there was little to take. It was more the ridicule that the family back in Hungary had to go through and even if they thought, "Good for them for leaving, well done". They had to say, "Those terrible people, very bad Hungarians and very bad Communists, shame on them". Uncle John kept quiet, he knew that there was no return but he couldn't and wouldn't say a word. Boarding a plane was one thing, but to board a massive 747 Jumbo jet was another. It was overwhelming for people that have never seen one, to now be in an airport and seeing this amazing plane in person for the first time. Before the days of shoe bombs and smoking restrictions and locks on the pilot doors there was the fun days of flying. JD and his wife were impressed, the kids were bouncing off the walls at the excitement and looking forward to their first flight. This was not JD's first flight, nope, that came in the army. The wonderful three-year mandatory service in the Hungarian army was JD's first flight.

This was of course on another level. This was a Jumbo jet, the two-level luxurious jetliner that was nearly 10 years in service already. But to this family it might have been put in service yesterday. This Jumbo Jet was the plane to a new life, a new beginning and for the journey of unimaginable proportions. For this small group of four people this was a life changing moment that very few people could comprehend.

The way of the airlines back in 1978 was to engage and please the customer and it was not a torture to fly and a pain to go through customs. The kids got little gold colored plastic wings to pin on their shirts, small packs of Lego and once the plane took off, they even got to go up and to the pilot's cabin. My how things have changed.

Today if you approached the pilot's door the plane would be grounded, and the SWAT team would show up. But not that day and not back then, back then they still gave out metal cutlery and most people took them home and had complete collections of airline cutlery. They went well with TV dinners or small desserts. The days of flying in smoke filled cabins was still prevalent and this was no different. JD's wife was a smoker, and, in the end, it would be part of her demise.

The flight to Canada was amazing. Looking out the window at 33,000 feet and being on top of the world was exactly what JD needed. This is how it felt, this was the exact feeling that a well-executed plan felt like. He had won, they had won and the Commies had lost. Now there was no way of holding this man back. He was set to run and run he will, with all the energy and all the excitement of a kid on his birthday or Christmas Eve. The flight was nearly 9 hours but it was nothing, it was merely seconds in the span of 6 months and nearly two years of planning. The flight was exciting and uneventful, the landing was a whole other story. When you fly into the massive country of Canada, you first fly over Newfoundland and then Quebec. In December both of these provinces are snow covered expenses of land that you fly over until you reach Toronto.

Flying into Canada and knowing that this is now your home. This is the country that you chose. Both of these things are a little overwhelming when you come from a small country like Hungary. Looking down at the grey and black roads and highways crisscrossing the snow-covered land beneath you. There was not much to see and even less to see when the winter days are short, and darkness sets in around 5 pm. By the time the Toronto airport came in to view and the plane landed there was nothing to see but city lights and at the time the tallest freestanding structure in the world. The CN Tower is a marvel of engineering and to see that on the grand entrance to your new country is incredible. It shows you right there and then that you have arrived at a much more advanced place than where you came from.

The landing was exciting. Even more exciting was getting off the plane and heading proudly to Immigration with all your papers in hand and telling them that you are legally entering this country and you are here to stay. This was a different type of excitement, there was an anxiousness to get things going and get things done all before even setting foot on Canadian soil.

Stepping off the plane, experiencing a different type of world was nothing short of exciting and scary. The language barrier was one problem and the new environment was another. Those things can be learned, and people adjust. Now it was time to head over and hand over all the paperwork to be able to enter one of the greatest countries in the world.

This was a blur, and JD was too overwhelmed to recollect what happened but getting out and meeting his sister and thanking her and her husband for all their help during this crazy time was first on the list. The second was getting dressed and warmed up because Canada was cold.

None of the family could stop themselves from looking left, right and up and down and taking in this new place. The cars, the buildings and the people, the way they dressed, the behavior was all new. Everyone was smiling and happy, wearing different clothes and acting so differently than their Hungarian counterparts. This just gave everyone a push to fit in as quickly as possible. But not before getting into a brand new 1978 Lincoln Continental. This... this was one of those things that made you feel important. It's a materialistic thing. It's not something that JD needed or wanted but it was something that was different and something that was so American.

Yes, this was Canada, but it didn't matter. This was a Ford, a Lincoln and something that was so vastly different. It meant you have arrived. With its black and burgundy paint job, its plush tufted interior along with a plush ride. This was some way to be picked up and driven home from the airport.

The drive home to the 100-acre farm was a pain, not the type of pain that hurt. It was a head spinning type of pain.

Everyone looked left and right and answered questions and comments from each other as they drove through the city and out towards the countryside. Once the city vanished, darkness set in and a calmness also set in on the family in a new land called Canada.

The drive through the countryside was amazing. Long stretches of road ahead with nothing but the Lincoln's headlights lighting up the darkness. At the time, the farm was so far out from the city that it was really in the middle of nowhere.

The paved road turned to a snow packed gravel road that led deeper into the countryside. This was a sight the kids had never seen before. The amount of snow and the trees on either side of the road were not a usual sight for this family. This new country called Kanada, or Canada was very different indeed. There was quiet excitement from the family that planned this moment years ago. Everyone was waiting and anticipating the next turn, the next unusual sight.

When the family arrived at the farm it was another unusual event. Two large gates had to be manually opened, and two German Shepherds greeted the family. One large black and tan and the other was a white one. The white one blended into the snow as it ran in front of the car headlights.

Piles of snow one to two meters had been piled up by the tractor. With the moon out, the reflections and the shadows, the farmhouse was barely visible. There were a few lights on inside, and since the color was white with a stucco finish, it too blended into the snow. This place was old, the farmhouse was very old and when everyone got out they noticed the very large century barn that is so typical in the North American countryside. It towered over the farm like a wise old intimidating old man. The dogs were quickly locked up as they were not used to kids. No one knew how the kids and the dogs would react to each other, since there were no kids in this household and while visitors were common, they were mostly adults.

Unloading was quick. It's amazing how the lives of four people can fit into a few suitcases. The most important things were the birth certificates and school documents that proved who you were and where you were from. The rest were materialistic things, yes clothing is essential, but you better have the correct documents if you want anything else.

Entering the old farm house was an eye opener as well. While it was old on the outside, the inside was very nice. Modern two door refrigerators, a microwave and a hood over the stove for ventilation. Yes, it all makes sense, and this was normal for people living in Canada but not for people from eastern Europe.

Many places in eastern Europe still didn't have running water in the house and no hot water unless you made a fire and fired up a boiler for a bath. Canada in 1978 was decades ahead of eastern Europe and especially the villages that still used coal to heat their homes.

Phones in each house, central heating and cooling were stuff that dreams were made of for a person in an average or below average household in nearly all of Europe. Coming from a country where a car would take years to order instead of being able to walk into a dealer and drive it off the lot the next day was a shocking idea.

No wonder that this place as old as it was on the outside, was mind blowing modern on the inside. Entering the house led straight to a hallway that led to a large kitchen table and that opened up to the kitchen. From there a right turn led to a very large family room. The room was the size of the family's old apartment.

This room was big. Two large sofas and a large bookshelf on the other wall with a big television and a very large coffee table in the middle and enough space to still have room for at least 8 people to sit on the floor by the fireplace. The room was very comfortable and warm. There was no need for a radiator to kick in and take an hour to give off a little heat. No, this place was a pleasant temperature and despite the snow and cold outside there was no sense of cold in here.

This being the first night here for the family called for a drink, for the adults that is. The overwhelming part was for the kids. JD's sister brought out several drinks like Coke, Sprite and orange juice for them. It was like Christmas had come early. Then when she brought out snacks, chips and cookies it was a birthday celebration and Christmas rolled all in one. There was no turning back, no going back, Canada was the place to be, even if it was only for the pop and cookies.

The buzz around the family was unusual. JD and the family were tired, excited and blown away. JD's sister and brother in-law were used to having visitors, but not having a family move in overnight. They were certainly not used to having kids around. No matter, everyone had to adjust and learn. But now it was time for bed and this family surely needed the rest.

That night was incredible, the two kids were used to sharing a bed while JD and his wife shared the other. For the first time in six months the family slept in separate rooms. The kids had their own and so did JD and his wife.

Having a bed and a mattress was not something JD was used to now. It's been a while since he was in a bed and years and years since he had felt a warm body beside him in bed. JD, saved as much money as he could. There was no spoiling yourself on the street except for the occasional KFC when he felt he had been given sufficient money for the week.

This was interesting because way back in 1978, JD and his family didn't know what KFC was. Seeing a KFC bucket full of meat was a dream, it could not have been real. In Hungary, they would use meat sparingly and cook chicken soup one day and eat the bits of meat the next with potatoes. Since war time meat had always been expensive and few people could afford it. So, seeing piles and piles of meat with crispy fried batter was a dream come true, it may well have been heaven. Seeing the TV commercials for KFC, McDonalds, Burger King and Pizza Hut along with Woody Woodpecker, Scooby Doo, Daffy Duck and the Flintstones cartoons was truly a kid's dream come true.

Never mind all the delicious looking cereal and toys the kids would be teased and enticed with. Don't forget the icing on the cake. There was a choice of 100 TV channels and they all had different programs. In Hungary there were 2 channels named TV1 and TV2. So much for originality, the other thing was the commercials... They were far more interesting than the programs. These commercials were for clothes, cars, toys, food and toothpaste. All this is available to buy? All this is in the stores? All this and central heating with hot and cold running water?

To the average person in North America this was normal. But for a family that had landed in Canada this was an alien world to live in. The days after when the family went from one store to another and one mall to another, a whole new world had opened up for them. Each day of suffering, each day of stress, the agonizingly long days and weeks of waiting for paperwork and medical results along with the fights, the tears, stressing over money and the kids was all clearly worth it. No one in North America would think or accept anything less than what this family saw. However, for this family this was all new.

Accepting this new reality was easy... Learning the language and getting a job to get things going was the next step. Nothing is hard when you put your mind to it. Arriving before the Christmas holidays and just before school break was great timing. The kids needed to start school and it was just enough time to settle in a little and get ready for the new life in this now even more amazing country. Everything was new to the family, there was a Dominion grocery store in a place called Orangeville nearby. This was a town that had everything, even though it was only a few thousand people. In a small rural village in Europe these things would not be available.

A Beer Store, a Liquor store, a grocery store, hardware store and even a large hospital nearby to service the rural area that has a few hundred thousand people. All this was unusual, so many services. Even a theater for entertainment, fast food and locally owned family restaurants all within minutes of each other and all fully stocked with whatever your heart desired. No shortage of bread, butter or milk. A pharmacy stocked with medicine that serviced the local hospital. All this changed for the family with a 9-hour flight on December 2nd, 1978.

When people talk of the land of opportunity... well this right here was the land of opportunity. You can work one job or two or three or whatever you have the energy to take on. Here you can work hard and also buy the things you want and need. That was the big difference. People didn't walk around with sulking miserable faces. People smiled and asked "how are you" each time you turned to someone in a store. The people were alive. The kids, the adults were happy and full of joy and not the miserable existence that loomed over each and every "happy" Communist that couldn't get an orange or a banana for two reasons, one they couldn't afford it and two there was none in the stores. Whereas in Canada you could load a station wagon and take as much as you want and the store would restock it as needed.

This was something special. Not a single soul would believe this by telling them, they would need to see it for themselves. They would think these were made up lies, Western propaganda against the Communists that had an iron grip on Eastern Europe.

The next few days went by quickly the kids needed to be registered for school and JD and his wife needed to work. JD and his wife were eager to work. The kids were less eager to go to school after nearly 6 months off, but it was necessary. For JD and his wife, it was a pleasant surprise that jobs were waiting for them. JD's sister worked at the Hudson's Bay Company or The Bay as it was called. She was an accounts receivable manager and JD's brother-in-law owned a small furniture company.

The small furniture company was called Gerard Bedding and it was about 18,000 square feet, maybe a little larger. They made upholstered furniture, mattresses and wood furniture such as beds and bunk beds, tables and the like. It was big enough that they could handle the extra two new employees and small enough that it had a nice family atmosphere to it. On top of that, they had a couple of Hungarian people working there that made communication and learning English a little easier.

Coming from Hungary, JD and his wife expected the company to be nearby, but this was not Hungary and it was not Europe. This was a massive country called Canada and the distance from the factory to the farm was well over an hour drive. This was not common in Europe. But in the grand luxury of a wonderful 1978 Lincoln Continental this was a drive that was to be enjoyed. Commuting for work in North America has always been and always will be a topic and it was less of a topic back then than it is now. Back then, less traffic, less pollution and the gas being very cheap made America and Canada what it is today.

The great rail lines that were put in to crisscross both Canada and the USA were all to help develop and grow the automotive industry and to be able to ship all the manufactured goods anywhere as fast as possible. In Europe people go to get bread every morning from a local bakery. Here you bought it, froze it and reheated it because if you lived in the country the grocery may have been a 20-minute drive away and not a short walk or a short bicycle ride like in Germany for example.

Understanding this is easy, but for a newcomer it was different. The hour plus drive to work was great to take in the roads, the buildings and the vast variety of cars, houses and factories of all kinds.

Both JD and his wife worked in a large company where JD played soccer and worked in the machining department. While JD's then girlfriend worked in accounting, they met at the company while playing ping pong. Oddly enough JD's then girlfriend was in charge of handing him his pay at the end of every month. From day one until the day she passed away she always knew how much money JD had or didn't have. This skillset and the fact that JD was a hard worker made them a great team. It was a skill and attitude that helped them ease and settle into the new reality of Canada.

When most immigrants landed in a new place, they would do the jobs that the locals didn't want to or the low paying jobs that most people would start out with. This had been repeated over and over in history, but this was not JD's reality. The hand up came, he didn't need to start pushing garbage cans around or clean toilets as a first job. Being given a job and being walked through the plant by the owner and a relative was not the norm for most people.

These were little things that JD and his wife had and was a tremendous help and push to a brighter future. Admittedly this was good luck, good planning and sometimes you get lucky in life when other times you get completely screwed over, but that comes later.

Entering a furniture company was an interesting sensation. Away from the metal, oil and industrial manufacturing of a truck and bus part plant with massive smokestacks and guarded iron gates. This was a palace, filled with the smell of stains, new fabrics, sewing machines and cutting machines that neither JD nor his wife had ever laid eyes on. Sanders, gluers and filling machines lined the floors of the factory.

Shaking their heads and thinking to themselves *this is a new life indeed.* The language, the people, the place and the lifestyle will all need to change to be able to integrate into this new reality that they have woken up in. As overwhelming and daunting this all was...

"There was absolutely no doubt and zero hesitation in JD's mind that he could learn, he could do and complete any and all tasks given to him in this building."

Reflections:

Being in any country at any time is interesting. I have had the pleasure of visiting many countries all over the world and a few are still on my list. But traveling to a country and visiting is very different from living there.
How do you decide that this is the country I want to live in and I am willing to risk it all to live there? While we moved from house to house and place to place because of the business, it's not something that everyone is capable of.
My dad must have been a cheerleader for all of us, to keep us motivated and make this move happen. Once we were here, he had to work his ass off to make sure the dream he sold us would come true. The dream did come true, it was his dream and we fell into it. What I would have done with my life or what my brother would have done with his remains a mystery. I love cars and wanted to be a mechanic and most likely that's what I would have become. Instead, we fell into the business that made up this story.

Chapter 5. The massive surprise

There are times in life when you are down and you are up. Being from a Communist country you just are. There is rarely an up or a down. You are there as a worker for the state, you eat, drink, sleep and repeat.
In Canada, you lived. You felt alive in Canada. Therefore, things are different and as many people know, most of the time hard work pays off. With hard work comes a little more money and along the way you occasionally get a tiny bit of luck.
This was certainly the case for this family. Having a job when you arrive in a new country is unreal. Soon, JD's sister was able to get JD's wife a job at The Bay and because it was an accounting job, the language barrier was less of an issue. Numbers were numbers all over the world. So, while JD and his wife had jobs it was going to be a bit of a commute for them each day to get to work. However, as luck would have it, that was not to be the case. No, this family had a bit of extra help that few people get.

One morning, the new immigrant family got up, they were told that they would be making a trip to the city as a family. This in itself was normal, they have had outings before. Piling into the Lincoln once more was something everyone enjoyed and looked forward to.
The now normal long stretches of roads were easily gobbled up in comfort and before the group knew it they found themselves in the

area of Dufferin and Eglington. This was a predominantly Italian area where there were many Italian bakeries and barbershops. Driving through here was wonderful even though it was snow covered. All the houses had front and back yards. Some had attached and some had detached garages. They all had some sort of Christmas decorations up in the windows or on the front lawn.

All the driveways were shoveled. The piles of snow were high on both the left and right sides creating tunnel-like roads to each house. This was a mature neighborhood with large trees lining the roads. This was an area of mostly older people. The older Italian immigrants from the 1950's to the early 1970's.

Making a turn on Bowie Avenue, the name was unpronounceable for the new family. Driving a short way down the street, they turned into a narrow single car driveway and the car came to a stop. At the side of the driveway where the front lawn would have been was a SOLD sign. This too was a foreign word to the family and so no one thought a thing about it. They all headed towards the modest all brick two story house. JD's sister opened the door and once everyone was in the house she said "Welcome to your new home"

Well this is what would be called a surprise. But it was far, far beyond that. Kicking off their shoes, the family looked at the hardwood floors, the old solid wood door frames and the bits of real stained glass in the real wooden frames. The house felt warm and welcoming to the new immigrant family.

The front door opened up to the family room that led to the dining room that led to the kitchen. From the kitchen there was a door to the basement but that was saved for later. Heading up to the second floor was a narrow solid wood staircase covered in a black rubbery material and sure it creaked a little but that was part of the charm. There was no way of holding back the smiles, the laughter and the joy in this family. When the kids got up to the top of the stairs they immediately asked which was their room.

The upstairs contained three bedrooms. The master and two smaller bedrooms that were huge to these kids. This was a three bedroom one bathroom home with a small narrow yard and the driveway that extended from the sidewalk to the back leading to a small green and white wooden garage that ended in the backyard.

A backyard! JD thought to himself as he made his way north on Yonge street. Oh, how sweet that backyard was. Oh, how wonderful that day was when they were handed the keys to the house. The house was not a gift, it was not an outright "Here you are, we bought a house for you" type of surprise. This was a gift and a responsibility. JD's sister and husband made the deal and co-signed for the house with a down payment for the house… With JD and his wife also having jobs, it was up to them to make the payments and make a go of this life in Canada.

Also, at that time when you immigrated to Canada, JD's sister and her husband had to sign a document to say that the family that they sponsored to come to this great country would not be on social assistance for the next ten years.

That was the kind of help this family received upon entering this wonderful country named Canada. From here on, the wellbeing the prospering or lack thereof would be in the hands of JD and his wife. It was an incredibly generous offer and gift from JD's sister and brother in-law. There was no way the family could thank them enough for their generosity, their kindness and support. Yes, at one point they too were immigrants to Canada but without kids and in different times. Their story was also interesting and intriguing and they didn't have anyone in Canada to give them a hand up. So, for them to help family members was a pleasure.

The fact that a house like this would never have been achievable in Hungary. Knowing that this was a gift of such magnitude that they may never be able to thank JD's sister and her husband. In the empty house the family's footsteps echoed throughout. The dated wallpaper, the old feel of the house was evident and it must have been 30 to 40 years old back in 1978. The area was set for development in 1924, and that made sense. This house was older than its occupants and surely it had the warmth and confidence to take in this new immigrant family.

The house didn't echo with emptiness for long. The move in date was close and with only the suitcases from their arrival with them the house would have been rather sparse. As luck would have it they were surrounded by several generous and welcoming families who were also immigrants to this land. They were established immigrants who have settled and made a great life for themselves here. One was a doctor, one was a professor, others in sales and engineers.

JD's brother-in-law is an engineer, he worked for McDonald Douglas and helped design the wings for the DC-8, DC9 and DC10. The family doctor friend who became the family doctor and all these people who knew very well how it felt to be immigrants, chipped in to furnish the home with second hand, hand me down furniture. Everything in the house was second hand except the beds because they were manufactured at the small furniture factory where JD was learning the ropes of the furniture industry.

The neighbor on the north side of the 124 Bowie Avenue residence saw the family moving in. Since next day was garbage day, he had hauled his solid wood cabinet black and white television to the side of the curb that evening. He asked if they had a television as this one worked but he said the tube inside was not very good. The television took a few seconds to warm up and if you turned it on and turned it off it may not restart for about 5 minutes. A working television was better than nothing. So, the old television made its way into its new home where it served the family for years. A black and white solid wood encased old TV that was hooked up to an antenna somewhere on the outside of the house and it could still catch 30 stations or so. Moving in was a surreal experience.

When the final preparations were done, JD hugged the family and knew that he was well on his way to make a life for their family in this new and amazing country called Canada. Sleeping that night was impossible. New life, new adventures and all they had to do was work hard and make the payments on this house. They even ended up being gifted a silver 1976 Peugeot 504. It was a manual transmission French car that was built like a tank. There it was, all second hand, all gifted. The family was ready for a new life but not before celebrating their first Christmas on the farm where they first set foot.

This wasn't any Christmas; this was a miracle Christmas. This was an amazing experience for the family but mostly for the kids. JD's sister and husband were well off, and to be able to make the kids happy after 6 months of stress and years of planning was most important. It was the calm before the storm of fitting in and learning a new language and a new way of life. To get down to business and work hard, learn an incredible amount and be able to fend for yourself.

Interestingly nothing had changed for JD. He was still fending for himself. Partly by choice and partly by circumstance. Christmas came and went and celebrations were not worthwhile. Sometimes a candy cane could be found and sometimes an odd gift card but this was different.

That was hard work and providing, growing, expanding and moving forward with the willpower of a bull and the strength of a horse. The hard headedness of a fellow Communist comrade. There was something positive about the Communist life JD laughed a little as he made his way past the Tim Horton's.

This was not the same, this was survival and like before the choices he made were his. Unfortunately, this choice was handed to him, die or take the alternative. The big YB and its evil employees went on to live their lives in the lovely and very false brainwashed bubble that they lived in.

There was such anger each time JD remembered the YB. It would be a welcome Christmas gift if their stores went up in flames this Christmas. Terrible thoughts, but after being burned and pillaged, any normal person would feel some sort of anger. This being Christmas it was supposed to be filled with happy thoughts and back in 1978 it was all happy and positive thoughts.

Being on the farm with the sun shining and going outside with the dogs and wandering over 100 acres of sheer white landscape dotted with evergreens was mesmerizing. The reflection and brightness of the snow made it difficult to keep your eyes open. In the forest at the back between the naked trees, footprints could be seen from deer, coyotes and raccoons. The wildlife out here was wild, not just cats and dogs but real wildlife that JD's brother in-law sometimes hunted. Using a snowmobile to get around the property was a first-time experience and the Arctic Cat snowmobile was something no one in this family had seen. A machine that is made to travel on the snow with ease made it fun and exciting to get around the 100-acre property to check out the swamp, the forest and speed down the wide open previously harvested farm fields.

Spending hours outside in the winter with the dogs, making snowmen and digging tunnels in the snowbanks; were all new and interesting experiences and there was no way the kids would be the only ones having all the fun. Everyone joined in, for JD's sister and brother in-law it was also a unique experience. Having no kids of their own they had never spent such an extended time with kids. This was the beginning without an end this new experience for them. They too were surprised at the energy level of kids and the joy the little things like a tunnel in the snow can bring.

Watching kids laughing and smiling brings joy to any adult. JD and his wife were beyond words, they have never seen their kids so care free. Seeing this alone it was already worth the escape, if they can make a go of this and they can make this new world their home it was worth every ounce of effort and energy. Seeing your children happy gives you energy and strength. Watching them grow, prosper and develop is what every parent wants. The Christmas holidays and the leisure time before the hard work began, wasn't planned, but it all came together perfectly.

The kids were old enough to know that Santa Claus was not real. In Hungary it was Jesus Christ that delivered the presents, so this was a slight switch in the spirit of giving. In Hungary at the time the gifts were small and no matter how small they were they were welcomed. This Christmas Santa was sure to be extra special and bring extra gifts.

Since this was shaping up to be the most incredible Christmas ever in the history of this family all the giving should have been over with. A down payment on a house, the gifts to furnish the house and a car would have been plenty. But this Christmas was going to be super special for the kids. It will be a Christmas that JD and the family will cherish for the rest of their lives.

The Christmas tree was set up and decorated by JD's sister. She was always dressed to a T. Her nails, hair and makeup were always done perfectly. She dressed her part at work and knew how to act her part as well. Yet she was fun, funny and always ready to smile. Her attitude and personality was loved by the kids. She was always ready to be a little naughty and have fun. Her husband was much more reserved and had less of a smile and was a much more serious man. All this was a time of adjustment for everyone. Having two little rug rats around and in your life every weekend was unusual.

The tree was set up and ready to accept all the presents that could possibly fit under it. It is Hungarian tradition to celebrate Christmas Eve. In Canada it is tradition to open presents Christmas morning. This was one tradition that was not about to change. Christmas dinner was being prepared and because the family arrived early enough there was plenty of time to bake, cook and have the most amazing Christmas ever!

The tree was very big and tall, in an open concept living area with high ceilings. It had to be with all the presents being stuffed underneath. After finishing the traditional fish soup which was a Hungarian tradition along with duck and other Hungarian side dishes, the kids were eager to dig into dessert. The family enjoyed this meal and this time together tremendously. It was something new and exciting for everyone. The anxiousness from the kids could be seen and felt, waiting to run to the living room and find out what "Santa" brought them was all that was on their minds. While the kids wrapped up dessert in the dining room JD and his brother-in-law stuffed the dozens of presents under the tree. The place looked like a river of presents had flooded from under the tree.

Having a separate dining room, was a blessing and all the presents made it under the tree before the kids couldn't be contained any longer. There was a fire in the fireplace, several candles were already lit and of course the lights on the Christmas tree were on when the kids rushed in to be blown away by what they were seeing.

This tree had massive boxes under it. Two gigantic boxes with so many other small and medium size boxes that they had no idea what to expect when the names were going to be called out as to who and from who the presents were. What could possibly be in those boxes, the two large ones, they are huge, what could be so big? Questions the kids will never forget but were sure to get the answers to within minutes.

This was a memory that JD will never forget. Because at this moment he knew that his push and eagerness to come to Canada was worth it. This thought touched his soul to this very day. It melted his heart and gave him a reason to work his ass off and to show the people back home that he left for a reason. A better life for himself and his family.

When the kids dug into the presents everyone smiled and laughed. The one big box was a train set. It was a very, very large train set that needed a ton of room. The other box was a car racetrack that also needed a lot of room. These were big presents for big boys and big places. Among the presents were radio-controlled cars, clothes, Lego and smaller items that had the kids mesmerized. Some of the toys were not available in Hungary and for that matter maybe never even seen by the average person.

Explaining this to someone back in Hungary would have been impossible. There was no way that even photos could bring to life the excitement in the room and the feeling of warmth from the fireplace. As all the wrapping paper was burned the fire roared with massive flames and gave off heat at an alarming rate. When the kids were somewhat settled the two dogs were brought in and they too were given presents, a pack of hot-dogs each. While this was unusual it was what it was. Let everyone be happy, merry and giving at Christmas.

Spending these days on the street meant that one hoped and many begged for the kindness of others. These days are different, wages are lower, the focus has shifted to phones, social media and the latest tweet from that "bellowing" Trump character. Joy today was finding a half -eaten burger and hoped it had not gone cold. Joy today was a cup of coffee from Tim Hortons and this made JD think.

Reflections:

Admittedly we had help from my Uncle Joe and my Aunt Livia. Though Aunt Livia's health is not so great nowadays and Uncle Joe takes care of her as much as he can, the memories with them are wonderful. Growing up partly on a large 100-acre farm and having the freedom to roam, play and explore are things not available to everyone these days.

Having them in our lives is wonderful. While there are many great memories, I will only touch on two.

Aunt Livia and I went snowmobiling on a sunny day. In the vast open field, she didn't see the snowdrift and we hit it at considerable speed.

We both flew off the snowmobile and in her panic, she reached around to grab me. In the process, she pulled her groin so bad she could hardly walk for a week. We both looked at each other and once we realized we were ok, we looked at the snowmobile that had kept going for about 200 meters before it came to stop at the farm fence. Then there is my Uncle, oh Uncle Joe… Aunt Livia was easy to get used to. Uncle Joe always seemed distant and despite having been a teacher he was not as approachable. I do remember working with him or helping him do electrical work. Uncle Joe always made things interesting. He followed the news and kept up to date on most events. Connecting with him on a personal level was never easy.

As he got older, he too needed help here and there, interactions got much easier. Besides Aunt Livia was always there to be the buffer if things were getting out of hand.

Chapter 6. Hamster wheels

What is really important in our lives? Looking to the past many of us have worried and still worry about the future. Today the only thing JD worries about is having enough to survive today, tomorrow no longer matters.
Today he will have a few generous people look at him and donate a few cents or a few dollars. There will also be a few people who will give him dirty disgusted looks. All he needs to worry about is getting through the day, sleeping through the night and only then does he worry about the next day.
It's not easy to live like that. Most of us worry about our investments, our kids, our parents and our jobs. To shed that way of thinking is nearly impossible. We worry about mortgage payments, cell phone bills and subscriptions that come up for renewal and car payments that must be made.
Running on a hamster wheel is what society has trained us to do, we all do it. We knowingly run and run until we die; or have a breakdown. Only then do we slow down.
Looking back on the many Christmases and gifts that brought so much joy, albeit expensive joy. Today the gift of waking up is enough. No need to have the newest toy or cell phone.

So, the days that we feel are so valuable and so extremely important are not so important. The new phone, car, that purse or jacket are all eye candy and they feed our sweet tooth to the point of driving us to mental instability. The rise of mental illness and stress levels can be directly attributed to the rise of social media and anxiety.
Body image issues, girls with curly hair wanting straight hair and Asians stressing over skin whitening creams. These are all advertiser driven anxiety inducing weapons of personal destruction that people in the know have fed us. They have given us the carrot; they have given us the hook line and sinker and we fall for it every single time. They know how to press the buttons, from the young to the old we all know what triggers us and yet we let them. Have another spoonful of hate, another helping of the Kardashians and maybe another glass of whiskey because that is how you are choosing to destroy yourself. Let's not forget the pain, oh yes, the pain that we live with. In our heads, our bodies and the prescriptions we must have. The kickbacks for the doctors for stuffing opioid and oxycontin laden painkillers into us, because someone told them it works the best to ease the pain.

To all the people on the wheel, get off and take a look around.

This is a wonderful outlook on life. When you have nothing, you realize that there were and are so many things in life that you never needed but wanted. The things you never wanted but kind of felt you were obligated to have. To upgrade that phone even though you never used half its features in the first place, but your girlfriend upgraded so you need to as well. This was evident in everyday life. We all want to lose weight but we all know we eat too much because the food is there. It's sitting there calling out,
"Eat me, eat me! You paid for me; you can't leave me on the plate. Eat me and stuff me in your mouth even though you are full."
Today JD may have a coffee and a sandwich of sorts, maybe a snack and some water and he will be alright. He may not be the healthiest person on the planet, but he is not obese that's for sure. Even in this state he is most likely healthier than millions of people on the planet. He lives without the stress of everyday life, he lives without burden. What he lives with is regret and wishing for that Hot Tub Time Machine to appear so he could go back and fix a single bad decision…

"Making decisions with your pride in mind and the way you think others will see you is wrong."

"This goes for the phone, the meal, the car, the drink, the ring, the clothes and the oversized house you are about to purchase."

So, the most wonderful Christmas ever… Was that allowed? Would that be alright to splurge and set an example that all this makes sense? No, it does not and it does not make sense but we will all make exceptions. That Gucci watch or the Christian Dior purse for $10,000 does that make sense? If you have millions in the bank and you get that money back in a week or two sure it will make little difference to you. But if you are saving up for a $500 purse or a $1000 watch it's not for you.

Reaching deep into his pocket, JD pulls out enough change for a tea and when he orders it he feels a little bit of satisfaction. It's as if he is having his own mini Christmas morning, but this is a regular morning. Being grateful for the little bit of warmth and imagining the warmth of the fireplace and the old house when they first moved in. The importance being placed on everything but our personal well-being is ruining society.

As the tea touched JD's lips and the sweetness of the sugar and milk touched his taste buds it gave JD the warmth and satisfaction he needed to get on with the rest of the day. It made him forget about the regrets in his life, the ones he was really bitter about and the ones he thinks of often. The ones that make him angry and relives the days of the tortuous YB web that he and his family got tangled in. For now, the tea relieves the pain of the old deep open wound.

Back then JD and his family didn't know that their lives too would end up on the hamster wheel. It didn't seem possible or even plausible and the thought of such things would never ever cross the minds of people working hard and trying to get by.

As the days passed, the new house took shape and the family finished off the holidays with school registrations and exploring the neighborhood. Meeting the generous neighbors was also nice even though communication was held to a bare minimum. In the evenings, the family would gather and watch some television in hopes of picking up more of the language. The kids were nervous about going to school. They had never been confronted by such change. JD and his wife were also nervous but it was different for them. For them it was learn what you need to learn so you keep the job that was given to you and work hard. Work hard and work harder so you can make this massive adjustment and make money to buy food and provide for the children. This was more than motivation for the parents. This was a must, they had received so much more help than others, that they had something to live up to.

There were no written expectations but there was the looming possibility of failure and that failure could absolutely never happen. There was too much pride and too much at stake. They have worked so hard and planned so well that there was no way they could fail. Learning English, learning new jobs and learning a brand new way of living, shopping and conducting yourself. So much learning at the age of 33 and so much more education to come.

Getting on with daily life in the new country was a big learning curve. JD's goal was to learn the furniture trade inside and out. From cutting to sewing, frame making, springing, preparation and upholstery. Even the packaging and shipping had to be included, after all the process was not finished until it was in the customer's home.

Little did JD know that learning the basics of any business should begin the way he was. Learning as an apprentice from the ground up was the way to begin. Learning how to cut a piece of fabric was a simple thing. But having industrial size scissors in your hand and cutting expensive fabrics was serious learning. Slowly being trusted to cut with an industrial cutter that had a blade height of 10 centimeters that would slice your fingers or hand off in a split second was very serious.

All this came easily to JD, he was eager to learn and prove himself. During lunch and breaks he never waited around. He finished and walked the factory, inspecting, watching and taking in the process of furniture, mattress and finishing. He was a sponge, he absorbed everything. Slowly with determination he began to understand, and the knowledge sank in quickly because he was eager to learn. This was all the practical aspect, the hands-on doer approach that he needed to learn for manufacturing.

On the weekends, he came in with the kids. It was a time to learn even more. Check things out and learn the different stages of production as people left things half prepared and half finished. The kids were "allowed" to sweep and learn as they went through the plant. It was unknown to them but being exposed to this at the age of

7 and 10 they too were learning. Throwing long fluorescent light bulbs from the second floor woodshop was not smart or safe, but it was fun for the kids. At the end of a fun Saturday the kids would hear the coffee truck buzzer and they would eagerly await the payment for the day, hot honey buns off the coffee truck. This was a rare treat that stuck around for a long time.

In the meantime, JD's wife was learning English as fast as she could at The Bay. Her environment in the office was much more personal. With many other women around and the office being inside one of the Hudson Bay stores, it made her day more interactive. Dealing with numbers during work was fine, they spoke an international language but learning from co-workers was fantastic and so she picked up the language much quicker than JD.

While the common goal was the same, their daily goals were different. JD wanted to learn everything and do more. His wife wanted to do her job well to keep her job and pick up the language as fast as she could. This worked out and as the days and weeks passed, they both flourished at work. They didn't have much, but they had a hard-working family that was making a go of it and that is what mattered.

The kids went to school at West Fairbank Memorial. It was within walking distance. No bus routes were needed, and the two kids went to the same school. They went in the morning, came home for lunch and went back after lunch. Today, having kids at home alone at the age of 7 and 10 would most likely be looked upon as child neglect and the next-door neighbor would call child services, the cops, the local newspaper and post about it on Instagram and Facebook. Back in 1978 that turned over to 1979 it was normal. The kids had keys to get in the house, they had lunch prepared in the form of a sandwich or they ate cereal. The kids lived off of cereal back then.

It was the time of cartoons, cereal, TV dinners and episodes of Gilligan's Island, The Six Million Dollar Man after school and the Flintstones during the lunch time at home.

Not sure if it is a shame that we do not raise our children that way anymore or if today's way is better. No matter, JD and his wife didn't have a choice and the kids understood that they could not have a stay-at-home mom. The kids didn't need to be babysat, they were mature and of all the days at home nothing ever happened that would have caused their parents to be worried and that was great for their piece of mind. It let them focus on providing and by providing they were taking care of the kids. Slowly the family was getting things in order.

There were very lean times though, times when certain expenses exceeded the income of the hard-working family. Times when the kids had holes in their shoes, times when new pants or new shirts and underwear had to wait. Kids are kids, they played soccer and took part in extracurricular activities after school such as house league soccer, baseball. All this was causing wear and tear on the clothes and shoes and of course these active kids had to be fed.

This forced mom and dad to work harder. They had to make more money and so JD and his wife made do with what they had. Being an accountant, JD's wife was good with money. Slowly she managed to save and they made a plan. Buy a van and they would do deliveries on the weekend instead of the furniture company hiring an outside firm. They would hire them to deliver the finished goods. Anything from mattresses to sofa beds or bunk beds. This extra income helped the family but also left the kids home alone longer.

Many times, mom would ask them to prepare and mix the hamburger meat; or put things in the oven. These were gigantic responsibilities for the kids. This was before the time of the electronic babysitters. No iPads, X-box, and PlayStation consoles. This was a time of Lego, racetrack and train sets. This was a time to create. Keeping themselves occupied by making paper airplanes, boats and being creative. A time of playing with matchboxes on the old cast iron tub that came with the old house. Or actually go outside and ride a bicycle or play basketball.

An interesting thing happened when JD and his wife began to deliver furniture. Many customers began asking for their furniture to be recovered, reupholstered and asking for new foam cushions for their existing furniture. This led to a spark in the entrepreneurial spirit that JD and his wife never knew existed within them. They didn't know how to reupholster a sofa or how to price out the work even if they did take on the work but now the spark was there.

As kids this was super embarrassing… Having your mom and dad pick up a couch from the side of the road that was left for the garbage collectors and put it in the van so they could take it home and practice on it was embarrassing. To mom and dad this was homework and along with the homework came experience and more learning that they were now adapting to. How long does it take to take something apart, how did it come apart and how can I put it back together?

Whether they knew it or not at the time they were learning the skills of costing things out, preparing cost sheets and figuring out how to make a buck on their own. This was learning, working and growing as a form of survival, as well as a form of income. Anything JD and his wife didn't know they could find out from the factory or ask their brother in-law. But that was kept to a minimum, they wanted to make it on their own. Slowly JD and his wife picked up customers and private cash business on the side. This made life much easier and eventually with hard work comes luck and with luck came opportunities.

One day a friend of the family offered a small business to JD and his wife. He was an old salesman that sold to hardware stores in his retirement. He was going to retire from his retirement business and offered the small business to JD and his wife. This little business was $150 back in 1979, the equivalent of about $600 today. He would remain on as a salesman and slowly hand over the business to JD and his wife. For the $150, they would get 150 customers in and around Toronto and as time went on and they got the hang of things the old retired friend would hand over the business completely.

The other things that came with the business was the one style, one color small carpenter apron with a pattern and samples of the buckles, rivets. A small riveting machine and a sewing machine were all part of the deal.

There was a hiccup in the plan, neither JD nor his wife knew how to sew. This didn't stop them from saying yes to a business that they knew nothing about. But isn't that the entrepreneurial spirit? Never say no to an opportunity, never give up, learn, work hard and figure it out. With very little experience, the family took on the business. JD and his wife involved the kids and were open with them. With laying out $150 meant they had to save, $150 was a whole lot of money and the kids would have to not ask for anything for a while. They would also have to chip in and help.

This expectation does not or would not fly with most North American children these days. In Europe and most Asian countries it does. As the world's concern about child labor grows, most people don't understand that there is a difference between forced labor of any kind, forced labor of children and the labor of the children who to this day guide traffic, collect garbage and furniture on the streets of Jakarta, India, Africa and the like.

The purchase of a business for $150 and beginning to manufacture a single style of apron was the undertaking of a lifetime. Trusting someone to hand you a way into the future that you would never in a million years, dream of. There goes the time machine again, if only you could jump forward and check how this would play out. JD's wife learned to sew and JD learned how to cut, make the patterns and so on to be able to produce this little apron.

This is where the kids came into play. No arguments about kids working at the age of 7 and 10. They were helping the family to make a living. Homework came first, then helping mom and dad. This was not work, this was helping and working for a living. Knowing and understanding that if we get this order and that order out, we can put food on the table, and we can all enjoy life and make small improvements to our lives. This was not child labor and this was not forced labor. This was an immigrant family who were making a go of it and learning the business on the fly from the old salesman.

While he was a family friend, he was a businessman. An old Hungarian Jew that taught JD the ways of the business. JD and his family were not Jewish, but the teachings of the wonderful old man were never forgotten. After being slowly introduced to the many customers JD did something that the old man had grown tired of.

He listened… JD listened to the customers. They wanted different styles and colors. Grey was old and the one style was old. They wanted more. The customers wanted more, and JD and his wife delivered. Slowly new styles and colors emerged from the basement at 124 Bowie Avenue.

A true business was born and the family began to take on more and more business while working in an office and a furniture factory. JD and his wife did deliveries, the kids riveted and pulled buckles on to the aprons. The kids took apart furniture that was to be reupholstered and helped where they could to prepare the foam. Slowly the little basement grew. The weak electric staple gun was replaced with a pneumatic one. The piece of plywood and wood horses that was used as a cutting table had been replaced with a ping-pong table. This made for a rough ping-pong table but made a wonderful cutting table.

Slowly the business grew and as things were picking up and the family was starting to feel secure, life happened. Life happened, and the ever so slightly thriving family would face decisions and circumstances that they never thought they would need to face. While things always look good from the outside, it's the raw guts of the business you rarely see. Gerard Bedding was to close. JD didn't have enough experience to see that the company was slowly being robbed blind by employees. JD didn't know that the company was bleeding money and that his brother-in-law who was an engineer by trade may have missed a few things in the production world.

So, the small furniture company was forced to declare bankruptcy. The people that helped to realize the dream of coming to Canada and signing papers that this family would not be seeking social assistance and government help for 10 long years were now in hardship as well. This was a dreadful situation. The family was learning English and the kids picked up the language quickly, but the parents were busy working and the language skills were still developing. Find a new job? How? Who would hire them? They were faced with real immigration problems and this was a very uncomfortable feeling. Asking for help from anyone would have been a sign of complete failure.

"Failure was not an option" and JD and his wife had to figure out how to make ends meet."

Reflections:

Stop and smell the roses... Take a moment out of your day to breathe, relax and understand where you are going and why? Why do you do what you do? How are you going about doing it? What are you sacrificing? Is it worth sacrificing for?
Knowing what I know today, knowing what we know today, would we have done things differently? Absolutely we would have, but we can't go back.
Taking what I have learned and going through the experience that we unfortunately lived through; it makes me think of the many people who sacrifice their lives, families and happiness. Why do they do the things they do? What is the motivation?
Is it greed? Is it the drive, the excitement of the next deal? Yes, it's in most of us to have more, do more and get more done. The fear of not having enough, the drive to want more is how we ended up in business in the first place.
But stop... ask yourself... Why am I doing this? Am I hurting anyone in the process? When is enough, enough? At some point, enough is enough and after that it's a stretch for the next milestone, a sacrifice for the next plateau. As people in business, we knew we had to do better, be more efficient and make that next deal. To show up the next morning and fight the fight so we can achieve what we think we want to achieve. Now, I look back and wonder, I often wonder what I would do different and each time it's the same conclusion. It's not what I would do differently but what have I learned from all the crap that we went through and how I will try to make wiser choices going forward.
That's the point here... The future is in your hands, choose wisely.

Chapter 7. Get up, stand up, start again

One thing JD knew about life, from being in the army, playing soccer semi-professionally and the escape itself was to never give up. Never lay down and never surrender. These were not options and the kids learned this, they knew the situation. JD and his wife always shared what they had or didn't have. They shared the financial part of life as well because the kids needed to understand why they cannot get all the things the other kids may have had.
The loss of income, the loss of a job brought immense problems to the family. The loss of income meant the loss of everything. The little business was not strong enough to sustain a family of four and there was no knowledge of growing it fast enough.

"The situation was dire, JD and his wife never let on to the kids how bad it was until many, many years later. For now, this one problem had to be kept to the adults and would not be shared."

It was a typical problem for an immigrant, looking for a job without speaking English fluently and without guidance on how and what to do. Where do you look for a new job? This part was missed by the family because the job part was taken care of upon arrival. They were super lucky to have these big problems taken care of. But now, they were faced with a very typical immigrant concern.

At the same time JD's wife was moved to part time at The Bay. It was a double tragedy but one that came with perfect timing to test the family and test the strength of their relationship. This was a test of a marriage and the test of how strong this family was.

It was time to further tighten the belt that was already pretty darn tight. All unnecessary spending was put on hold. Little did they know at the time but these were lessons in not only life but running a business. This was learning on the job and cutting spending, cost cutting in all departments and an accountant's nightmare to stretch every penny, to account for every penny spent and pay the right bills at the right time. Don't pay this for 5 more days, pay that a few days late. The phone bill would be last, the mortgage would be first and the electrical and oil bill would and could wait till early next week. Oh damn, we need money for gas, yes that would need to come first but only put in 5 dollars.

Wait, the insurance bill came for the car, the younger son has a birthday, we need to get him something.

The life they were building was coming to an end. The glory of escape was coming full circle to an amazing crash landing. It was a full court press on getting orders in and out and picking up as much reupholstery business as possible.

While the small business was registered, another name was added to the name in the form of "upholstery" Every chance JD and his wife had they passed out business cards in hopes of landing another customer. This was as close to knocking on doors for business as it came.

As with all things perseverance and life lessons come and go. With a few dollars in their bank account and not knowing how to make ends meet JD took a chance.

While his grasp and understanding of the English language was marginal he picked up the Toronto Sun newspaper and saw an ad for the cutting room at Bauhaus Furniture.

Having thick skin, he decided to go and apply for the job right there and then in person. These were different days and in many ways JD was a different person. A man with nothing to lose and everything to gain. When you have nothing, you have nothing to lose. While this was not the case, the house, two cars would need to go, so there was a loss to be had but it was all or nothing.

When JD arrived at Bauhaus, he had no idea at the size of the place. Several hundred thousand square feet of production and warehouse space pumping out several hundred pieces of furniture a day. Not several pieces like Gerard Bedding.

This was a shock to JD. It was before the time of the internet. It was not a place you could check out online and read about. This was the old days, a phone number and a map in hand, JD arrived at this great production monster that ate raw material and spit out truck loads upon truckloads of furniture in a day with hundreds of employees. The sheer numbers were unknown to JD, the extent of the job was unknown to JD. He went in with as much confidence as he had or pretended to have and tried not to be totally overcome by the size and scope of this behemoth manufacturing machine.

Chain driven, in ground pulley system for the carts that had the furniture frames on it. Springing and preparation and upholstery to finishing and packaging and forklifts running back and forth. The number of people in the plant looked like a colony of ants and while he had no idea about the role of each person, the machine was pumping out goods by the truckload.

There was no way of understanding this overwhelming sight of production in a matter of moments. He was led to the person in charge and headed in for the interview. This was so out of the ordinary, a man who barely spoke English, applying for a skilled job that he could do. How and what he was expected to do, not knowing before he walked in how big this place was, well that was another story.

After being told his duties and understanding most of what was being said it came down to the wages. JD knew that he was underpaid at the previous job. Underpaid was a little harsh because he was paid but not paid upward to the knowledge that he now possessed. It didn't matter because that job was gone and JD decided to go for broke. He asked for one and a half times of what he was making earlier at Gerard Bedding.

That night when JD arrived home, he came in with a bucket of KFC. His wife nearly killed him and threw him out of the house. But this was no time for anger, this was a time for celebration as not only did they hire him at what he thought was a ludicrous amount of money, but he was to start right away. JD's thick skin paid off, the good old Jewish businessman that taught him to go in and do cold calling on potential customers paid off. He learned well and the education paid off. Breathing a massive sigh of relief, the family enjoyed the best meal ever.

"This was a lesson, not all business will survive and not all businesses will succeed."

Even successful businesses can go through times of drought and distress. How the business reacts to the distress and how its leaders react to the problems they face will determine its course.
The financial strength, the business's past performance and cash on hand will also determine how long it can hold on. Other possible scenario's; a hard-hitting quality issue or the company is being directed by their largest customer, after putting all of their eggs in one basket. These things also play a large role in the outcome.
After dodging a bullet, the family was able to breathe again and get on with growing this little business and focusing on getting back on track with life. JD's wife learned to sew and do other tasks that the small business required. Balancing the books and keeping track of the profit and loss was a small and easy task. All the government taxes and filings were handled for the time being by the old Jewish friend of the family.
Learning the ropes from the ground up. The family was working, learning and growing together. There was closeness because of communication and openness. There was strength, as the little business grew and each family member developed a responsibility. The younger son was pulling buckles onto the aprons, the older son was putting rivets in and they took turns on helping JD with laying out fabric and marking patterns on the fabric while mom learned to sew and operate a sewing machine.
Everyone was learning, from registering a business, to invoicing and filing of paperwork. This was learning as you go. Learning the job and doing the job at the same time. Doing your regular job at Bauhaus, The Bay and working late into the night each day to keep the small business customers happy.
The little 4-person company flourished, several different styles of aprons were born, and a few colors expanded the collection. Deliveries were made on the weekends, the van loaded up with aprons and the reupholstered pieces that were done in between regular work and sleep. The small business had 150 customers that needed to be serviced, visited and on occasion deliveries were made early in the mornings or late at night. Even before and after work time was used as efficiently as possible.

Time management skills were also being put to good use. All aspects of things you would be taught in school were used. Secondary education on a very different level. One was a must, it was the survival of the family. Profits were made but most of that was reinvested for raw materials. Since the family didn't know many suppliers it was a blessing to work in the furniture field. Slowly other suppliers were found for less expensive thread, fabric and new fabrics.
Once again, this was a lesson learned, profit margins increased. And there was a little more breathing room. All this education was taking place on the fly and the family was learning the ropes of business while working regular jobs.
In the meantime, life continued… Just as it does for JD. It's the same on the streets and in real life, survival is the utmost important thing. These lessons of survival were engraved into JD's head.

There was no giving up.
There was no surrender.
Can't let them win.

This was also the competitive edge that was carved in stone in the army and in playing sports.

Train, play hard and win.

This is a lesson from long ago. JD and the family not only stayed afloat but flourished. They got stronger, smarter and made money at the same time. JD began coaching soccer part time while working two jobs. It seemed insane but once more, you make time for the things that are important in your life.
No one that wants to spend time with you will say they are too busy. No one that wants to meet you will refuse to meet you. It's the same for dating, business or any other aspect of your life. People may postpone, shit happens and things come up in life that you can't avoid. A car breaks down, an appointment cancelled or rescheduled. Major disasters can happen at work but the person that wants to make time for something or someone… will.
Fill your surroundings and friends list with those people.
The soccer aspect grew in the family as both kids got into sports and that made life more hectic but this was real life. This was the life that

they came here for. Where you can work hard, play hard and make a living. Make a living and make a better living and put money in your pocket.

All this time, the family had been adjusting. The new job for JD turned out to be an amazing move. It was the break that was needed and deserved. JD's wife learned to sew, invoice, balance the accounts and slowly the small business had a big decision to make. There was not enough business to keep JD's wife home full time, not yet, but it was beginning to grow to an extent that it was going to be a decision that will need to be looked at.

The family adjusted and put in more effort on the weekends to push out orders. They also made time to go to the farm on the weekends, even if it was just for a few hours and not staying over. These small breaks were important. The kids got out and the family had a break. Work/Life balance… We preach that all the time.

JD's sister and brother in-law also adjusted to their new reality. Another lesson learned and they learned it much later in life. JD's brother in-law went to Humber College and became a teacher. He had all the qualifications as an engineer. He now didn't have to run the business but had to look after students and his classroom. JD's sister continued to work at The Bay.

There was always something to do on the farm. The large lawn, the pool, gardening and the vegetable garden. The massive barn always needed something fixed. A door, a window, the tractor needed maintenance and the garden had to be looked after, cleaned and the vegetables collected.

This became a hobby and while it was not directly business related all this was lessons in planning. Planting, nourishing, taking care, checking on the progress and collecting the goods. These were also lessons for the kids. Some old-world lessons were taught in the fields when strawberries were picked, and made into jam. When the pickles were pickled and sealed in jars and put away for the winter. When the peppers and peas were cleaned and frozen and put away for later. These were old world Hungarian traditions that JD and his wife learned from their parents. They learned the old traditional ways of making sausage and pickling things. This was also a way of saving money, make it yourself and you know it's fresh, it's good and your little garden worked for you while you took care of it all summer.

Gardening and pickling foods also brought the family together. After the hard work, there was amazing barbecues and incredible sunny days by the pool, playing soccer and playing with the dogs. The family was coming together and enjoying the first summer in Canada. Where the once snow-covered landscape was, wonderful green hills and valleys of the countryside emerged. Canada was very different in the summer. Many uneducated people south of the border believe that Canada is a snow-covered country all year round. They are often surprised that we do not all live in igloos and we do not hunt and fish all the time and that we do not all own and ride snowmobiles 365 days a year.

Canada is cold in the winter and very hot in the summer. So, the pool and the breeze in the countryside was a fantastic escape. The meals and laughter shared by the family was something to be cherished. The family learned a great deal. They both had a fall down, get back up again type of year. It was the first full year in Canada and they have already learned and adjusted to new things and new ways of life. One part of the family was older, and they needed to make a shift in a new direction. The other part of the family was still a fish out of water but learning to swim even if it was against the tide sometimes.

This made the family proud. This gave strength to each member of the family and during the days at the farm, friends and family would gather. Eventually they all settled into weekend gathering and everyone made time to come, eat and play cards, swim and enjoy each other's company.

This was a wonderful environment for the kids. They had a large group of people to call family even though they left most family members behind. The Canadian family were the very same people who donated clothes, furniture, pots and pans to the family. They were also close friends, who were always curious on how things were developing for the new arrivals. They were always kept up to date by JD's sister. She was very proud of her brother and how he and his family prospered in this new environment. How they were truly making a go of it despite slight setbacks.

Many people immigrate to a new country but not all succeed. Many come and expect a handout and wonder why they didn't succeed or why they didn't manage to achieve the American dream. When you land in this great country or any other, there is still an awful lot of hard work that is needed. Not all will have family businesses. Not all will be successful and rich, but if you put effort into your job and don't spend your money on useless things you will succeed. You will be able to succeed at anything if you keep plugging away, keep learning and make adjustments in your life along the way.

With each weekend, the family learned the value of friendship and family. Despite the crazy amount of effort and work, they made time for soccer and the weekend. Soon the little business that could, did and managed to grow. This business was a basement industry. It took up no more than a few hundred square feet and it needed a little more room for fabrics and raw materials. The idea of buying more at a lower cost and paying COD for things was also learned. These were baby steps. But some of these steps required room for stock and room to store goods.

Some customers ordered the same thing every month. Bell Hardware was such a customer. 320 aprons every month. It was worth cutting a thousand at a time and making them all at once, becoming more efficient. The family didn't know it but they were making smart business decisions in efficiency and cost reduction. This would benefit the company in the years to come.

Keep in mind that this family had arrived a year and a bit before and learned all this on their own with little guidance. They didn't go to business school; they didn't take online courses, nor did they have background in business management. This was all learned on the fly.

Soon they knew that if things kept up expansion would be needed. But survival came first, so for now the little basement with the ping-pong table and the one sewing machine and that small hand operated riveting machine will need to stay where it is.

Reflections:

Survival is key. No matter what, no matter how, when you fall down get back up and keep going. Contrary to the previous chapter, there are times when you need to be humble and when to go and fight and work as hard as you can. Being a fighter is what brought my dad this far. Being a strong family and always sticking together is what brought this family success. Knowing when to stop was not something any of us knew how to do. All we knew was how to work hard.

We all learned on the job and those little lessons in life brought us a very different type of education. Business planning, financial planning and such were not in our vocabulary but we were doing it on a day to day basis.

My mom would do financial planning and forecast how things would look in a week or a month. She was a financial controller and knew what we could and could not spend. These are lessons they do not teach in schools. Planning went into everything and to be as efficient as possible in all things was key. All this trickled down to lessons that we would use in production in the later years.

Many times, fresh out of university students that worked for the great Yellow and Blue would come with brilliant ideas on how to do things and we would say:

"Please, we have been doing that since were running the business from our basement."

Goes to show you that just because you finished university it doesn't mean that you are smart, but you can be if you learn a little more.

Chapter 8. Kids being kids

While the kids were involved in all aspects of the business, they were also involved in all aspects of the household. Mom was busy with her part time work at The Bay, her sewing in the basement and dad worked full time at Bauhaus and part time at home in the basement.
The kids were asked to vacuum, clean up and do some of the chores around the house that mom didn't have time to do. For many kids this would not be possible. Their parents would not be able to make them understand why this is important. Doing the little things like cleaning and tidying up was a great help for mom. She would call ahead and have the kids mix the burger meat or take out the small Hibachi barbecue that the hot dogs would constantly roll off of. Prepare the charcoal and get it ready for dad to barbecue so that dad could get the chicken and burgers ready.
All this added up to being more mature kids than their ages indicated. The youngest was pulling on belt buckles and helping with layouts. These are tasks that require a sense of understanding. It was not fun; it was not exciting but having the responsibility and understanding at such a young age was incredible. The family was hard working and so the kids picked up the traits and learned from the decisions and from the examples that their parents were giving. It was not easy to be kids with a family business. Things were generally rushed and having the business in the basement meant that

"to go to work" meant you going to the basement. Often taking an apple to mom and making her a coffee meant the world to her. Coffee was easy, one spoon of Nescafe instant coffee and add boiling water. Mom liked her coffee black and cold. She didn't mind it going cold beside her sewing machine and sipping it a little bit at a time. She often had an apple beside her and she worked away at the sewing machine like a pro.

Memories of the good old days filled JD's head. Little bits and pieces often came back to him when he let his mind wander. He didn't like taking too many trips too far back in time. They were painful, they were full of endearing memories that he needed to leave where they were. Knowing they were safely stacked away on a shelf, they were classified with good memory inventory labels. Reliving the memories during this time was hard for JD. Tears often filled his eyes and his heart felt as if it was being torn to shreds by touching on certain parts of the past. But this story had to be told he felt before it was too late. Before all the details slowly vanished from inventory. Some of the fondest memories in this story were the summers the kids had. While they worked and helped with the business and the chores, there were amazing times that were most likely the story of many at the time and the story of few for the present time. These two kids were still part of the generation that grew up in a very old fashioned way. By old fashioned way it is not meant as pioneers. However, they still experienced village life in Hungary where there was no running water, but there was outhouses and horse drawn carriages.

They experienced life in the Communist world and understood the restrictions to a degree. They escaped from a world that was restrictive ending up in a free world on a farm and a house in Toronto.

The farm was located in Caledon at the north west corner of Kennedy Road and Beechgrove Sideroad. Looking at it now on Google maps, the location is overgrown with huge trees. As much as JD would love to see it, he also wants to leave it as is and avoid disappointment by revisiting the past. But back then when the family went out to the farm, the kids were free. They were free to roam the 100 acres with the dogs following and taking off then returning as they felt.

The traffic on Kennedy Road was little to nonexistent. It was a dirt road that intersected other dirt roads. Most cars took Airport Road and Highway 10 up to Highway 9 and headed to Orangeville, so Kennedy Road was not used much except by the drivers who were drinking and wanted to avoid the cops.

The little-known unadvertised fact about Kennedy Road was that there was a money-making opportunity. The kids knew that beer bottles were returnable. They went for walks and hopped in the roadside ditch and came back with a few bottles until the entrepreneurial spirit struck and they went out collecting beer bottles by the bags. The more they walked the more they got and so on a weekend a few dollars were to be made by heading out on the road and taking advantage of drinking and driving. This is by no means making light of drinking and driving but it was a money-making opportunity. While most of the money the family made went to a common account this was money for the kids.

Whatever money the kids made or had because of the beer bottles was theirs to split. These weekend excursions were bonding time for the brothers. Along the way they would see deer and farm animals as well as get an amazing amount of exercise. The long summer days were spent outside, the parents never worried about things such as being kidnapped or taken away. No smart phones to distract the kids or to keep in touch with. The kids were out and when their stomachs couldn't bear the hunger or they were thirsty beyond belief and the bags were full of beer bottles they headed home.

Before they dropped the bags of bottles off they always had a few things they needed to hide. Along with the bottles there were plenty of adult magazines that the kids would come across. These were the bonus items that the kids would gather on the long stretches of open road. Most magazines were wet and in the ditch but on occasion some pristine ones could be found and they were worth hiding in the big old century barn.

This particular part of Kennedy Road had a very small airport that was a few kilometers up from the farm. Always a good walk, and the kids got to see airplanes taking off and landing. The little airport is gone today, but just up the road on google maps it goes by the name of Skywood Park. There the two strips are still visible even though the asphalt, concrete and building are gone. That small airport was to be a place where cottagers could fly into and out of. Now this area is residential and farms while cottage country is way up past this area in Muskoka.

A small credit that does belong to this area is that Police Academy, the first one and supposedly one of the Rambo movies was shot here. In Police Academy the farm is visible from the hot air balloon scene. While the Rambo scenes are not for sure, all the kids knew is that one day on the way past, the burned-out carcasses of the planes and helicopters were visible and explorable.

This was a kids dream come true. Rummaging through exposed reels of film and burned out planes. Climbing in and on the burned out aircrafts was incredible fun. This also meant that dreams of the small airport growing were gone.

Another dream was up in smoke, but the kids had the most amazing time and could go back to the place on weekends and when time permitted. Since this was the days of the gadget free era no record of these outings was documented. These memories were ones that are kept in a safe place as warm memories of the past by the kids. These wonderful and amazingly long summer days were spent exploring and enjoying the things most kids are not encouraged to do.

On occasion a car came by, the dogs knew to move out of the way, the drivers slowed down and cared about the kids and knew about the country life. Different times indeed. When the kids were not out and about; they were flying a kite, swimming, or throwing a Frisbee, baseball or kicking a soccer ball.

All these things are now taken over by gaming consoles and smartphones. Nothing wrong with these gadgets. These kids ended up with them too when they came out. But the little money they collected from the beer bottle sales went to the really fun entertainment of the time.

At the corner of Dufferin and Ronald Avenue was a donut shop. Surprisingly it is an empty parking lot now, but at the time it was a donut shop that housed the most technologically advanced video games. It was not an arcade but it had Space Invaders, Galaga and Centipede and other games that was the start of all the gaming that is enjoyed by billions on earth.

Along with the video games, the occasional donut could be bought. Since things were pennies back then, the collection of a few dollars on the weekend made for great fun for the kids. It was cheap entertainment and a little bit of splurging in a household where every penny was counted for many, many years. These little things made the otherwise hard work fun. This generation of adults will remember the emergence of the Pac-man, Frogger, Donkey Kong,

Mario Bros, Street Fighter, Duck Hunt, Pole Position and many others that came later.

The background music in the donut shop spun out tunes from the late seventies to the early eighties. The Rolling Stones, AC/DC, Ozzy Osbourn, REO Speedwagon, Rod Stuart, Def Leppard, The Scorpions, Pink Floyd, Iron Maiden, Depeche Mode, The Cure, Motley Crew, Pet Shop Boys, Culture Club, Aerosmith, The Bangles the list could go on and on. These bands along with the crazy 80's television shows shaped this generation. It was the crazy hair, the crazy music and the entertaining show of the 80's that made this era so, so, so memorable.

Growing up in the emergence of technology mixed in with the old ways of being free in the country and exploring was a wonderful mix in these kids' lives. Being exposed to everything from fun, to business and to the city life along with the fun exploring in the country gave the kids and the adults a good mixture of work/life balance even though the work was a grueling and the stress could be overwhelming at times. It made life fast, often hectic and even too much, but they managed to juggle all the balls, even if one was dropped now and then. This lifestyle and this mixture of work and play was needed. But less work and more fun for the kids would have been beneficial.

Sports were also important in both kids' lives. Track and field with soccer, baseball and basketball at school were after school programs. These were the days when teachers stayed after school for sports, music and arts programs. The days when one teacher Mr. Dawson still stands out to this day. A grade 3 / 4 teacher who sang songs like The Chattanooga Choo-Choo, She'll Be Coming 'Round the Mountain and Sentimental Journey and the like. People who liked to teach and wanted to teach. People like that stick around for years and years in one's mind. Unlike the school principal, who years later was arrested as a pedophile.

Needless to say, there are good and bad people everywhere. This included the good neighbor next door who gave the family the black and white television. Of Scottish descent he still had his accent and so did his wife, though his wife was harder to understand. He was an older gentleman who would be out tending to his flower garden and beautiful roses at all times in the spring and summer. He was a wonderful kind and caring old man that always had a smile on his face. In the beginning it was communication by waving and smiling.

Later on, when the family picked up the language, he was a man who loved to talk and often had the kids over for lemonade and hot chocolate.

On one particularly snowy and cold winter day the older son was out shoveling snow when his younger brother came out to help and when the door closed behind him the kids realized that the key to get back in the house was... well it was inside the house. They went to the house next door and he invited them in, but the older brother decided to go to Mom's work and retrieve the key instead of staying there all day.

Either way the kids experienced kindness without giving a second thought to the fact of having bad people around. The old couple even paid the kids to mow the lawn later on when he couldn't do it anymore. It was a wonderful arrangement, the neighbors kept an eye on the house. They knew the family went to Caledon for the weekends and there was never a chance for anyone to rob the place. This was an era when you could sleep with the doors unlocked in the great city of Toronto. Sure, there was crime and such but good people kept an eye out for each other.

They took care of each other and as the kids gained friends they were introduced to long lasting friends as well. One such person was Tod Febbo and another was Mark Basciano who taught the older son English in the school hallway between lessons while the teacher made sure they also got their school work done. Such different times, so much more trusting and caring. The friends used to ride their bikes in the streets, play road hockey, skateboard and run around without the bylaw officer coming and handing out warning tickets and getting in fights with police officers.

Often the kids would have sleepovers and not be home for a night or two. All this before smartphones and constant communication with parents. There was trust from the kids and trust from the parents as well. Sure, kids must have gotten into trouble, but it was different. Now when JD looks up from the street it's a constant barrage of dings and dongs in between the tweets and texts coming in and going out. The likes and dislikes of social media that is clouding the brain of each and every person both young and old. The way of FOMO and the amazing like button that has ruined the world and changed it for the worse. There up in the massive flashing jumbo screen at the corner of Yonge and Dundas flashes the newest app, the newest phone and the newest mind numbing ad that is sure to be the next hit amongst the teenagers and adults alike.

Shrugging off the thought, JD thinks back how it was better that this and all this crap was introduced to his kids later on in life. He didn't have to think of the online digital menace, a different app to run everything that society lives with today. Surely studying, friendships and daily life is ruined, enhanced very little by what kids are dealing with today. The real benefit comes to business and the new world of influencers. Spoken or thought as a good older man would, life was better in the old days. At least if there were bad people around or news that happened in the world it would take a little longer to reach the masses and stronger and more intelligent thoughts would prevail instead of mass hysteria.

The kids grew up with a much better balance of tech and old school beer bottle collecting instead of growing up with... "will there be a signal there?"

The mind numbing new tech rules everyone as JD looks up. Every single person is on the phone and is online. Smiling, frowning or crying to a screen attached to a smartphone being operated by the masses.

As JD pondered this, he remembered how rock and roll and heavy metal music was blamed for suicides, and how TV was going to make his kids generation the dumb ones. He knew that the small rant in his brain didn't make a difference to the world. Technology has helped as much as it has hindered. In both business and his personal life technology played a big role. His business would not have been what it was prior to the technology and prior to automation and that was a trickle-down effect to all industries. Automation in all industries plays a large role in price reduction and mostly benefits companies that want to have the least number of employees and the most robots.

This was too much thinking for JD right now as he had his eye on a man in a suit and watched him making a deal on the phone. The man was wheeling and dealing with a client and he didn't know JD was listening. It reminded him of the good old days when he used to feel so good when he closed a deal. Today he feels good at the closure of each day when he can sleep with a semi full stomach.

He always hoped that his kids would never go hungry and he made sure of that. The kids never went to bed hungry, they always had what they needed even if it was not everything they wanted. The kids knew this and there was never a question of having enough. Sure, there were days when there were holes in the bottom of a pair of shoes or days when KFC was not the choice for dinner. But the kids knew and understood. Tonight, JD wished he had some KFC. He kind of felt like eating KFC tonight. He looked in his backpack and checked his paper bag and saw that the collection of the day wasn't as good as usual. KFC will have to wait.

Making his way back to his favorite spot he saw Romeo and Juliette back on their favorite spot and that made him feel good. He looked at them as if they were his kids. He looked at them as if they were his responsibility. Even though they weren't, they were part of a routine to check on the people around him so they do not end up like Peter. It was a comfort zone for JD. It was the check list of the day, the kids, the bum at the fountain down the street and the beggar who plays guitar a block north of here. The routine gives the day meaning. Like kids need routine when they are small this is all part of the day. A checklist of the surroundings that helps pass the day.

This had become a bit of an OCD thing for JD, there are things that need to be a certain way. Same as kids, if they get knocked off a routine, the rest of the day is also ruined. A terrible cup of coffee can throw an adult off track in the morning as well. JD doesn't worry about his kids, he knows they are well, they are well adjusted. Growing up they were given proper instruction and guidance. They were left alone enough to make their own mistakes and yet they were guided enough to have been helped and led down the right path. Other than a few speeding tickets and a small accident here and there, the kids were always well behaved and kids to be proud of. There were twists and turns along the way in each child's life but both turned out well.

Reflections:

Although I cannot speak for my brother; I am glad that we grew up when we did. I am glad to have had experienced an outhouse and a horse drawn carriage in my dad's hometown of Ujlengyel and my aunt's place in Szigetcsép. I am glad I was able to grow up on a farm and experience having cows, horses, chickens and a vegetable garden.
These small experiences taught my brother and I many things. I for one loved cutting the grass with the tractor and always had great ideas develop as it was a form of relaxation. Our parents didn't hold us back and say, "No you are not old enough" if you think you can do it, go do it. If you get hurt don't come running to me.
Today kids live in a bubble, and I try hard not to shelter my kids from the experiences they can have because some other parent may think that their kids are not old enough.

"A kid's ability will surprise you; you just need to let them try".

Most parents do not give enough credit to their kids to let them try and fail. Our parents let us do whatever we felt we were capable of and let us try things. We never lost a finger or broke anything trying new things. Yes, we both had plenty of injuries but that was due to soccer and other sports. We are both in our early 50's and we seemed to have survived quite well.
I am pleased to have grown up before the time of cell phones and social media and I commend all the kids that are growing up with the use of social media and peer pressure. Hats off to them as I may not have been able to cope...

Chapter 9. The growth

Time moves along, the days turn into weeks, months and years. Time, we all wished we had more time, more time to do things. Mostly more holiday time and working hours when deadlines loom. Time, we all have it and we mostly waste it. Time flies and so did the weeks and months for the family. Between work and the business, the kids playing sports and the struggles of each day and looking forward to another and another and another the family didn't even realize how much time passed. The tension that had built up with JD and his brother and his wife's family eased. The government of Hungary sentenced the parents and not the kids to jail. If they were to return to Hungary they would be imprisoned but the details were sketchy. The government was more upset that the kids had left more than the parents.
However bad it was family is family. They worked out the differences through letters and phone calls and like all things time and distance became the healer.
Unknown to JD, his wife had a secret little savings box. Not to hide from JD but extra savings where she put away a dollar here and dollar there. A dollar back then bought a few liters of gas, lots of sugar and bread. This little savings grew and as the family was getting more and more established, picking up the language and getting a bit more financially secure JD's wife was struggling.

She was homesick and not homesick for the country or the way of life. She was not fed up with the hard work. No, she missed her family. While this was not known to the kids, she was struggling. There were phone calls here and there but the calls were very expensive. Video calls were non-existent and while photographs could be sent it simply wasn't the same. This little slush fund was for her, her secret savings to bring her parents to Canada for a visit. Interestingly enough she felt that no matter how much she told her parents and her sister back home, she felt that they thought she was not telling the truth. She felt that there was reluctance in believing that she and the family were good. There was a reluctance about the business, the house, the car and that life in Canada was truly better. There was a sense that they thought it was all a ploy to make them think she is fine. She was homesick and this made it harder. When she had enough money saved up, she let JD know that she felt they could afford this. They could afford to bring her mom and dad here to visit and experience the reality of Canada for themselves.

First of all, JD couldn't believe she saved the money. She managed to scrape together every penny and every cent. She managed to keep the household afloat, feed the kids, pay the bills and still save a little here and there to be able to bring her parents to Canada. There was a very important question and a massive "if." If they get a visa. If they managed to get a visa was questionable, but older people are welcome to leave since they are a burden. If they defect it's not a big loss for the country. If they managed to stay in Canada well then so be it. That was the reality. That is exactly what happened.

While it did take time and it didn't happen overnight the family was to be partly reunited. JD and his wife would be able to have her parents visit Canada. Show them and prove to them that all she had said, mailed and all the photographs were indeed real. It was the Canadian life and the Canadian dream. This was no lie; this was a dream come true in a very different way than the dream to come to Canada.

These times and this year was a time of growth. The kids were growing, the family business was growing. The whole family was growing roots deep enough in this Canadian soil that they were able operate on their own. Throughout the first year and the second they felt they still needed to have their hands held. What is this? What is that? How do I do this? Where can I get that? How can I manage my taxes and so on? Now they were growing so to speak.

Another surprise was that JD's wife got her license. This seems like a simple accomplishment. Most people have their license except for the fact that she was afraid, no, terrified of driving and the worst part was that she had to learn on a manual transmission car. Again, not a big deal but she decided she needed to learn because with the business growing and her parents coming she had to overcome this hurdle. She took lessons and managed to pass on the first try.
While JD knew she was practicing, and he too was giving lessons he didn't know she was going for the test. She wanted this accomplishment or possible failure for herself. She needed to focus and do this on her own. She needed to be the big girl she knew she was. Her parents coming to visit was just the motivation she needed to complete this daunting task. The motivation paid off and this was a relief. She could now go shopping and go do things on her own and not wait for JD to come home and waste time. She will also be so much more flexible to take her parents around when they come.
This was a time of growth for the business and personal growth along with personal achievement. This was a time the family was blooming. The kids were busy and settled in, the family was able to speak and read English. Interestingly enough prior to this the kids would often need to translate government letters that came in the mail. Or if the parents were not sure about certain documents they needed to ask friends and relatives and this was always embarrassing no matter how much those relatives and friends understood.
JD's sister and husband were also in a time of change after closing the bankrupt factory and both of them working regular jobs. As the saying goes, the more things changed the more they stayed the same. Everyone adjusted and everyone thrived. The families were strong and had the right mental attitude and focus to be able to move forward with passion and hard work. It is always easier when you see the fruits of your labor.
JD's sister and husband took a big risk, they were responsible for this family. Two adults and two kids in a strange country and a brand-new beginning. Lucky for them JD's sister knew JD well. She knew she bet on the right horse so to speak. In this time of expansion, the kids had more friends, more sports and the little business was moving forward as fast as the Chattanooga Choo
Choo.
Picking up steam and growing with the right attitude and in the right way. Sure, there were mistakes and misunderstanding. Lots of

arguments and fights; but through the process came standard operating procedures. Little kinks were worked out along the way. The "We know not to do that again" type of comments came up often. Finding out how to reach out and talk to each of the customers and becoming a sales person, a CEO and the janitor at the same time is not easy.

Having a start-up company is not easy. Today the words "start-up" are thrown around every day. Back then you were starting a new business and funding came from your pocket. How well you managed determined your growth. Those rules apply today but building a business from the ground up is not easy with the barriers that this family had to climb over.

By the time JD's mother and father in-law came to Canada the family was no longer as poor as church mice. They were not rich but they were managing. Managing enough to take some time off and be able to afford not to work day and night and take their relatives places.

They still watched every penny that was spent and wasted none of their money on useless things. When they were at the airport awaiting the arrival of grandma and grandpa the excitement was unbearable. JD's wife was on pins and needles to see her mom and dad.

Juliska and Frank were in their 70's. They were both in good shape for their age but 9 hours on a plane is 9 hours on a plane and no matter what they were not young. It's been years now the family was separated.

It was a surprise to everyone that they had a passport and a visa in a very reasonable timeframe even though it seemed like forever at the time. The moment of truth was about to come. The moment when JD and his wife can prove to the rest of the family that they were telling the truth. It was hard for a regular Hungarian to believe that in a short time you can have two cars, a house and a business. That all the things you ever dreamt of and even the things you didn't know you wanted, were available in the store.

From the crazy commercial on channel 29 that can be caught on the wonderful rabbit ear antenna that advertised everything with the words "But wait! There's more" Or to the local channel 57 in Toronto that later became City TV. The movies and the commercials were all true. All the rumors you heard in the East about the West was as advertised or even better.

So, when the doors opened at the airport and JD and his wife along with the kids set eyes on Juliska and Frank it was time for tears, hugs and moments of truths…
Meeting your parents after a long time apart is always emotional.

"This was more, there was a touch of betrayal, there was a touch of disappointment and a whole lot of forgiveness along with love and more tears than it was imaginable."

Holding your son, daughter, mom, or dad always feels good. Holding them in your arms after a relatively short time by expectations and a very long time in reality was amazing. There is no way to describe the closeness the family had and the warmth that was never lost in the time apart.
There were hugs, cheers and long moments of silence and just taking in the moment and the reality that this family was together once more. As soon as one lands at the airport in Canada the world changes. As it did for JD and the family, you cannot help but do a double take on the world around you. There is no way to tell people how it is. Sure, you can try and send pictures but when you see it and feel it your eyes open a little wider and your brain needs a moment to recalibrate to this world.
Sitting in the car, heading home, the 20 to 30 minute drive was a nonstop question and answer period; where no one could finish a complete thought or sentence. There was so much to show and explain and so many questions about how and why the family decided to leave and questions of the past that needed to be cleared up.
So many questions were unanswered because the Hungarian government monitored letters and communication between the families. No one could ask yes or no questions and so the superficial is all that could be touched upon. No hard questions could be cleared up and the family knew this because it was clear on all mail received and the ones that were sent that they were opened. The Communist spies as much as it was hard to believe, were opening letters and monitoring conversations.
This family had no ties to any sort of spy agency, no ties to German or Russian intelligence… yet there was monitoring of phone calls and letters. The family knew why, well they suspected why. It had to be JD's brother. He had been under investigation and in the

Hungarian police force this was frowned upon. He was getting grilled and, in the process, he ended up being demoted. This was the biggest repercussion of the whole defection process that the family experienced. JD felt sorry for his brother, but they did move out of his jurisdiction for that exact reason. In the end the reach of the government did find its way back to him and he was punished.

After the grandparents opened their suitcases, it was very, very clear that it was a good thing that Customs didn't check these old folks. Everything from Hungarian Salami, to ceramics and toys as well as chocolates were pouring out of the suitcases. Some toys and chocolates the kids have never seen or had forgotten about were gifted and funny enough many of those chocolates and gifts are still remembered today.

The questions poured from grandma and grandpa. There were so many things to ask and answer and take in. As it was planned from the beginning the grandparents were to stay for a few months. It was a time of retirement for them and it was time off school for the kids. It was the perfect time for the kids to brush up on the Hungarian language that was nearly lost. The family was so busy working and learning English and even taking English lessons that the kids were getting very rusty with the Hungarian language. While not forgotten, it was a great time for the grandparents to come and keep them from forgetting their mother tongue.

Time with their grandparents was very much overdue. They had plenty of stories from the past and the childhood of both kids. It was a wonderful mix of old and new. Newly discovering the grandparents and the grandparents getting to know the kids that had grown like weeds.

Grandpa was a huge soccer fan and going to soccer games and practices was something he adored to do. He would advise the kids on how to play, what to do and mention his favorite team and of course the famous Puskas, the enormously well-known Hungarian team in the early years. It was a wonderful time for the family. Not only for getting to know the family again but also understanding the reasons behind the defection.

Going from store to store and place to place it was completely crystal clear that the stories, the letters and the phone conversations to the family in Hungary were all true. There was no fibbing or lying. There were no white lies or truths that were stretched. In fact, it was the opposite. It was the difference between seeing Niagara Falls in person or seeing it on a postcard. You can completely understand the beauty in both but cannot take in the beauty of the Falls the same way.

The understanding behind leaving was sinking in. It was a process that came in small increments. The house, the cars, the stores, the working conditions for people and the general mental health of every person was another level. The country was on another level. One cannot compare Hungary today to the Hungary behind the Iron Curtain in the 70's. The cold war between Russia and the USA was full on. Hungary managed to fair quite well on their exit from under the Russians and today it is a completely different country.

Back then though JD and his wife had something to prove. They had to make the grandparents understand that this was a better place to live. Though they tried hard they didn't have to. The wise old grandparents could see the difference. They have lived a hard life…

Being through and living through the war was no easy task. Surviving it and thriving afterwards was a tough task indeed. Grandpa told stories of the war that the kids loved.

How he and the others would play cards in bomb craters because the chances of the bombs hitting the same spot twice was a million to one. How they were laughing at how crappy and loose the Russian guns were when you picked them up, right until all the Hungarian guns froze up when the Russian winter kicked in.

Interesting stories of all seven brothers going to war and all seven returning alive was unbelievable. Despite the fact that he was captured and released as a prisoner of war because the doctor took pity on him. There was a sense of compassion and it showed that many didn't agree with the war, they were only doing their job. In this case Frank and the doctor's little girl took a liking to each other and seeing this the Russian female doctor had enough compassion to see the love and care this "terrible" soldier had within him. Over time their friendship came to an understanding and they knew that the "terrible" Russians were not all bad and that this was a byproduct of war. Eventually she signed a letter stating that Frank is very ill and will die. With that the Russian's released Frank.

Frank was a big man, tall and now a little fat around the belly. However, at the time when he arrived home a single spoonful of mashed potato satisfied his hunger. These men and women went through hell and back. The people that fought for the freedom we enjoy today must be thanked each and every day. We just hope all this freedom lasts and does not get wasted.

Understanding hunger was something JD was in complete understanding with. He too was a soldier and even though he never saw the front-lines himself he had an understanding how it was. Dealing with hunger in the modern times is very different. The Russian's didn't steal his food. The Government didn't come around and take your livestock or strip it from you in a form of taxes. No, this hunger was caused by the YB. Let's not forget JD… His life hangs in the balance of the YB and the pain they caused. Strolling downtown and poking your head in the garbage cans as inconspicuous as you can is embarrassing when you first get there. After a while hunger takes over and you don't care anymore. Being a prisoner of the street was a very small reminder that freedom also has its downfalls.

At the time of growth and at the time of the grandparents' visit JD couldn't even dream of thinking that far ahead. His life revolved within months of the present time. Thinking forward only to the next month and making sure the next month and the next and not to the yearly forecast that his business was going to get in the years to come.

Right now, it was a two-month window he lived in. Meeting and greeting the in-laws and hoping that they understand, forgive and have a good time. Going to all the famous places was something all visitors do. Centre Island and The CN Tower in Toronto, Niagara Falls and Marine Land were all on the list. But it was clear and very evident that while Juliska and Frank loved the attractions, the main attraction was the kids and the family.

They simply wanted to spend time with the family and despite being guests they chipped in and became part of the small business. Juliska was a seamstress all her life. Sitting at the sewing machine for her was second nature. The only difference was that this one was electric and not powered by your legs and feet. The little business bought another sewing machine and the two machine sewing room was now called the sewing department. While this was a joke it was wonderful to see how they had taken joy in helping out and this gave the family not only a little boost but more time to spend the well-earned free time together.

As far as the kids go they saw how this work ethic was not only engraved into their parents but the grandparents as well.

Juliska and Frank also loved visiting the farm and working in the garden and taking on DIY projects at the house. Soon with the little bit of time here and there the old wooden garage got a new lease on life. In Hungary most people know how to mix cement, build and make things with their own two hands. No Hungarian's hand was manicured. They were all hard working rough and tough as they were from the old school… No wimps allowed back then. You had to be tough and do things on your own. This work ethic and this attitude was passed down to the kids. The example they had was all hard work mixed with determination and knowing that if you work hard and keep at it good things will happen.

The white and green wood siding single garage was stripped down and painted, a new roof and shingles were added and there with the one project many, many projects began. Good old fashioned elbow grease and a good attitude created a new patio and that led to repainting the front porch. This was not looked upon as work, this was fun, it was fun and family bonding was brought together to create amazing memories and learning how to do things around the house.

The few months that the grandparents spent in Canada were passing quickly. One day Frank and JD sat outside on the small patio that they made and spent a little time alone. Their conversation slowly led to the defection and the new life in Canada. Frank being a hard-core Communist all his life took a deep breath and looked around. There was a small but nice backyard before him with the small freestanding garage and two cars in the driveway. Behind him was a house with three bedrooms and a wonderful family inside. Despite being disappointed and admittedly very angry at JD for stealing his daughter away from him and convincing her to escape Hungary and causing all the problems with the defection… He was also man enough to admit that JD did the right thing. That he would never be able to achieve such things in communist Hungary and that for sure the life for the kids would be better in this country.

This was a huge admission from him and these words were very welcomed by JD. He knew his decision to leave Hungary was the right one. He knew he could and would make it work. But regardless he needed to hear this from his father-in-law. This moment of acknowledgment was much needed, well deserved and welcomed by JD. It was good to hear from a man that was not only his wife's father but someone who had a change of mind about the west. He was man enough to come for a visit and see for himself, and man enough to admit that he was wrong after decades of commitments to his country's political views. This put an end to the Communist versus the West discussion in both JD's and Frank's mind. There would no longer be this push and shove when it came to political views. Besides Hungary was always a little more progressive in moving forward and out from under the Russian rule but that was to come later.

As the time grew near for the grandparents to leave the mood in the house saddened but they did agree that the families would spend a few months together each summer. Even though this was a year away it gave everyone something to look forward to. Saying goodbye is never easy, see you later is a little easier.

As the grandparents looked forward to leaving there was one very interesting thing that happened. By being in Canada, they too were liberated. Not in a political sense but in a personal one. Grandpa was getting ready, feeling and looking 10 years younger. He arrived wearing the same dress pants and dress shirt that he wore all his life. He was so used to wearing his "uniform" that he never thought about shedding it. It was the usual outfit of shorts and an undershirt. It was the typical older "Hungarian, older people outfit" But what he noticed was that the older people here wore jeans and golf shirts and he flirted with the idea of trying on a pair of jeans.

"To our disbelief, Grandpa never wore jeans and a golf shirt in his life."

This was hard to believe but it was true, at the age of about 76, grandpa put on a pair of jeans and a golf shirt. As unbelievable as this was not only did he put it on he saw the difference it made in his looks. From the stuffy old dress shirt and pants to the stylish casual look he now had. Grandpa looked and felt like a brand-new man and he would never in a million years have tried something like this if it wasn't for his trip to Canada. It just went to show that your surroundings can shape you. For the good or the bad your environment does and will affect you. That first trip to Canada changed both grandma and grandpa for the better and most likely added a few years to their life.

Reflections:

Having growth in business is one thing… Having personal growth is very different. I was lucky to have my grandparents in my life. Even though we were living far apart, having them in my life for 3 months out of the year was amazing. Learning from them and listening to their experiences from the war and their life was always amazing.
At the time, I had no idea how this experience would affect me later. My grandparents were always calm. Not much shook them and it seemed that even the biggest problem was looked at with logic and calmness. Maybe it was their experience through the war, maybe it was the fact that they were thankful for whatever they had and were happy with that.
They never fought or seemed to argue and if they did, they hid it well. So, this time with them was more than the growth of the business. This was personal growth and the sharing of experiences that they brought to me and our family.
Their wit and childlike curiosity was amazing. One experience I had with my grandma was one I always tell. Admittedly I love cars and yes, I was a bad apple when it came to street-racing. I never got caught racing; but had plenty of speeding tickets.
In this instance we were in my 1988 Ford Mustang and a Chevrolet Camaro pulled up next to us. I looked at my grandmother and said,

"That guy wants to race us; are you ok with that?"

My grandma smiled and said, "Yes, let's go." The light turned green, and we took off… We raced and won so I backed off the gas and had only one question on my mind. When we got home, I asked my grandma if she was afraid, she smiled, "No as I am sure you wanted to stay alive as well"
I guess what she meant by that was, I too didn't want to die racing. She trusted me not to get us killed. Who says a 75-year-old has no spunk? This was very funny at the time, and it is one of my fondest memories of my grandmother.
So, the growth came with personal experiences as well as work experiences and a good balance of both helped me become who I am today.

Chapter 10. The move

After the family visit, it was time to focus and get back to business and the businesses at hand. It was very clear that the business was growing and that this little business needed more room and more production space. The small basement business was not big enough to support the family, the extra income from both mom and dad was needed. But the business was outgrowing the small basement.
The plan was eventually for JD's wife to stay at home and grow the business to the point where it could support JD as well. To have enough business and to make enough profit to make it worthwhile meant the business would need to at least triple in size. This also meant hiring some part time workers or outsourcing some of the sewing. Planning at this point was planning, and while this was not a business plan on an Excel sheet accompanied by a flashy PowerPoint presentation it was scribbled on pieces of paper and looked over several times very carefully.
At this point, property prices were rising and moving out of the city to Brampton a 35-40 min drive away was a logical choice. It was between Bauhaus and The Bay. Driving would be extra but it was also much closer to Caledon where JD's sister lived. Brampton, Heart Lake, it was with great hesitation the family made its first move of many in this wonderful country. The new house was also three bedrooms but with an extra bathroom and a side split

configuration that gave the small company much needed extra space.

The move came quickly… Soon the 68 Braidwood Lake Road house was occupied. A little quicker than hoped as the house was brand new and it was finished on time by the builder. The kids were still going to school for a week or two before the summer holidays. Something that would be unheard of today, a teacher offered to give a ride to the kids because he too lived in Brampton. Mr. Jemmett offered the kids rides in and JD or his wife would pick them up. Today this would probably not fly, but back then it did. Interestingly enough, Mr. Jemmett was by reputation one of the meanest and strictest teachers at the school. He had this "if looks could kill" attitude and no one ever misbehaved in his class. However, once you got to know him he was a nice man and when he heard of the predicament he offered the rides. Never judge a book by its cover.

The new house was the very last subdivision at the time, a few houses down was nothing but farm fields with rows upon rows of cornfields being only 6 or seven houses away. The new house was much more spacious and its unique back split configuration was perfect for the business. It had a nice size backyard and with the fields and Loafers Lake recreation center being only a short walk or a quick bike ride away it was a great place for the kids. Like all kids, the kids complained about the move and the loss of their friends. This was temporary and now the kids had so much more room to roam that the inconveniences were quickly forgotten. Besides, this was the first or many moves the family would go through, they just didn't know it yet.

Moves not only happened in this family's life, it also happened in JD's sister's. She was retiring from The Bay. She had a few health issues such as falling off a ski lift, knee surgery and a very unwelcome heart attack. Slowly things changed for their family but JD's family was now closer and so it should be. As these changes slowly took place others did also for JD's family.

JD's job at Bauhaus ended. The company was on strike, the fallout with the owners meant the company decided to close up shop and head to the States. Quickly JD managed to find a job at Sealy Upholstery, the same family that owned Sealy mattress at the time. Billy Natheson was the owner and JD quickly secured a job running the leather furniture manufacturing area a new division for Sealy.

Having gained much needed experience from Bauhaus, Sealy was smaller and large scale manufacturing was easily implemented in this growing company. Sealy was at Steeles and Fenmar. Billy was from a rich family and he always had his Ferrari parked out front. It was either the Ferrari or the Mercedes. He didn't have a Rolls Royce like JD's previous boss, but the Ferrari was good enough that's for sure. With the new space and the old connections at Bauhaus and the new ones at Sealy JD was able to outsource some work to home sewers. This eased the burden a little on JD's one and only sewer, his wife and along came an opportunity that would change things in so many ways. One good deed deserves another, the saying goes. Since JD's wife still worked at The Bay under a new manager and now being able to communicate clearly in English led to an opportunity. The new manager's son had an import and export business and he was let down by a supplier. She knew that JD and his wife had some sort of a sewing and upholstery business. A supplier from China had shipped Rattan chairs and the seat pads that were supposed to fit in the chairs were an inch too deep. A few seat pads had to be reworked, cut down and reupholstered.

This seemed easy enough and so they were delivered to the house. Since this was a different time they were simply told to unload the seat pads in the garage and so they did. What they didn't mention is that the few seat pads were actually a few hundred for the Hotel at the Toronto Convention Centre that was newly built at the time. Of course, like all things this was needed by Monday and it was delivered on a Saturday. Either way the job was done and completed and this small, but enormous favor led to this little business's next large step forward.

The new step forward meant more investment and capital up front that was not available to the extent that was needed. With new business coming in, their personal line of credit was used to purchase fabric. This new business of cushions for the very popular craze of Rattan furniture was very big. Once samples were made the orders came rolling in. Within a short time, the business escalated but the profits were marginal because this business required much more fabric and foam that had to be paid for upfront. The little business didn't have much credit yet, it was still a little basement business. A very young and small player in the fabric, thread, zipper and foam world.

The kids helped as much as they could but with school, a flyer route and a newspaper route it was hard work. A part time sewer was hired from a few doors down, more home sewers were hired and even on occasion a cushion stuffer from Sealy named Ken would come and help. Ken had one eye but always had a smile on his face. There sure were some wonderful people that were hired along the many years in business.

The move turned out to be great. The little business grew and soon JD's wife had to make the very scary choice of staying home and working full time or the business would suffer. The business was big enough to take on one person's full time salary after about 5 years. This was a critical and carefully measured step. So much was riding on the continued expansion of this small business with the new Rattan cushion manufacturing. Luckily word spread and companies like Angel International and Camilla House became large customers. The small company also attended trade shows. Apron styles as well as new colors and the addition of leather electrical pouches made the growth possible. Adding customers from Montreal and more from Mississauga helped immensely. New upholstered furniture with Rattan arms rounded out the lineup. The business flourished and JD was now itching to stay home with his wife; to help this business that was started with one sewing machine, one riveting machine and a whole lot of sweat and tears grow.

There were amazing opportunities but some could not be taken. Even the possible loss of a steady income from Sealy would be detrimental. That was a big company and while Billy upgraded from a 328 Ferrari to a Ferrari Testarossa, JD and his wife were still buying second hand cars because a new one was not possible. The family was doing well. Gone were the days of holes in the shoes and not being able to afford the next meal. Things were comfortable now. The hard work didn't stop. The hard work never stopped but it was paying off. Picking up some cut and sew business with leather cushions from Sealy itself meant even more expansion and more cutting and sewing for sling chairs were in the works.

Soccer and Judo made the family even busier and added travel to Ohio and Washington to the already busy schedule of Rep Soccer that took the family all over Ontario. From Niagara Falls to Windsor and out to Scarborough for weekly matches. JD was busy with work, soccer and the home business. This was life in the JD household, school, work and sports was the life for the kids. While at times it was too much, they did see the difference in what the family could now afford, and it was worthwhile.

The life for the kids was not "normal". Not many kids went home from school, did their homework, had dinner and went to the basement to work. It was not a small amount of work. Home by 4 on the bus, homework, eat and work until 9:30-10pm and go to bed. This was not, come home finish your homework and watch TV or play video games. This was work… Help dad do a layout, help mom with the aprons, fill cushions. Prep a sofa or install a bed mechanism, cut this and make a pattern, oh and don't forget the paper route and the flyers that the younger sibling took care of.

Having your own business is hard work, working as a kid from the ages of 7 and 10 onward, the kids learned everything from the ground up. How to take apart a piece of furniture to recover, not to damage the fabric too much so patterns could be made from the old covers. How to spring a sofa and how a bed mechanism could cut your fingers off if you put your fingers in the wrong spot. No this was not a normal life for kids in grades 7 and 4. This was hard work and the family couldn't sit back and enjoy life, not just yet. One salary was fully paid by the small business, while one was still paid by Sealy.

While other kids were out messing about, these kids were in the basement. A day out was going out to do deliveries with mom or dad. A day out was soccer practice or a game.

While it wasn't a struggle, it was not easy, it was never easy. With a bigger business comes a bigger responsibility. The family always looked at this small business as if it could end overnight. There was great emphasis on the steady stream of income from JD and Sealy. There were many nights filled with arguments between JD and his wife about JD staying home and making this small business a bigger business. JD's wife was very conservative and very calculated in everything, especially finances and as much as JD would hate to admit she was probably right 90 percent of the time. Those odds were all in her favor and anyone would take those odds on any given day. JD had to wait, his dream of working in his own business and running his own business full time will have to come later.

There were rewards of course. With the time at Sealy the cut and sew business was taking off. More sewing and more products were now being offered. New fabric selections and even a catalogue was drawn up of all the styles. Marketing materials were made available and even a different business card was designed. Gone were the days of cream and brown and replaced with a fresh blue and while color scheme.

The move to the new location meant faster and easier deliveries and more production. More production meant more money and in the process the old Peugeot was replaced with a Nissan Sentra and the old van was replaced with a VW Vanagon that happened to be white with a blue stripe around it. It was the courtesy van for Bramgate VW and quite possibly that sparked the business card change.

By now the family was far more comfortable in their skin, there was more confidence in the little business and soon there was a need for growth once more. This too was very well calculated. Never were things taken lightly in this household. Not in Hungary and not now. The little business had to make do with the space it had, the garage was now fully used to house raw materials and not the cars. Winter or summer the garage was full of foam, fabrics and frames.

The furniture business was improving, the reupholstery business was still booming and things were snowballing. Things looked up and positive. When they do you need to look forward to the next pitfall and unexpected costs like a very expensive engine rebuild on the VW. Just when you think you are ahead something pulls you down. This was normal and that is why JD and his wife were conservative about things. Sure, some chances had to be taken but some didn't. Thinking back to those days JD sits on a park bench and feeds his furry friends and tosses crumbs to the pigeons. How lucky and how free they are. Not a worry in the world but stuffing their faces with as much food as possible at every turn. The rain comes down and JD seeks shelter under a bridge where common folks also huddle at the unexpected rain. The unexpected is what is scary, the unknown, unseen monster under the bed is far scarier than the one you see and can avoid, or run away from. It's this unknown that you make calculated decisions for. Most businesses do not have a bridge to hide under and weather the storm. No, they are exposed to the elements the same way as JD is. The winter cold that freezes your toes and nose. JD knows full well that some situations are impossible to account for.

With the rain coming down he is not afraid to shed a tear for the past. With the rain coming down, he is not afraid to admit the mistakes that were made because he can blame the rain for the tears running down his cheeks. Unfortunately, the rain cannot wash away the past or wash clean the present. You can wait for the sun to shine and hope there will be rainbows to make you smile. JD has not smiled for a long time, what reason is there to smile?

Thinking back and peeling back the layers and layers of memories are like tearing off bandages from a very sensitive wound. Each layer goes deeper and deeper to the heart of the matter. The closer you get to the heart of the matter the more you want to scream and yell. But you have done that and no one listened. You have cried and no one cared. You have begged and people turned away. So why bother with thinking back and opening up this partly self-inflicted wound?

Because people need to know that this little company didn't fall on its own sword. This little company didn't grow and grow and commit suicide. This company was hung by its balls and left to bleed by the big YB. This anger is what drives JD to tell his story so that others may learn and not be led to the slaughter by YB or other massive companies that come along to offer them the carrot and then beat the crap out of them with a stick.

Ah but the carrot sure looks good, doesn't it? Somewhere on the carrot there is a fine print that the jackass doesn't see. Oh, it's there, it clearly states that I will screw you over left right and center and you will be my bitch. Except the jackass already ate that part of the carrot...

So yes, this little company that could, did, and grew. Slowly it picked up enough momentum to be able to say to itself that it was a good little hard working company and was making money. It feels wonderful to say those words. This little company is making money. Every business needs to hear those words so when the company van needs its guts replaced the little company does not run to the bank for a loan. It was one of the favorite things that JD and his wife were able to claim. Except for the lifeline at one point in this businesses growth it was working without a loan.

While most businesses rely on some form of capital injection this business grew from profit. It may have grown slower than if someone came along with a plan and a forecast. But this business was built carefully, by people that didn't have a clue about running a business. To their benefit, possibly they tread very lightly with the money they relied on for their next meal. It was not money that could be tossed around and burned. This was personal money coming from their pocket and not some rich investor or public money.

Just then JD reaches into his pocket and takes out the paper bills. He opens his backpack and places the bills into his paper bag. He takes the change and counts it carefully. He looks up and sees his reflection in the glass at Tim Hortons and winks at himself. It was a good day, he can afford a chamomile tea today. It's the little things in life that matter. Work hard for what you want, that's the bottom line. Working hard was never the problem. As the members of this family managed to work hard at more than one job, work hard at school, play soccer and slowly climb the social ladder. People around them knew that they were destined for greater things.

There was a sense of success, because things were carefully calculated and dissected a dozen times there was a process in place. Risks were assessed and major decisions were slept on for more than a night. The high road or the low road, which one to take? Make a left or make a right? There was very rarely a wrong turn. This security and decision making was nearly faultless.

This is what CEO's get paid for… This little company had great management. It had hard working people on the "board of directors". They were hands on and watching every penny. They were not tossing money away on useless crap or spoiling themselves with lavish gifts. No, these people took care, took very good care of every penny and made sure they invested in proper equipment and in themselves.

It is amazing to see how people without a background in business can make a go of it and succeed. So many examples of this at flea markets. People managing to make deals and grow businesses as they learned from their parents or on their own. Such was the case with the younger son in the family. Whether he was paying attention, picked it up without knowing it or it came naturally to him. But as a kid he saw an opportunity and he took it. He opened up a small stall to sell second-hand Nintendo or Sega video games at the Flea Market. It was the most basic of businesses. Just like trading stocks, buy low and sell high, sell it at a profit. So, he went, with boxes of second-hand video games that were traded in at a friend's computer store. Stock was bought up and taken to the Flea Market. It was a well calculated business. The store didn't want to go to the Flea Market, but the young entrepreneur did. This was another example of how this little business was now creating a new entrepreneur and a person that is being groomed to be in business as an adult.

Reflections:

There are plenty of personal and business decisions to be made in life. I feel that this move was the biggest. It was a life altering decision and one that sent this business into a higher gear. It was always a terrible thought as a child to switch schools and make new friends. It is the nightmare that kids do not want to think about, and I remember each time we switched schools very well.

However, this was a business decision and one that would make the greatest difference in our lives. We didn't know it at the time, but it was an amazing move and investment into a bigger house, a good business decision for growth. Putting the kids aside for a moment, our parents made a decision.

Once again, they didn't know a thing about growth and planning. Not officially and not by formal education, they were learning on the fly and therefore we were all learning, growing and expanding. We did what every CEO or owner does. Evaluate the situation, learn from your experiences and base your decision on what you think will give you the most profitable or favorable outcome.

Mom and dad were learning, but this was not shareholder's money or a public company. Every decision affected the family. I remember my dad buying a skid load of beige checkered fabric. I recall my mom freaking out and until that skid of fabric vanished, she was always on his case. It was a bad buy; the fabric was not pretty and since it was a big deal, I remember it to this day, it was sometime in 1985.

While the move was great and it set us on a path that we never expected, we were not perfect, no one is, we did our best and that is all we could do.

Chapter 11. The move to?

Each summer the grandparents came...without fail each summer for 3 months. After visiting each year for the first few years there were very few places that they had not visited. Trips were taken to Ottawa, Montreal. The grandparents didn't come to Canada to go places, they came to Canada to spend time with JD, the kids and their daughter. It was interesting as grandma looked forward to sewing and grandpa looked forward to fixing things and helping wherever he could. They became part of the machine and rooted for the success and growth of this business. Each time they came they checked out the new inventory. New sewing machines or a new cutting knife or the semi-automatic riveting machine that grandpa got attached to. In Hungary, grandpa would tend to the vineyard and water the flowers. There was little to do because they were retired. They would maybe visit friends but mostly they stayed home. Here they were part of the workforce. No one asked them to work, they could have sat on the sofa, watched TV, gone for walks and taken the dog out to play fetch. But they wanted to feel useful and help. They so were proud to be able to go back to Hungary and say they were part of this and that and show off the photos of them operating a sewing machine or helping take apart a sofa. Their mindset was amazing and very different.

JD's sister and brother in-law were also retiring, and their idea of retirement was very different. They gave up the farm and built themselves a house in Caledon on a few acres rather than the 100 acres. They went to Florida every winter and JD and the family would look in on the house once or twice a week. The winters in Florida were filled with days of golf, swimming and sunshine. Very often JD and the family would hop down for a long weekend or a week. These little luxuries were now affordable. Grandparents coming and going, trips to Florida and in 1985 the family was able to purchase their first ever, brand new car.

It was the first new car after a long line of absolute shit boxes. Cars that were mostly rusted out and in dire need of bodywork. This was their first new car. Though riddled with problems that Chrysler never wanted to pay for even though it was new. This new car was quickly in a small accident at a tennis court when it was rear ended and it also hit a small tree in the front yard at the hands of the older son. Maybe it wasn't worth buying a new car after all.

Soon it was clear that considerably more production space was needed. Though there wasn't enough business to keep JD home full time, the business needed more employees and those that can come to a house and work full time. It was time to expand and hire people. The family began looking for a new house once again. This was not because they needed or wanted more space themselves or they were not happy with the current house. They needed to double the space, but the business was not ready in their minds to move out and rent. Renting a thousand square foot building would have eaten away the profits in a considerable way. Why pay for square footage when you can work in the same space you live and pay a mortgage.

All this made sense to JD and his wife. It was simple math and JD's wife knew her math. That's why she worked out the taxes that were written off on gas and phone bills as well as some of the electrical, insurance costs and so on. JD's wife and the accountant worked it out and there it was. A bigger house was much more cost effective than the rental of a space that had its own insurance, heating and electrical costs. In Europe there are many companies that have the owner's house at the front and the factory at the back. In Asia many people live in the shop house that they sell from on the ground floor. By now there were a few employees that helped with the sewing, cushion filling and packaging. This house had a walkout basement and the furniture could be brought in and out of the house around the back. This was far more convenient than coming up through the house and far faster.

The house was located at 62 Barr Crescent in Brampton and was a 3000 square foot house. It was large and it indicated that yes, this family is growing and making money. It was a bit of a stretch financially, so the family bit off a little more than they could chew but it was planned with growth in mind. It was planned for more production and more employees. The cushion and furniture businesses were growing. More and more work was coming from Sealy and before the family knew it, they were shipping van loads of leather cushions to Sealy.

Billy agreed to sub-contract the sewing and stuffing to the family. This was great, good solid paying customers and van loads of goods, the type of customers everyone hopes to have. The leather pouches and the cushions increased in sales, so did the profits and so did the planning to make sure things kept going as smoothly as possible.

One drawback of the extra mortgage costs and the extra space was that JD's income from his full-time job was still needed. He was dying to work in his business full time and stay at home to join his wife. This was not about to happen, not yet.

If anything, this was a constant argument in the house. There were many, many nights when the kids would hear their parents arguing. This arguing was mostly business, at times they were close to saying they wanted a divorce, but more from the business than each other. JD's idea of working in his own business must come true. The business had to make enough money to support this family on its own soon or he would go crazy. This was his drive to make this business profitable and big enough to handle the family.

JD's position at Sealy was good, a company car, gas paid, and a decent wage. This was a load that was not bearable by the little company. Little is a relative word, it was little compared to many and bigger than some but it had a vision from JD to be more. He worked at these large companies and all he really wanted was to work in his smaller company.

When the furniture business picked up and sofa beds became a much bigger part of the business, the family ran into a problem. The company delivering springs and sofa-bed mechanisms was not allowed by law to enter the subdivision. Normally this did not pose a problem because these things would be picked up by the van and brought home. But to get better prices on goods, larger quantities were needed. Was it time to move again? This was a tricky question and one that didn't have a clear answer. This move if it were to

happen would need to be a different one. One out of the city, closer to the country with a little bit more space and a place where trucks would be allowed to enter for delivery drop offs and pick-ups.
As usual JD led such things with great enthusiasm and soon it became the talk of the family once more.
Having been in Canada since 1978/79, it was 1987 and the family had lived at three different properties. By now the kids were in high school. The high school that they went to was in Caledon. Caledon was the place to move to next. The older son got his license and loved driving the Sealy provided Camaro. It was never really JD's choice for the Camaro but since he was driving the van to and from Sealy for the deliveries, his older son took the Camaro as often as possible. This was one of the perks of working for a large furniture company.
The kids were incredibly busy now. Heading to high school both kids now went to Mayfield Secondary School. This school was in the middle of nowhere back then. It was a country school located in Caledon East Ontario. It was a 20-minute bus ride from home and straight out to farmers fields and apple orchards. This area, 20 years later was surrounded by a Walmart, a bank and donut shops and not to mention thousands of homes. A school plan that had an amazing amount of foresight.
Unfortunately, back then you needed to ride a bus or be able to drive or possibly hitchhike to and from to. The closest small restaurant was a 45 min walk and not many kids took on the walk unless they were skipping classes.
While JD was eying moving out to the country, the business had to continue and they needed to assess the situation. If they were to make this move JD wanted to be able to work from home. They were in a massive house and all for the size of the basement. Moving out to the country would mean a less expensive house with truck access and that meant they may be able to afford for JD to work from home in his own business. Calculations for the wages, the loss of a car and future profits had to be made.
Another interesting decision had to be made as well. The government charges were dropped against the family and the family was able to return to Hungary unpunished. This excited JD's wife. She wanted to go home and visit the family. There was one worry... She had to take the younger son with her because the older one was just at the age of being drafted by the army and army service was still mandatory. This

was something JD and his wife looked at closely and the decision was made to go back to Hungary with the younger son. Nearly 10 years after being away and not seeing Hungary and the immediate family, it was time to return to the country of birth.

This was an easy decision to make, get on a plane and go. But with the business only being on holidays during Christmas it had to be a Christmas trip. That meant that for the first time ever the family would not be spending Christmas together. While this was sad it was manageable and it was a different kind of Christmas gift. A gift of holding down the fort at home and two family members working through the holidays while the other two went for a holiday. There was nothing wrong with this decision, it was always a family decision. Everything in this business and home was decided together and therefore everyone knew where and how things would be going. Many families do not work together well. Up to now this one did. There was strength and unity and togetherness because there were results. It is hard to work and work without results. The kids were never paid for their time and effort by giving them a paycheck. They were given cash to go out with their friends and everything else they needed. Sure, there were some things that other kids may have had. Designer clothes and brand name shoes or clothes.

These kids had family time with sports, everything they needed they had. Did they have everything they wanted, probably not. But the kids didn't behave like other kids. They knew very well what the family could and couldn't afford. So, the kids didn't ask for more than what they really needed. This was most likely the situation that they were brought up with. They had a clear understanding from mom and dad, they also knew that if by chance there was something they really, really wanted it would be provided. This Christmas was very different and Christmas dinner was held much earlier than usual because this way everyone could be together. It was unusual but it was the way it was.

JD remembers this Christmas very well for a few reasons. He and his older son were alone for nearly two weeks and the actual Christmas Eve dinner was just the two of them. His sister and brother in-law were in Florida, so dinner for two was a roast in the oven and potatoes prepared by his son. Unfortunately, the roast turned out to be very, very salty and it became a joke for the longest time that the Christmas dinner was not the greatest without mom.

All in all, the past few Christmases have sucked for JD. Losing everything and not wanting to remember the good old days has its consequences. The joy of 35 years of hard work has been sucked out of you and a company that you were proud of and poured your blood, sweat and tears into is gone. Clearly every memory attached to your life is attached to your company in one way or another. Every holiday, every decision in your life hung on the wellbeing and profitability of the company and each decision was made with the family in mind. The family was the company, it was the heart and the heartbeat, the heart and soul of the business.

From 1979 to the day it died, the day it was taken off life support and lay in pieces, ripped apart, pillaged, broken and destroyed. JD broke down in tears. He had to stop, he had to stop torturing himself by remembering. This is why he chose to distance himself from everyone. Each person in his life was attached to the business. Every friend, every acquaintance and every employee. Each turn in his life he would bump into the past. The people that would look at him as someone who had something and now has nothing. This way he could hide out alone and be happy that he didn't need to face those people.

Some of the happy memories like this one with his wife were bearable because it had deep meaning for the first return to your country of birth. Not your home country because Canada was home. Canada will always be home no matter where he ended up in this world. It is the country he made something out of himself and made his dream come true.

Now this was an achievement. To go to Hungary knowing you are successful. Not as a big shot, big mouth. But to be able to send his wife and son home knowing they have made it. A wonderful house. A house you would no way, no how, ever be living in, in Hungary. Driving with the family to the airport was something to be proud of and sending them on their way was a very satisfying feeling. It was so much more satisfying than he ever thought it would be. His wife worked hard and deserved this trip. A woman who worked in a truck factory, returning to Hungary as a successful small business owner and does not need to watch every penny she spends anymore. She has enough money to give to many relatives and share some of her wealth with the less fortunate.

That is hard to say… It reminds JD of YB. How the YB earns billions and yet do not even have the decency to be fair. Shame,

shame, shame. This rocked JD back to reality and he sat down on a curb. How many successful people are in Dundas Square right now? There must have been a few hundred people there. Let's say only 10 percent are successful, successful as in have money in the bank and very little debt. It's not much and maybe only 1 percent of that 10 percent is rich, like really rich. None are as rich as the YB, none at all, they are in a class by themselves. Yet the average "non successful" people are the ones tossing coins into his hat each day. What a wonderful world we live in, where the less fortunate support the even less fortunate and the rich? Well they may or may not. But percentage wise the less fortunate support him daily. This is just a thought, there were no statistics, but in JD's mind this was just a hunch.

When JD's wife and son arrived in Hungary it was an eye-opening experience but in reverse. Everything in Hungary seemed smaller. The cars, the old apartment and the places JD's wife used to frequent as an adult. Even the very large old bus and truck factory shrunk in comparison to the Canadian manufacturing plants. There was no comparison anymore. Even though both of them were born in Hungary this was no longer home. It felt strange being at "home". This place was memories and nothing else. They were not so good memories in most cases. They were average adulthood memories and quite good teenage memories. As a teenager one has a different outlook on life and thus the fun times were so much easier to recall. On the trip most people had nothing good to say besides you look good, it's nice to see you. Other than that people seemed unhappy, miserable and complaining about this that and the other thing. It was nothing but illness with this and stress with that and the economic conditions that make it hard to get by. If it were one person it would have been understandable. But everyone singing the same tune was getting stressful and repetitive. There was very little happiness and therefore the trip was bittersweet. In all fairness the situation did improve in the years to come but the first and the most exciting trip was lackluster to say the least.

It was nice to be In Hungary and wonderful to see everyone but family, happiness and home were back in Canada. As much as she recalls being homesick and crying herself to sleep at night, she now saw that it was a great waste of energy. But this was something that she had to experience for herself. It was in many ways the way Frank had to see Canada she had to go and experience Hungary on her own.

In many ways she could hardly wait to get home, sit down at her sewing machine and join her team to get orders out. That became her happiness and satisfaction. Put in a great day of work and leave with a sense of accomplishment rather than the doom and gloom she landed in. She often thought about the business and the family back home. Though she knew it was all in good hands she wanted to check on things and relax.

At home JD held down the fort just fine, and after the trip was over and the family was reunited it was clear that the trip back to Hungary was very worth it. In ten years, what had been established and accomplished here in this wonderful country of Canada was absolutely no way possible to accomplish in Hungary. This fact alone was satisfaction enough for this couple that they made the correct choice despite the fact that this here was nowhere near easy. When she recalls meeting her old classmates in Hungary they seemed older, stressed and with a very different mindset. She didn't want to be them, she wanted to be herself. Full of life and positivity. It was good to be with likeminded people again. It was good to be with the likeminded and hardworking family members.

Spending the time together with the family is how this family thrived and there was nowhere else she would rather be. Even though there was a little bit of jetlag, she had to visit the shop and take in the sight, smell and look around at her accomplishment regardless how small it is it is her accomplishment. She would never have been able to achieve this without the three other family members around her. This is her life, this is the life of the family and no one can ever take this away. She was so right and yet she was wrong. Fortunately, she was not around when it was ripped away from the family.

Reflections:

Living in North America you cannot help but have a different outlook on life. Things are different and when reflecting on the good old days, mom and dad never looked back to Hungary. Their good old days were here, all here in Canada. Hungary very rarely came up in everyday conversation. As mentioned, we almost forgot how to speak Hungarian. Thank goodness for my grandparents that we can speak another language.

My memories of Hungary are old. My last trip there was in 2000 and I cannot believe myself when I say that, because I should be ashamed of myself.

We always feel we have so much time until we run out of it. I guess my trips to Hungary were rarely a vacation. They were trips that involved rushing from one relative to another and so when I had time I would rather go on vacation.

At the time though, it was super important for my grandparents to come and visit and eventually for my mom to go back. She had to know she made the right choice and in retrospect she knew that despite the hardship, all the decisions they made were the right ones. There is a sense of accomplishment and pride knowing you did the right thing. It is that pride that continued giving the family the encouragement and push to keep going and grow the business. When the odds are stacked against you it is good to know that you made the right choice.

When my mom went back, she was very surprised as to how everyone was so different than her. Not being judgmental at all but they had different priorities and different outlook on life. Those people had done all they could and were stuck and Ann was not. She was a woman who ran a business and got to go back to Canada to continue, while her friends in Hungary were still living in the same place and doing that same job they started out with decades ago.

Chapter 12. The move to Caledon

The move to the lovely town of Caledon was the most significant move for JD and the family. The very careful and calculated decision to move to a place that was smaller but had better basement space was a perfect move.
Shifting from a 3000 square foot house to an 1800 square foot bungalow that had an 1800 square foot basement in a nice long rectangular configuration meant plenty of space for work. With the addition of the two-car garage, the small shop grew to just over 2000 square feet. No matter how you looked at it, it was a smart move. With the property market the way it was, the move from the city of Brampton to the town of Caledon meant that the family also had some cash in their pocket and a house with an acre of property where trucks could back in from the road. 14770 Airport road was a small house. The kids were not truly happy with the move, but it was a business decision and as with many business decisions they didn't always make everyone happy. JD and his wife promised the kids that this was for the greater good and to be able to have more later on, this sacrifice had to be made.
As with all things it was understood and soon the family settled into the new home and new workspace and hired two sewing ladies that lived close to the house. Both ladies were from Bolton, a nearby town that was a few minutes' drive, and they didn't have to battle traffic. One lady was named Ruby and the other was Rosa. Both

were ex Bauhaus employees and were happy to work in a very family oriented business.

The shop had a small office downstairs with a fax machine and a cordless phone. No more getting up and running to the phone. Those new cordless phones were something else, of course that is funny to hear today but at the time it was frustrating to have to stop what you were doing to run and get the phone each time it rang.

The ladies were happy to work with the family. While the whole family was not working together the plan was that with this slight expansion, JD's dream was also getting closer. The day was coming when he could work full time in his own business.

With the move came other sacrifices. JD decided to not take another company car and the Camaro had to go. He decided to take the extra money as salary and use the money to buy a new van since the old VW was costing too much in maintenance. The family bought a Nissan pickup truck and a Nissan Multi. Both these cars were good for deliveries and when the kids were able to they did deliveries sometimes before or after school. The family still worked together, but with kids being in high school it was harder. They had soccer, school and work. Weekends were non-existent. The kids usually only went out at night if they were not too tired. The older son had to drive and pick up or drop off his younger sibling because one of the drawbacks to living in Caledon was the lack of public transport. It was a rural property and everyone needed a car to get around. Caledon was a beautiful place and it still is to this day.

With this move the family had major changes and adjustments to go through. Employees came through the front door and down to the basement. Some of the privacy was gone and it was operating more like a small factory. Part time workers would come seven days a week. People came to help with cutting, sewing, riveting and cushion filling. These people were from Bauhaus or Sealy who needed the extra money and loved working with the family.

There was also aunt Edith, who was a friend of the family and also Hungarian but had lived in Canada for decades and decades. She was a stay at home grandma that was bored and so she came and learned to cut leather for the aprons. All in all, they were solid, reliable people that were hired and that was important because one person missing from 250 employees or one missing from 10 was a big difference. Soon there were sometimes two to three van loads of goods leaving the house each day and JD being JD, approached anyone that would give him an appointment.

Such was one of the more memorable stories in the growth of this business. There were big players in the hardware store market at the time and CO-OP stores, Home Hardware stores, Canadian Tire stores and Woolworth/Woolco stores. JD approached them all, none of these big companies knew that these goods of cushions and aprons were coming from the basement of a house located in Caledon.

CO-OP became a customer but never ordered much and always ordered the simple printed promotional type aprons. Canadian Tire would have been a customer, but their payment terms were 90 days and the small company would have not been able to afford a 3-month lull in cash flow. Home Hardware was a funny one. Some franchise stores ordered but they never became a true customer. They had too much red tape to go through and so the small individual stores came on board but never the big corporation.

One of the most interesting stories and one for crazy surprising growth was Woolco. JD had made an appointment to see the head buyer at Woolco named Mike. To the families surprise, he got an appointment and JD showed up with his thick Hungarian accent and brown briefcase and the samples.

Walking into Woolco was one of the biggest meetings to this point in the business' history. JD was nervous but it was not something he worried about much. He needed the airtime to be able to get in front of a buyer and he would make a sale. The meeting was late, but eventually he got the face to face meeting he was hoping for. Mike was a nice man and JD and he hit it off immediately. Interesting how that is but a connection was made, samples and prices were presented. Although no immediate sale was made the meeting ended on a promising note and both men seemed satisfied.

As most meetings and business go, things take time, it's not the old days when you met and shook hands on a deal.

However, a month or so went by, and one day a fax came in and JD got a frantic phone call at work. It was an order from Woolco, there was a small panic because Woolco ordered 5000 of a fairly expensive style of a double carpenter style apron. This was of course doable and it was the single biggest order ever.

This was a celebration of sorts and when JD got home and looked at the order he was in for a shock. With the order in hand he looked at it, then looked at his wife and said…

"This order is for 50,000 aprons."

Both JD and his wife were in shock. In her haste and shock she missed a zero. it's not a mistake she would make but at first glance maybe her mind did not comprehend that this order was the biggest single order in the small company's history. This was a call for celebration! The order was more than all the aprons this company had ever made. A simple interaction between two people and a sale that changed the company. Getting into a store such as Woolco with dozens of locations and big stores not only meant orders but also meant rules had to be followed.

This was not just an order but also packaging sizes, box sizes and delivery instructions. A delivery schedule had to be followed and due dates had to be met. This small step forward caused a number of things to happen. Better packaging and sealing machines for the bags. The packaging also called for hang tags and made in Canada logos. This order brought this small company into the big leagues. Now forced and ordered to meet new requirements the company looked forward to not only meeting but exceeding the customer's requirements. Failure was not an option and now, finally after all these years there was a way for JD to stay home and work for the company he founded with his wife.

"Quitting Sealy Upholstery was the most difficult personal and business decision up to this point."

This was a dream come true. It took 10 years of hard work and 9 years for the small company to grow big enough to support a husband and wife team. To be able to sustain, make a profit, carry a mortgage and two wages from a basement business was incredible. The small company gained a full-time employee and a productive one at that. Now it was time to focus and pump out as much product as humanly possible. Working seven days a week was normal. But now it was full time in their own business and they had plenty of work ahead of them. The growth that they needed and the security of a large company paying the bills was replaced by Woolco and the money that was previously coming in from Sealy would come from a customer and not an employer.

Indeed, this was a step in the right direction. Completely self-sustained and working in your own business was the things dreams are made of. It was for JD at least. From the day he landed in Canada on his first visit in 1976 to this day, ten years later the dream came true. Working from home on the first day was like entering a new company as a new employee. Sure, the familiarity was there as he worked there pretty much full-time, but the part time workers had to be rescheduled and adjustments had to be made. JD was a founder but his wife was the boss. The employed were mostly women with a few guys as part timers. It was not Sealy where he was the boss and told everyone what to do. The schedule was made by his wife, the work was handed out by his wife and people did what the boss told them to.

"There were differences in how to run the company and there was a bit of a power struggle that the family went through. JD and his wife had to learn how to efficiently work together."

These were minor things but effectively working together full time was different than working together part time. Up to now JD's wife was doing the ordering and the customers were used to dealing with her. Now the sewing room was buzzing with machines and one more person was added to this little basement business taking the total of employees with the kids to roughly 12. Part time cutters, cushion fillers, and outsourced sewing operators rounded out the count and the business was growing.

When it rains it pours, and did it pour! The extra work was needed, and it couldn't have come at a better time. The move to Caledon paid off. It took the biggest sacrifice from the family but with both kids going to college and having slightly less time to work in the business it was perfect timing. Oftentimes, making cuts and sacrifices are painful. Cuts and sacrifices were made, but it left the company with cash in its pockets and security to move forward. With the addition of a secure large company such as Woolco, it was now clear that the future was positive, and they needed one more big customer. One more company with secure work and not just the small companies with small orders that required a lot of attention and maintenance. At this point JD and his brother had started talking. The hurt from the past had been patched up. The brother that was previously very hurt both personally and career wise was now coming to Canada.

Time heals all wounds and time healed this one too. While they were brothers there was a very interesting and kind funny story behind this brotherly love. JD and his brother had the same father. JD's brother was born, and his mother died of cancer years later. JD's father married his wife's sister who was an identical twin. So, there are two brothers with the same father and an identical twin gave birth to JD 17 years later to the day. They share a birthday 17 years apart with identical twin mothers. The whole thing is a little bit weird and a little bit strange but it's true.

The brothers worked out their differences, over time through letters and even meeting in Hungary and the relationship completely changed. It was interesting that once the past became just that, the past and the brothers were together it was as if you had two kids around. The constant joking and playfulness of the two was often childish and showed a side of JD that could only be brought out by a brother.

Even though JD's brother was a hardcore Communist, the same as Frank, he too quickly changed his mind and acknowledged that the move and the chance he took was a good one. Having to take each relative to and from the usual places was fine. It was good to be a tourist once in a while.

Sitting down and talking after years and years of silence and after years of letters and phone calls it was amazing to see each other in person. Sitting out on the deck and enjoying the sunset and sharing a beer or two over great barbecue was enough to forgive each other. This was a big event for both men. It cleared up this monkey on their backs. They were able to move forward and be even better brothers than they had ever been. Back in Hungary JD's brother was a big shot and acted as such, so the relationship was not good. After JD left things got worse and now it was back to better than ever and when the brothers parted ways, they were able to hug and embrace each other without even a slightest hint of resentment.

This was one of the happiest times in JD life. It's one that he looked back on during the many stunning sunrises he witnessed at Queens Quay. This is a lovely spot in Toronto. It's the best place to witness the birth of a brand-new day. The view of Centre Island and the beautiful view to the East always brought up strong pink and dark purple colors that looked nearly impossible to be real. Some sunrises looked like someone spent a great deal of time photoshopping the sky.

Each day was filled with hope for JD in the 1990's. Not like today when the only thing beautiful about the day was that JD survived and got to open his eyes to a brand-new day. To be grateful that he got to witness the amazing colors and think back to the truly good and the truly amazing days when he was in his prime, when he was so full of hope, energy and confidence that no one could have beaten it out of him. Today he is older, a little frailer and that burst of energy, that locomotive that roared inside him had been sidelined and is no longer operational. Now he is content, he has accepted that the rest of his life will be dull, boring and mundane. There is no spark or roar that can wake the working monster that was inside him in his younger days. The voice that once roared had been muted by the YB. This hurts and the wound refuses to heal. It splits wide open when the anger inside him boils over and no one gives a damn. Thinking back to the good old days puts a Band-Aid on and helps stem the bleeding that had been created.

Those days when one worked hard came with rewards. Little did the family know it but luck and hard work was paying off. They were about to come in contact with the evil itself. Since JD left Sealy there were other offers and opportunities that were knocking on the door. That's the way it always is isn't it? Make one decision and hope it pays off while you get similar opportunities that also offer significant gain but which to choose.

There was no way JD would leave this little business and there was no way he would leave to work for someone else again, not when he was working for himself. This was the dream, to own your own business and work for yourself. However, there were other opportunities that came knocking and these were from old contacts and friends.

An ex-employee was a supplier to the YB. At this point in time the YB was expanding and actively seeking new suppliers and new factories to work with and expand its business with. A company called DuBarry Furniture came calling one day. Not being one to lose an opportunity, JD jumped at the chance and the new opportunity that the little company was in need of appeared out of thin air.

"Thinking back... that one phone call changed this family's life. If that one opportunity was to be missed who knows where this family would be today."

Showing up at DuBarry Furniture, JD met his friend from Sealy and reminisced about the good old days from both Sealy and Bauhaus. DuBarry was about 30,000 square feet. It was a modest size compared to Bauhaus and Sealy that spanned hundreds of thousands of square feet.

There he was presented with a set of patterns and some leather and asked to make a sample that was prepared for YB but it would be contracted out to JD and his business because DuBarry didn't have the capacity to do the work. It was an all leather seat back and headrest and it was the most popular sling chair model that YB had called the P#*ng chair.

The orders were huge, they had a yearly forecast and it came in two colors with a stool and the chair cushion. It was just the thing that was needed, it was absolute perfect timing and a perfect fit for the little company that could. As usual they needed the sample yesterday and so the family put together the sample very quickly and presented it to DuBarry who neglected to mention that the blueprints given were finished sizes and not cover sizes. While the sample looked perfect it was small because of the stuffing. It was a small error that was fixed quickly and then it was presented to the technician from the YB. This is where the very first encounter happened with YB and one of its technicians, Bob Hibbert.

He was a technician from the YB that oversaw the YB products coming out of Dubarry Furniture. The YB products came with specific instructions. There was proper labelling, packaging and stuffed articles act criteria that had to be met. The Woolco setup was a perfect introduction to this. These were very technical and detailed documents that had to do with the YB brand. Instructions in several languages, packaging, and product delivery that had to be perfect as the end consumer was picky. The YB had a certain level of customer satisfaction to uphold. This was the first time that JD met YB and one of its many employees.

From day one all the YB employees were the same. They all had a certain demeanor about them that was pretty much the same as a Men In Black movie. You could always spot the agent by the black suit and the glasses. They also behaved a certain way all the time. Only telling you what you needed to know and not what you asked. JD didn't care, the business was there and the deal was made. All DuBarry said was, we will ship the leather for the first orders.

Another customer landed, security for the family and the business was another call for celebration. The hard work was paying off and the rewards were amazing. This particular business was absolutely perfect. DuBarry was providing the leather and the labels as well as the lining material. All JD and the company had to do was cut, sew, pack and deliver. No upfront cash, no money out of pocket and they were to get paid in 30 days. No better business venture could have come their way. It was the perfect fit for the company to help with the growth. It did require the family to invest in new heavy duty Juki walking-foot sewing machines and to hire more people to operate those machines for the final operation that called the sewing of a very thick seam. It was a small investment that was taken care of and after adjusting the production layout in the basement the family was ready.

Or so they thought. One day an 18-wheeler arrived with the leather. When the driver opened the door, the truck was half full of boxes upon boxes of leather. The boxes filled up the two-car garage and suddenly the place that was allocated for finished goods and shipping became a fully stocked receiving area. It was a shock, when they said "we are sending the leather" they meant we are really sending the leather. This time and the crazy amount of the chair pads for the CN Tower job were two times this little business was very overwhelmed. Both situations were a cause for laughter later on but shocking at the time.

This house was one of great things… The business boomed here, it partly burned down and was rebuilt. It was a place of forgiveness and a place of truths. Uncle John and Aunt Gabi visited one summer. The family enjoyed dinner and the topic of leaving and escaping Hungary came up. Somehow the conversation led to the night before, the night after and the day of crossing the border. The planning aspect of the defection came up and JD had said, "Well Uncle John knew". This set off Gabi, Uncle John's wife. She couldn't believe that he had kept a secret, even after things were ironed out; he didn't even tell his own wife that he knew about the code word. Even when the post card came that the family will stay longer in Bamberg, he never said a word. That is a trustworthy man, not many people like Uncle John around anymore.

Reflections:

The move, oh the dreaded move. To not only move a house but to move a business. How many times we went through this and how many times we did this afterwards was not funny. I am sure somewhere in our past we were nomads. We should have been nomads because we moved around so much that at times, I don't know how many houses we lived in and often forget one or two. Switching countries and houses, we should have had a moving business instead of making furniture. With each move came the challenge of growth and the challenge of making it work. This was no exception and while I stated that the earlier move was a life changer, this was life altering because of what was to happen next and not so much of this move. But this move enabled us to take the next step, the next gigantic leap ahead in our lives.

From here there was no looking back. We were invested in ourselves and the company so much and things were honestly looking too good to step on the brakes. No this was pedal to the metal, full speed ahead from this point on. When the iron is hot you need to keep working it and shaping it and this was that time for the Zsemba family.

By now both my brother and I were able to help out in many ways and despite losing part of our childhood to the business it was all working in our favor and we saw the good the business was bringing, and the opportunities that came with it.

Chapter 13. Partnership

The family was in good shape now, with orders coming in the shipping was constant. The Woolco orders were ready to ship and the day the small van showed up at the Woolco terminal, the small company was made to feel even smaller. With the large trucks and trailers lined up the van seemed rather unprofessional.
The small van made its way down to dock 29 and backed up between two large trailers. The door in the receiving door swung open and the receiver was rather shocked that this small van filled with boxes was delivering to such a big company that unloaded containers and trucks all day with forklifts.
The receiver had to get a skid and physically unload the goods onto the skid. This would have been normal but not at a large company such as Woolco. Though feeling very small the delivery was made and completed. Once the deliveries became a regular occurrence the feeling of being small didn't matter so much. It became a bit of a joke that all the goods came from a basement. In time JD and Mike became friends and Mike was invited to the house for dinner.
Since the orders were on going, being delivered on time and without fail it was time to reveal where the goods were coming from. Mike and the family developed a friendship, therefore where the goods were made didn't matter but Mike did find it amusing that a small company like this would supply a multi-million-dollar outfit such as

Woolco. Mike and his wife joined JD and his wife for a Hungarian meal complete with Hungarian wine. Their friendship grew and the orders kept coming. The size of the company didn't matter, as long as the deliveries and orders kept rolling.

A similar thing happened with DuBarry. The DuBarry product was ending up in a very large company that would eventually be the demise of companies such as Woolco. Maybe not directly but indirectly the YB was responsible but only because Woolco did not see and react to the threat from companies like YB in time. At the time both companies were sending orders and that's all that mattered.

Working with both companies felt comfortable and it felt like a partnership. Good communication, good people and a very good fit with the family even though they were dwarfed by the companies they were working for and working with.

Eventually Bob Hibbert was told of the subcontracted work that the family was doing and when the news came that DuBarry would be moving across the border to Buffalo New York the family was shocked and worried.

The move was instigated by YB. It was no risk to them, they wanted the supplier to move to the States and take advantage of the cheap labor and less shipping costs from across the border. Buffalo was not a pretty place at the time and it's not a pretty place in many areas even today. This was the first time JD saw the YB flexing its muscles but this move and the reason behind it was not known until much later. It all seemed like a DuBarry company expansion move and they did keep both companies operating for a while.

Would this mean the end of their relationship with the supplier and would this mean the end of the business that had been so well received? Well no, not yet and not for a while. DuBarry did move and they did open up in Buffalo and business went on as it should, there were no changes at all to production or the way business was conducted.

By now the kids were older and the interesting fact was that the kids never got a paycheck. So, it was time to be more mature as a company and the kids started getting paid because the company could and so it did. Both kids had their licenses and deliveries and pickups were done by all. Contract sewers were still being utilized and the machine hummed along as it should.

This seemed to be the peak for the company. The furniture manufacturing was still happening, reupholstery was kept to a minimum because of so much other work coming in. The small customers that paid well and ordered regularly were kept and others were just not pursued. The fact was that the company was growing and had big orders to fill. The good paying customers were always serviced, the ones that were not, the ones that were a headache or small orders were slowly pushed away. This was normal, this meant growth and the growth continued.

Things evolve and things change. One day there was a phone call from an old friend who ran a frame shop. Irving was a character. With a cigar that was sometimes lit and sometimes not but always dangling from his mouth called JD. This was a surprise and since Irving ran a frame shop it had to be furniture related.

Irving mentioned that he is now making wooden furniture frames for the owner of a group of companies and his name was Pasquale. (Pasquale has passed away and I wish his family nothing but the best) The furniture companies in the area were numerous. But the few that rang a bell were the big ones. Palliser, Sealy, Bauhaus, and then there were big outfits that were under the radar and supplied Sears, The Bay and other smaller chain stores that added up to plenty of production. Such were Distinctive, Superstyle, Statum, DHU, Direct Home, Decor-Rest, El-Ran, and others that were more boutique high end such as Euro-Design and many more.

Irving entered into a partnership with Pasquale and they were looking for a partner to open up a leather manufacturing facility and they needed someone to run the place. The last thing JD wanted was to leave the family business he had fought so hard to be in, but there was an opportunity there. The family business was moving along very well, and the thought of leaving and being partners with someone was not at all appealing at the moment.

They had great suppliers like Valle Foam, General Foam, Cansew, YKK, and on and on it went. The credibility and the on-time payment from the family company went a long way. In the years and years of business there were no late payments and all bills were paid, even ahead of time if there was a 10-day 2% reduction offered. This improved profits without affecting cash flow.

Unknown to the owners, they were well respected as a good paying customer that was easy to deal with and didn't cause problems. The name of the company and their money was respected. There are not too many things a company can be but being honest and paying on time is a great trait to have. This all took time and didn't happen overnight.

So far there had been bad news here and there but nothing like what was about to come.

The family was informed that DuBarry had gone bankrupt. This was a blow to the family and the news of DuBarry going out of business was shocking.

Who will fill this void and what will happen to the business? Fortunately, DuBarry paid on time and any outstanding funds were even with the leather inventory that was in house. No cash but the inventory was there and despite the bad news, good news came.

When Dubarry went out of business the YB needed desperately to replace the supplier and with the connections through Bob to YB an opportunity was born.

JD and Pasquale met and a partnership was born. JD would funnel all the business from YB to a business called Cuoio Designs and they would open a 30,000 square foot facility at Keele and Hwy 7 in Weston Ontario.

The facility was a turnkey setup because Statum Designs used to be there. Since that company outgrew the location, Pasquale wanted another company to move in. The setup was there. Airlines, electrical, the production lines and the hookups for the sewing machines and even the showroom and offices were ready to go.

This was quick and a decision that didn't come easy to JD and the family, but this meant the older son would join dad at the newly formed company and the younger son and mom would not only run the business but move out to 5 Edvac Drive in Brampton and rent a 1500 square foot facility.

It was indeed smaller than the basement that the business had moved out of. But the business also changed and with some products going to the leather factory and many more coming in it made sense.

The unit was not big. It was empty and needed electrical plugs installed for the sewing machines. A much longer and better cutting table was built by a few carpenters. There was no office to speak of, so some dividers were used to divide the office from the work area. There was a single washroom to be used by workers and visitors alike. The location was close, 15-20 minutes straight down the road on Airport Road that actually did lead you directly to the airport.

"This turn of events was not expected and did go against the whole concept of being together as a family, but opportunity was knocking…"

"The big YB was not seen as the devil at the time. They needed a cut and sew facility as DuBarry had gone out of business. Pasquale was offering a partnership with Cuoio Designs."

This turn of events made the small company an official YB supplier on or about 1988. It also made Cuoio an official supplier for the YB. The YB got a cut and sew operation that replaced the now defunct DuBarry. Bob now became the technician for both companies and without skipping a beat, the supply chain was not only replaced but strengthened because Pasquale gained a leather plant. The YB gained a financially strong partner and was able to build on it further by the companies that were owned by Pasquale, Statum Designs, Direct Home, DHU and now Cuoio Designs.

This was a total flip in the family business and once again the family was separated by opportunity of growth. The small business expanded in many ways. It took on leather cushion production that was later passed on to Cuoio designs and gained the cut and sew line up of goods from the YB.

The cushion covers and the kid's furniture lineup all came from the YB to the small company that gained thousands and thousands of dollars in business and a trusted, well paying customer. The one thing the YB had going for it was that like this company it paid its suppliers on time.

Working with them also raised the quality level, the details of packaging, and production levels to new heights. Eventually both companies were once again growing. Cuoio Designs manufactured furniture for The Brick and a number of other retail stores that Pasquale already serviced with his other companies in fabric furniture. His customer base was established and the big two customers paired well with the many custom orders that Cuoio had taken on.

The family business was very busy, churning out thousands of items for the YB and at the same time for a company called General Foam that was owned by the Woodbridge Group. General Foam was also partly a YB supplier and the cut goods ended up there for filling and distribution.

In this switch all parties benefited. It was a win-win for every party and that is very rare in business. The deal complimented both the big players and the small ones. It offered growth to YB with solid supply and established companies. They were always looking for credible solid suppliers because they had very big expansion plans in North America. With the Canadian dollar always being weaker than the USD it was always in their favor to go south from Canada.

The plan for them was to service the northern parts of the States from Canada because shipping up and across the USA was very costly. They searched and found good partners after the venture to open up in Buffalo went sideways on them. The YB always has plans years in advance and sometimes they let the plans be known and sometimes they don't. In this case the suppliers felt that the plans were shared because they needed everyone to play ball. Bob was instrumental in this and the Scandinavian MotherShip (MS) was letting things out of the bag because their growth in this country was a strategic one for further expansion into the North American market.

Their relentless pursuit for lower prices at the cost of companies was not yet evident. Their ruthless ways were brewing but not yet implemented in the brainwashed souls of their current employees. The MS was fully aware of what was about to come but with their market share depending on well-paid suppliers and global manufacturing was not yet the talk of the town, it needed to wait. The current strong and well established business model was working and products were being delivered without fail. This credit went to Bob and the suppliers he was working with. In many ways Bob was the key.

"He and the suppliers were able to make small changes to the products despite having blueprints."

"This is crucial to remember because many times the blueprints were wrong or didn't work with material sizes in North America. For example, ½" inch is almost 12mm but it's not, it's 12.7mm and so on. The drawings were all in metric and the sizes of lumber in North America were in imperial sizes. Therefore, the overall product dimensions on the outside were correct but all internal dimensions had to be changed.

I am saying this is absolutely crucial because many times larger, more expensive lumber had to be bought and milled down. This added cost, so it was either deal with the strange conversion sizes, make North American drawings or pay more so the lumber could be dressed to size."

By the time the family moved out of the basement it was 1989/1990 Christmas. It was the first time in years that the garage was able to be used as a garage and the cars were able to be inside and not out in the elements. Sadly, that New Year a fire developed in the fireplace and caused nearly half the roof of the house to burn. It was a blessing in disguise since the cars were able to be moved and luckily no one was hurt. Interestingly enough it made the papers, not because of the fire but because at about 2am someone woke the family up and he also called the fire department. The fire department was down the road and was able to save the home. Later the newspaper did a story on the fire and that is how they were able to figure out who the mysterious person was. A fireman on his way to his shift recognized the chimney fire and saved the family from certain death. A chimney fire is distinctive because the inside of the chimney is effectively on fire and it's not smoke that is coming out of it.

While the family never met the person who saved them, they were grateful, and the house was rebuilt in the same spot. These days were unique and interesting. The house was a house, the basement was finished and was now used as a recreation room with a bar. Where production took place before there was a ping pong table and a wall for the trophies that the kids had won during the many games and tournaments they attended over the years.

Life was normal. It was a lot of hard work but no longer did the family say, "I need to go to the basement and finish this or that" The family had family time and they could spend time together from Saturday afternoon to Sunday. The family was split in two during the week but the weekends and evenings were free.

Both parties worked most Saturdays. It was a normal thing but at least evenings could be spent watching Star Trek and the X-files. Both were favorites on the list for shows to get home to. It did make for eating much more KFC and other fast food during the week because it was no longer possible to cook something or to throw something in the oven, now that the shop was not in the basement. These were things that the average family never thought of or gave a second thought to. Both parents run their own business and both kids help out in the different but rather relatable businesses. It was a unique time, with the growth of the family and the kids done school. There was never a question on what the kids would be doing after they finished school. Their future was there waiting for them if they wanted it.

Reflections:

While this was one area we had absolutely no experience in, it turned out to be an experience that was one to learn from. When one gets into partnerships with people who have more money and more experience than you do, things will rarely go in your favor unless you hold some very special cards. The only cards we held was the ability to work hard and deliver on our promises. We thought it would be enough to take what we knew and make it work. Were we naïve? Oh, hell yes, we were but we were too naïve to know it. It didn't matter...

We thought that there was nothing that could stop us and once again it didn't stop us, it educated us in ways we didn't know we needed to be educated in.

We went in blind, full speed and built a business for someone else. We ran the business like our business and worked as hard as we needed to, not seeing the big picture. We saw what we wanted to see and thus we were blind.

Chapter 14. Say no to partners

As with nearly all marriages and partnership things start out strong and with great intentions. So did the partnership with Cuoio Designs. It was a fantastic start for the first year, lots of new business and loads of work, a good core group of employees and acceptable production for a newly established company.
The YB business was taking over and the business that JD handed over to Pasquale was much more lucrative than The Brick. The Brick was a one trick pony with one style of furniture and very little profit and hundreds of returns due to its pig skin and vinyl match construction. Vinyl was cracking in most places and slowly The Brick went ByeBye. The company was running on the YB and custom orders for the most part. JD was supposed to get commission on the YB business and slowly it was forgotten by our partner. The rift began after the end of the first year and continued from then on in. Pasquale would use the business money for building enhancements and things that he as a landlord would need to take care of.
Essentially the partnership that involved 4 people was run by one, the majority shareholder. JD, his son Marcelle and Pasquale were the partners but there was always just enough money siphoned away from the company so that no profit could be shared at the end of the year. It was the roof, the heaters, the washrooms or the purchase of

vast amounts of leather before the year end. The company was always at a loss but the inventory was there.

Slowly the years passed and the company operated as it should but Pasquale had other plans. He didn't own this building and decided to buy another building. A 40,000 square foot building that he was eyeing would be the new home for the business. 40 Ormont drive was to be the new home for Cuoio Designs. Despite the fact that "we made no money" Cuoio paved the gravel driveway and painted the complete interior of the 40,000 square foot facility white. The place looked magnificent and sure it was a better facility, but it had to be wired, compressed air and hoses needed to be run and machines needed to be moved.

This was a costly move that set Cuoio in debt. As a company they had to climb out of it but it was getting to be too much. JD and his son were left with a sour taste in their mouths since they were working as a family in all aspects of this partnership.

The leather furniture business was costly. The inventory and materials used were costly. It needed careful attention to detail and slowly the push for production was causing quality issues.

The YB was giving more work but they demanded more and more as far as quality and materials. Everything had to be upgraded, with the new push for the environmentally friendly stains and polyurethane ingredients. The world was waking up to water-based paints, glue and the slow understanding that fire retardants were killing people. The cost of removal of these hazardous materials were causing prices to rise.

In between the move and the cost of the move came a recession. Orders dwindled, workshare programs had to be implemented and people had to be laid off. The timing of it all was terrible. While the other business kept on going and in general the YB business expanded during the recession because they were the go-to source for decent inexpensive goods. The YB business never halted but the rest did.

It all made sense, a Canadian company shipping to the States during the recession meant that the Canadian dollar was low and for people buying with USD the goods were a great deal.

The YB could turn down the tap on the US supply and open the tap on the Canadian supply and make money on the exchange rates. This was so simple and smart, no one can argue the logic. The small business was very busy; it never skipped a beat.

The partnership had gone on for 4-5 years by now. It was a good 4-5 years of learning and it was time for it to end.
Like a divorce it is hard to get out of a partnership and so the oldest son left and went back to the family business that was still working out of the 5 Edvac Dr. location.

"But there was a plan. There was always a plan, everyone always needs a plan…"

The plan was to open V.P.T. Designs. A unique name that was named after a Rottweiler, Doberman and a Siamese cat. Vector, Prince and Tiny.

Around this time Valle Foam began venturing into the very lucrative home shopping network and the pillow business was in full bloom. They came to this well-known and well-established cut and sew operation to sew pillowcases. These were not just a few pillowcases but thousands a day. So many in fact that there was no way this could be done from the current 1500 square foot location.
It was time to quit the partnership and go back to being a family. First, the oldest son had to leave the partnership with JD and Pasquale. This was no easy feat but it was manageable. Taking about 6 months to iron out all the details, the first part of the now messy business with Pasquale was put into action. The reason was simple, the other business was growing and it was better to work for mom than to suffer with dad in a now rotting relationship where profits were not allowed to be made and partners were shifting money between companies.
It was not a fair partnership, feeling trapped and working your ass off for someone else was not the correct solution for the family business minded group of people. Was the partnership a mistake? Maybe, was the partnership a learning experience? For sure! With experience comes wisdom and that was ok.
At the same time the YB was once again looking for a company to fill small orders. Small runs and styles that were much more unique than the current run of the mill furniture. The YB openly asked if the family was interested in opening another place but the 1500 square foot location would not do. While this was being arranged a 13,000 square foot location was found minutes away at 10 Delta Park in

Brampton. Finally, a location with truck level doors and a proper space for the employees as well as an office.

This location was the perfect location, it was a manageable size and you could see everything from one end to another. It had a wonderful bright area for sewing and a door on either side for goods to come in and leave.

By now the younger son had moved out on his own to a small apartment, while the oldest son was still at home. Both kids had cars and a life, and while work was still with the family business, there was more space within the family.

The partnership was dissolving and further expansion continued on the family business side. Once again JD was left on his own in the other business. Somehow, he needed a way out and fast. He was jealous of the family expanding without him. He was stuck working for someone else and what was worse, he was a partner without rewards.

Details were being worked out between the YB and the new V.P.T. Designs company. This was not rushed, the place to move to was picked. The business plan was being worked out, and you need to give credit to the big YB because one thing they did well and adhered to very well was forecasts. They too were making changes and part of those changes was to develop more local supply.

Put in charge of this in Canada was Bob Hibbert and Chuck Smith. They both worked out of the YB building at Provost Drive near Leslie St. The building still stands today as it was part of the YB store at the time. At the time Donna Mercer was in charge of scheduling and the up and coming Rijan Salim was part of the team as quality control. The office staff was growing in anticipation for the addition of suppliers meaning it was a long-term plan for Canada.

The move for the family business was set and the new 13,000 square foot facility would be taken over in the summer of 1997. V.P.T. Designs would be established there as an upholstery production facility along with the well-established cut and sew family business. The business was up and running very quickly. The first yearly deal was signed for 1100 pieces of furniture and it was a new trend of slipcovers that would be changed or removed and washed by the customer, available in different colors.

This small location was now the test facility of removable covers that were attached with Velcro to the frame. This is now the norm at the

YB. They continue with their solution, not so much for the removable covers, but because they only have to stock a white frame in a knock down configuration. They can have several colors as covers only. This reduced inventory greatly. It reduced shipping and stocking costs. The first few styles with these configurations were born at VPT for the YB.

Slip covers were nothing new. They have been around for decades and were often used but not in this capacity. They were not used in mass production and not to the extent that they were intended to be used by the YB. Initially the covers were cut and sewn in one location, the same place the frames were made. Slowly this changed and the covers were sewn in Mexico and China. This left a whole lot of other challenges for fit or lack thereof, but they all started in this small factory.

Along with the YB business, the pillow business was taking off to the level that 10 sewing machines were humming along in two shifts. So far, the family had worked very hard to get to where they were today. Financially they were stable and now the growth was based on forecasts and looking ahead down the road. This was all possible with the YB. At this point there was a good comfort level. Working together, changing things and fixing things with the technicians. Always looking out for quality that trickled down to the other products made here. The 5000 pillow cases being pumped out each day were enough to cover the wages and overhead. Close to a million and a half pillow cases a year were produced here.

There was enough zipper used each year to go around the entire world. Staggering numbers for a small company with a few workers. It was a time for one partnership to dissolve and unknown to the family another one was to open up.

Finally, when JD was freed from the Cuoio partnership nearly a year and a half had passed. Time flies and the family once again is reunited. But as things went it was not completely united for long. One day a phone call came and oddly enough it was a cost control/engineer from General Foam who was desperate to meet with the family. Never refusing a meeting, the family met with a man who was visibly shaken and in terrible mental health due to a partnership he was in. If he got caught and he would be fired for directing business to his own company/partnership.

At this point the story didn't make sense but as he elaborated and explained the pieces fell into place.

His story was a curious one. The family business lost some of its business to a new competitor. It was a product for the YB and someone else had lower prices. That was normal, but it turned out that the man from General Foam was giving out costing to his partner and this came to bite him in the ass when his partner was stealing from him. Karma one could say.

After a long chat it was clear that this man was doing his own business with a partner and taking business away from the family and funneling it to his own side business.

Along with the cut and sew they had several foam cutting machines that the family business could take advantage of and cut their own foam and save costs. So essentially a man that was screwing the family came begging for mercy, to be saved because he would lose his wife and family if the company he worked for found out what he did. He used his influence to give business to someone else. In the meantime, he got screwed by a partner that was paying people under the table and stealing from him.

There was a huge advantage to cutting and selling the foam for the family business because this business was growing and it was money going from one member of the family to another.

Same as the original family business was charging V.P.T. Designs for sewing, the new foam business would charge the furniture business for foam. On top of all that the cut and sew business would gain back some of the cut and sew business that would be taken away from the other company.

So, while JD was coming back, the younger son was given the responsibility but it was his choice. He was asked if he wanted to prove himself and get into this new foam business that no one in the family knew anything about. Again, this was the family attitude, "Sure, we can do it" It was an attitude that was passed down from generation to generation.

This business opportunity was perfect, and the family was financially able to acquire this business. It was not an outright purchase but paying off the debt it had and continuing the business it was already doing and adding a whole lot of business that was about to come in. It is always easier to ramp up than to jump right in. This was a little bit of both. Funny enough, the younger son absolutely hated the feel of foam and constantly got goosebumps at the feel and sound of it if you ran your hand along the foam. He decided to take on this challenge, learning from the ground up.

Blocks of foam are like loaves of bread. Making a sandwich is easy, but efficiently cutting up blocks of foam to reduce waste was a learning curve.

This business was different. The majority of the shares belonged to the family and this family was fair. Even though John had diverted business with inside information on pricing and production numbers, he came forth humbly and honestly. When you see a man shaking and in tears begging for help and you are able to help and the business fits perfectly in your plans for growth, it was an easy decision.

The move to 10 Delta Park and the newly acquired business renamed and reworked called Design Variations Inc. or D.V.I. Was now the supplier for V.P.T. Designs. All of a sudden there were three businesses with the original family business leading the way.

It is never easy to jump into a partnership and this was as quick as heading off to Vegas to get married. But the fit and cost savings and the profit margins were staggering and with special block prices from a partner like General Foam and others soon to follow the decision was stupid simple.

There was a lot of pressure on both new companies. The two brothers had to work together but unlike before they were in different locations and each business had to make money and grow.

Growth was both business wise and personal. The "kids" were used to responsibility. They were not kids but kids to JD and his wife they will be forever. The kids knew the business from the ground up, they knew the grades of polyurethane and they knew what they needed, how they needed it and using all that knowledge to package all that common knowledge between them. They had to communicate person to person and business to business. Proper documentation was needed both for themselves and for the YB.

The YB did in all accounts bring all business to another level. Not because they were the YB, but because you were a supplier for a company that had success, and therefore they had experience on how to build up suppliers and how to ditch them when they didn't meet standards. The quality aspect was always number one.

"The YB customer requires zero defects."

This was the goal and any implementation in quality had a trickle-down effect to all the products. Starting off with the YB when you are small was perfect.

Going into a large existing business and revamping it to the YB standards was a difficult task. Adding the YB way to a business is an exercise in paperwork, training and standards that may seem rather strange and some can seem rather obvious. Growing with the standards was easier than later implementation.

At this location many things changed. Before this all the workers were in very close proximity to the owners. But this location was a move from 1500 square feet to 13,000 square feet. In the beginning the sewing area was the only part that was active because that fit right into one area with wonderful windows looking on to the street. The rest of the building had to be set up with a compressor for pneumatic tools. Tracks had to be set down for the wagons and electrical and air hose drops had to be set up for the upholstery and gluing areas.

There needed to be a good flow for production to reduce bottlenecks and doubling back over the flow of production. The sewing room was set up and when the workers showed up for the first day they felt a bit lost with the vast empty space that was being readied for the production to come.

The workers now had a lunchroom, they had their own washrooms and the owners had theirs. The biggest change in the setup was that at this location there was an employee entrance. This now differentiated and acted as a buffer between worker and owner. The employees that worked with the family in the basement were family, the employees that worked with the family at 5 Edvac Drive were family. But here, they had a separate entrance and no longer did they sign in on a timesheet. They had a punch clock and that with the employee entrance made them different... It made them employees, workers and no longer was the owner in close proximity at all times. Even though JD's wife worked on the floor and the older son was in close proximity there was now an office that they needed to enter and a slight barrier grew between the workers and the employees.

Another change was that the company had hired a few other workers. Strangely enough this business was run by a woman. This business was built by a woman and to the family this was normal and was never given a second thought. This was not an issue to suppliers or customers. This business had a female CEO that was in charge of production, finance, planning and growth. Sure, it was a family business but it was run by a woman who was a mother, a wife and the CEO.

The employees in this business were mostly women and it was not because the CEO was a woman but because they were sewers. Most of the sewing people in the industry were women and very few men knew how to sew. Well in this family everyone knew how to sew, but mom was the best.

When the company hired workers, most were men because most of the people who were in upholstery were men. While there were more women upholsterers than there were men sewers it made sense. When the new employees showed up the mostly female staff felt kind of strange. Slowly the close family ties were lifting and the employer/employee relationship was being established. However, because the owners worked in the business, the family was always on the floor as working owners. This is what made the company successful. The owners were not stuck in a fancy office and giving orders. They were part of the workforce and that was respected by the workers.

The family was also well respected by the industry. Paying your bills goes a long way in all industries. Being working owners you see and feel things differently. When employees come to see you and complain about something you are actively participating in and their feedback or problem is understood because they know you know.

Anytime suppliers came they were treated well and the family was loyal to its suppliers. There was no bullshit or lies, this is what we pay, this is what we need, this is what we are doing. There were no secrets or bluffing and the suppliers loved this. The suppliers knew that they were welcomed to share a homemade Hungarian lunch if they came at lunch time or a coffee at break time.

The family always, always took breaks, and lunches when the workers did. The buzzer went and they were back to work. This is what made the workers respect the owners. This is how the foundation of this business was established and in this location things took a drastic change.

At one point the business was bursting at the seams. The move that was not doubled or tripled in space was almost 10 times bigger. The business added the second shift. At this time the 13,000 square foot business was doubled to 26,000 square feet just by adding a second shift.

"This location was the most fun, the most satisfying and the location we worked the hardest at in our lives. The longest hours worked and the most money we had made up to this point".

This was one statement by a family member. Added to this was the fun they had. Even having to sleep at the location several times because there was so much work to do. The oldest son worked the evening shift. Hours were from 7:30am to 4:00pm and the second shift started from 4:30 to 12 midnight. The house was not far and so when getting home for him at 1 a.m. and seeing that there was nothing to do at home, most of the time the hours he worked was from 10 a.m. to 1 in the morning. This two shift arrangement went on for nearly two years.

By this time JD was at 10 Delta Park and the partnership that was a little messy to get out of ended and yet the close friendship remained with Pasquale. In fact, the family became better friends with him after they were no longer working together. It was like being really close friends with your ex-wife after your divorce.

One amazing thing that happened amongst the groups of companies that worked together was that a soccer league started up. It was a fun thing and no one recalls how it started. Statum, DHU, Valle Foam, Cuoio Designs and this one started up a small league. Companies that in reality were competitors; but had plenty of differences that they didn't directly compete and beat each other up for customers, played soccer together. These were fun times. These were times when you worked hard and reaped the rewards.

With JD back in the family business, the younger son very successful managing and growing the foam business. The furniture business was picking up, things were well on their way and the little company that could, did.

This location was a blessing, the business that came with this growth was a blessing and as time passed it was time for the company to make the biggest leap. A growth that anyone would be proud of, scared of and maybe even terrified of.

Reflections:

All businesses start out with the best intentions. They start out with amazing energy and the hope for growth and expansion. All this happened and then some. But like all marriages that start out with much the same intentions they too rarely last or stand the test of time.
Such was this partnership and the trials and tribulations that went with it. It's hard for people in power to be fair because they believe they built it all and they are the "stars." They started it and the employees helped build it. Most people forget this, and it is hard to keep a level head when you are making money and riding around in your Mercedes, BMW or Bentley. When you wine and dine your clients and make amazing deals.
However, all those deals and all those purchase orders are then filled by the employees on the ground. The worker bees that buzz and run around in the factories some owners refuse to heat in the winter… And the ones that boil in the 40-degree heat that the owners choose to ignore while seated in their air-conditioned office having lunch or drinking coffee patting themselves on the back. At least we tried we bought ice cream in the summer and efficient heating for the winter. Our employees didn't dress like they were going to shovel snow when seated at their sewing machines.
Yes, we were not those people and so the partnership slowly ground to a halt, and it was time for a divorce and get back to our roots, the family business.

Chapter 15. Together again

Number 10 Delta Park was the location that kick started the drastic growth. As the lease ended at this location, a plan for growth had to be made. This was not a plan that was taken lightly.
There were no bank loans or lines of credit. All this was to be with family money, personal money and business money. It was not money from shareholders to burn. Every penny was still accounted for and every single penny spent, the family knew it would be returned when the plan they made was executed properly.
 26,000 square feet was needed. They were running almost a full double shift and while the money saved in overhead costs by running the double shift was amazing, it was a tremendous amount of work. So, the decision was made to move. Move to what size was the main question.
This was a time when the family had a smile on their faces and it was not so much because of the success. They didn't feel successful in the way many businesses were successful. But when they began looking at buildings in the 30, 40, 50 and 60,000 square feet and looked around in those incredibly empty spaces and thought back to the $150 spent 20 years ago it made them smile. It made them take a deep look to where they came from.

Never forget where you started, never forget where you came from

After looking at many buildings, trying to figure out the costs associated with the move, and which building would fit the growth in this family's future was a difficult one. It meant two things. One was that they would need to move further from the house and into a more industrial area. The buildings that were near were either too big, too small or too expensive. 21 Fasken Drive in Etobicoke was chosen. It was chosen for a few reasons and they were all perfect for the growth of this business. The design of the layout was perfect because the previous company had added about 20,000 square feet to a 30,000 square foot building. A wall with fire doors was already up to separate the foam and wooden frames from the rest of the plant. Fire doors are heavy metal doors with a track like a large sliding barn door. These doors have a weight that hangs by a wire that would and would melt in case of a fire and the doors would close automatically. This separated the companies and yet the companies were together. Everyone was within a short walking distance to each other and that made communication and supply quite easy. This called for very good organization, planning and scheduling so the foam plant could stay within the just in time needs of the upholstery plant.

This location was 50,000 square feet, over three times the size of the current location. This was exponential growth and the space was ready to be filled by not only one but three companies. The decision was made to move the new foam fabricating plant, Design Variations Inc. V.P.T. Designs and the family business to one location to reduce shipping costs and to allow for just in time cutting of foam and the delivery of sewn goods to the foam plant.

By now the family business was sewing or had sewn, aprons, cushions, upholstery goods, trampolines, backrests, pillows, dog beds, slipcovers, kids furniture, medical device covers, neck supports, knee supports and also mattress covers. The mattress covers were going to play a big role in the future.

The 50,000 square feet was a vast emptiness to begin with. But when all the pieces were placed in the empty space and the foam plant components were integrated in the plan, the space filled absolutely perfectly. This building was rare by today's standards. It had 3 shipping doors at the back to receive frames, foam and raw material but it also had two shipping doors at the front of the building that meant raw material would flow straight forward and out of the factory. The sewn goods were coming onto the upholstery line from the sides and the layout was very efficient.

The move to this location had one other major plus. The YB was looking for a company to manufacture foam encased mattresses and they tried contacting Simmons, Sealy and other companies but no one was willing to play ball with them. No one but this company was. This company was open minded and didn't mind setting up a dedicated YB mattress manufacturing line alongside the upholstery line.

The reason the other big players didn't play ball was because this was an automated line capable of 300-400 mattresses per day with no more than 12 people. The Fill-matic line that was developed and manufactured in Germany would have put many unionized workers out of work. Sealy and Simmons were unionized and YB did not work with unionized companies. This was never disclosed openly but it was to the suppliers. If the union came in the YB would walk. This was always quietly communicated but it was a known fact and if this is double checked in the news it is evident even if they may never openly admit it.

The YB was also going through changes. The main Toronto office was to be closed and offices were to move to New Jersey and Philadelphia. There were changes in the air and the reign of the good old B.H. and C.S. was slowly coming to an end. It was an interesting dynamic. Out with the old and in with the new. There were talks of both men being compensated for some of their added work by the suppliers. There was truth to this. What would you give your friend for Christmas? A box of chocolates? Chocolates do not cut it at this level and afterwards the YB employees came accompanied by another policy. No gifting of any sort was allowed nor was any employee allowed to accept any gifts. Coffee and food were an exception of course. But lavish dinners were not allowed.

This was a new way of business, no lobbying of buyers, technicians or anyone of the visitors regardless of the position they held. Interestingly enough as the new people slowly trickled in they were educated people. They were young educated people who knew nothing about their jobs. This caused a big rift between the suppliers and the YB. Sending green new people to a supplier that ended up teaching the technicians how to do their job, and yet they were dictating to the suppliers what to do and how to make a certain product. No one had decision making powers... Every single question had to be called in, the MS oftentimes didn't understand and each time the technician came out a visit report had to be made.

As the mattress covers were coming in, the quality issues rose from the Mexican suppliers. The YB was ramping up other sewin and upholstery production and was banking on Mexico to be a very big player for them and supply the southern states. Shipping goods up from Mexico was easy, unfortunately shipments were delayed because customs would pull trucks in for inspection all the time. The search for drugs constantly delayed shipments, and it was not uncommon to find a dead scorpion or two packed in with the mattress covers.

The 1.2 million-dollar automated machine with state of the art hot-melt gluing heads and totally computerized sensors was in and the mattress line started up. This was at the time, the one and only fully automated box encased mattress manufacturing machine in Canada. It was doing the work of 60 people on a traditional line and pumping out an easy 300 mattresses a day.

It manufactured, stuffed, automatically packaged, sealed and multi-packed the mattresses in bundles of 3,4 or 5 depending on the style and size of the mattress. It was mesmerizing to watch and count the mattresses come off the line. Twelve people were feeding the machine, dropping pocket coils into the foam box that was being assembled by the machine and fed by its human counterparts. This was fun and very interesting to watch; the speed was constant and the humans had to keep up with the robots.

If a person needed to leave for a washroom break they would need the supervisor to step in and take their place so the machine would not stop. Henry Ford would have applauded this manufacturing line. The immense amount of foam used was all being supplied from right next door. Some mattress covers were sewn in house and all shared the shipping and trucking to the YB stores. The trucks were over 100 percent full. A line of mattresses would reflect 100 percent but the slip cover boxes were loaded on top and so on. On paper the trucks were 125 percent full. The cost of shipping goods with shared shipping to the same locations was amazing. One supplier was shipping kid's furniture, upholstered furniture, mattresses and slipcovers and other foam goods like chair pads and tufted cushions that were for the wicker style chairs.

One tufting machine that was used was a simple machine that sewed circles instead of tufting with a button. This machine was a very old machine once used by Chrysler to make tufted car seats. It is amazing how some of the old machines could still be used alongside a fully automated PLC controlled machine and the two worked side by side. With this tufting machine comes a short story of Happy.

"Happy" was the name of an employee and was the only and the one and only person ever to have been fired on the spot in the 35-year history of the company. That says a lot because while there was turnover there were many, many long-term employees. Happy operated the tufting machine, who was let go after he "accidentally" cut a half inch 675-volt power cord that led to the machine in half with pliers. Why he did it, and how he survived is a mystery. The thick rubber soles of his Converse basketball shoes thought to be the only logical explanation for his survival. He was fired on the spot and given his walking papers

"The only other tragedy was a shipper named Brian who had a heart attack in shipping. He fell to the floor and was given mouth to mouth resuscitation by the youngest brother since many of the staff did have health and safety training but as the paramedics explained it was a quick death and there was no way anyone could have saved him."

Those two were the only ones that checked out without giving formal notice or going through some sort of process before being let go or quitting. Even at this stage of the game the family were hands on. Working on the line was the oldest son, in charge of production. JD's wife still had a sewing machine on the floor and was actively sewing. The youngest son, in charge of the foam plant was cutting foam and had expanded by hiring a few workers and working with the other partner. JD was always jumping in to load a truck and making sure things were in order, creating the schedules and following up with the different lines that were running with different styles. This was no longer a "small" family business but it was a family business all the way without a doubt.

At this point this was a machine that was well oiled and well maintained. It was not just running well it was running very well. This was a fun time for the family, things were so well organized and so well executed and the orders were so plentiful that production and people had to be added.

The mattress line was now running with a night shift and upholstery was full on 6 days a week and growing. Unless the YB and the family were happy together things would not have moved forward and this was still a very amicable partnership. Things were communicated well, well organized and the YB had been very open with their plans and kept their promises. This gave the family security and in turn they were open with the YB.

The very interesting part was that the foam plant D.V.I. was also growing at an alarming rate. Partly because of the family business and partly because it was also well run and well planned. It too had built up its own line of medical products that needed covers, it too had its own mattresses for hospital and specialized covers were sewn for mold and bacterial resistant covers. This at the time was very advanced, they were the first ones to manufacture roll packed mattresses and vacuum packed pillows. They were building their own machines and were one of the first to utilize hot melt machines over the messy water-based gluing systems on a production line after the solvent based glues were switched out.

This little company that did now had locomotive force. Suddenly the industry paid attention and within two years both the foam plant and the family business needed further expansion. Having signed a lease here and not wanting to move there were no other choices but to rent out buildings nearby.

At first the foam company moved to about 35,000 square feet and the trucking was subcontracted to one company who was always ready to run around with a straight truck and later with a large trailer.

The company bought trailers for frame and machine storage. Some old machines were threaded in, others put in storage and they could be brought in if needs changed. It was time for expansion and the family business took over the back of the whole building at 21 Fasken drive and moved the foam plant to 44 Fasken drive. This was a very busy time, there was no looking back. Looking forward with all hands-on deck was the way to go.

The foam plant was doing pillows and underpadding, underlay and were specializing in hard to fabricate complex foam pieces that no one else could or would manufacture. Again, always saying yes and figuring out how to do it was a strength of the family. Having a good strong relationship with the customers and suppliers was always a good place to be.

Even though the company expanded they were still running on family money. No bank loans and no lines of credit. This was a very healthy company. At this point the company was stretching into unknown territory. The expansion was on a scale that is rarely seen in any industry...

"The most interesting part was that at this point this company had never spent a penny on advertising or salespeople."

This family business was always word of mouth. Business came to the small basement and continued to roll in years after. Maybe it was pure dumb luck, maybe it was the people, the family or the quality and the way the business was run. It may have been a combination of all of the above, that drove this machine, that was now chewing up raw material and rolling finished products to the shipping doors at the rate of 3-5 trailers a day. This machine was not about to stop. Several frame manufacturers now supplied the company full time. With about 70 employees now all together this was not a small business. Frame Tech, National Wood, and Traditional Frames were some of the larger manufacturers for frames for this company. Tri-star manufactured legs and other wooden components and some metal components were made by Da-Sh Metal and most of these companies are still around today.

The golden rays of the sun bounce off the water while JD treated himself to a soft ice cream. He contemplated his day while enjoying something he has loved all his life. Ever since he was a kid he loved vanilla ice cream. He would save up the pennies to buy regular ice cream in his town of birth Uj Lengyel, which was a tiny little dot on a map in Hungary. When soft serve ice cream came along, well that was a game changer. JD loves it and to this day he has a hard time to resist it.

This part of JD's life was about as good as it got. The family was well off, not millionaires and not Ferrari's or Bentley's but they were comfortable and things were very stable. Stable with wonderful growth and growing even more. JD didn't believe in getting a sales person because one was never needed. But now it was time to diversify a little. All the eggs were in one basket. Actually, there were no eggs, no basket, just one umbrella and the company needed other customers and other business in case things were not always rainbows and unicorns.

JD takes a lick from his ice cream and almost smiles. Not quite a smile but he remembers the good times. The push for production and seeing the challenges ahead he remembers the people that helped from day one. This company had its core strength because of the can-do attitude of the people. Because this family worked closely with all their employees. There was never yelling allowed on the floor, JD recalled the way supervisors treated the people like dogs, yelling and screaming and calling people names. That was never going to happen and never was a voice raised at anyone no matter what. In public or in private, no yelling and no screaming. JD had plenty of supervisors that treated people badly, supervisors that treated him badly. No one in the family ever yelled at anyone and that is a fact. To think back over the years and to think of how many people were able to afford new cars, new homes and sent their kids off to school because they were given a job is quite amazing. There is a sense of accomplishment and that makes JD happy as he enjoys his ice cream. How this family directly affected the wellbeing of not only their employees but the ones that worked for the frame, fabric, wood and metal suppliers that were directly or indirectly growing because of the hard work this family was putting into this expanding business. Back in the basement the family often wondered,

"Who is buying all these aprons? It was incredible to see someone using a product you made."

Later on, the sofas and mattresses were in people's homes and you would visit and you would say I made that. One of JD's favorite things to do was to check out the constitution of all furniture and he remembers one time in a store when he lifted up a sofa and knocked over a glass table behind the sofa. Yes, he had to buy the broken table and at the time it was hilarious.
Remembering the breakfasts that his wife would bring the family from a small diner that was on her way to work at 10 Delta Park. The wonderful bacon and eggs that they got there, always at the perfect temperature in the Styrofoam boxes. His wife would page the family in for a family breakfast. These were the amazing times that made it all worth it. Bringing donuts in for the employees or Tim Bits that he still enjoys when he can afford to splurge a little. At the time there was little reminiscing, it was full speed ahead and all hands-on deck.

With the growth came another move. The property on Airport Road served its purpose and it was time to move on. No longer was the family buying a house for the sake of the business. This time it was for personal reasons, not the size of the basement or how to get furniture in and out and checking if trucks may or may not enter. This time this house was for the family and it was something to make their own.

This time the move was to 12723 The Gore Road. A beautiful home that had a separate two-story house attached to it with a breezeway. The breezeway was essentially a hallway that connected the two.

This property was purchased and renovated extensively with a new kitchen and new bathroom. It needed some work but with three acres it was a fantastic home to come home to.

When the family came home, there was a rule that was rarely broken, no business talk. It was treated as a home. The family was very good at leaving work and work related topics at work. No matter what, there was nothing you could do to fix it when you were not at work. This house was the first home that was bought for personal reasons and not business reasons. It had white siding and grey brick, plenty of space and a nice view of the country in all directions. There were no neighbors around and even though it was close to a fairly busy road it was not that busy back then. The drive to work was actually closer than the old location and it made for a wonderful home that the family really enjoyed.

The addition was perfect for a single person and once again it was nice to come home and relax. This was probably the most perfect time in the family's life. These were secure, comfortable times that had some stress and also had good positive vibes.

In 1992 to this new home the grandparents were welcomed. They were getting on in age and grandma had Alzheimer's and Parkinson's disease. At the same time grandpa had throat cancer. He had been a smoker all his life and it caught up to him. He had to have his voice box removed and he had the hole in his throat to breathe and cough through. He could communicate but was very sad to see, yet they still mustered up enough strength to come to Canada and it would be the last trip for them. The trip was amazing, they got to see the family at a peak that no one had ever been able to imagine or predict when the family first defected from Hungary so many years ago.

This trip was a sad one, it was clear that they would most likely not be seeing Canada again and the family would certainly need to go back and visit as often as possible. Though this home was not bought with the business in mind, it was bought with convenience in mind. If JD and his wife wanted to leave, there would be someone at the house. The family always had pets as the name of the business indicated. This home was no different. Unfortunately, two members of V.P.T. had passed away. Prince had to be put down. He lived quite long for a Doberman, Tiny the Siamese cat vanished and never returned, Vector the Rottweiler was the only remaining member of the pet family. He was well known at work as he came and went with the family all the time.

The family replaced Prince with Zena a German Shepherd and Taz the Bengal mix cat that lived up to its name by being the craziest pet ever. The family had a new home with new pets. The continued growth of the business also required further hiring of people and even more expansion on a scale never thought possible.

JD also managed to purchase a 1994 Porsche 944. It was not new; it was not perfect but it was something he had wanted forever. It was a dream come true for him, an amazing splurge he was able to now afford. Over twenty years of hard work and he finally spent something on himself. The burgundy on burgundy leather 944 Porsche was something he always wanted. A little sports car that he could take out on the weekends and have some fun when he drove to work on a beautiful sunny day with the windows down and the sunroof open. It was not the Rolls Royce that the owner Marty Silver's mom from Bauhaus had or the Ferrari that Billy Natheson from Sealy owned but it was his little sports car that he was more than happy with.

He sincerely felt he had yet to deserve to treat himself. It was not as if he couldn't afford it earlier. It was not as if he wasn't allowed to purchase something for himself, but in his modest mind he did yet deserve it and was not allowing himself to buy a toy for himself. In his mind the kids and the family, the house and business always came before he did and now it was time to spend a few thousand dollars on himself. This was well deserved and while he always had a grin on his face when he got in, he never forgot the moment he drove that car home for the first time.

Reflections:

This time of our lives was quite amazing. Things were good and things were positive. It would be hard to knock anything at this time. The business was moving forward with such energy and such speed that we would have to think really hard to find a negative thing to say. If anything, the negative was to be able to solve the problems of growth which was a positive thing.

Sticking with the family theme we always had pets of some sort. When we lived in the country, we had dogs and cats as well as the odd found animal such as injured pigeons nursed back to health and baby rabbits that were raised and released.

At this time mom and dad took some time off and were able to enjoy life. Trips to Mexico and Cuba, taking some time off for the Field of Greens on Prince Edward Island and meeting up with Chef Michael Smith.

After the weekend, they became good friends and even did an episode of Chef Abroad together when Michael was interested in doing a real authentic pig slaughter in Hungary. Ann and George were in one episode of Chef Abroad Hungary and oddly enough we played the video at mom's funeral. It was not until later on that we realized that a pig slaughter was not the best idea at a funeral. The fact that Michael dedicated a recipe in his book to mom brought tears to our eyes when he presented it and to this day remains a very special moment in our lives.

But before her passing mom did get to enjoy life a little more. She made up her own hours and taught Donna and Sarah as much as she could. Often, we wonder how things would have played out if she were with us today.

Chapter 16. Change is constant

As nothing ever stays the same in life, this place was far from stagnant. The years at 21 Fasken Drive were amazing. Although it's referred to as 21 Fasken Drive, it was a sprawling business that had outgrown the location. 21 Fasken Drive was now also 30 Fasken Drive, an 80,000 square foot facility where all the YB production had been moved. At this point the two locations were producing about 300 pieces of furniture a day and this was not enough for the YB.

The previously mentioned sales person came on board and brought with him Steve Freedman from The Chesterfield shop and a few other stores. The family was expanding to custom furniture, piggybacking off the amazing prices the business was able to get from the suppliers of raw materials. This buying power was very advantageous giving amazing prices and amazing quality on custom furniture. With the addition of leather, the family business gained many customers from the local custom furniture market. Gone were the days of picking up furniture from the roadside and taking them apart in the basement of the Toronto home. The company now very rarely did special favors for customers, but even that was contracted out.

The apron business slowly dwindled with the competition from China and there were only a few customers that still ordered aprons on a regular basis. The business model had changed, business itself had changed and was changing. With the YB production moved more people were needed and Rijan Salim and Donna Mercer both ex YB employees came on board. The old team was being pushed out and "offered" jobs that they were not going to take and therefore they were forced to quit. The YB was and is slick in their ways. At this point frequent flyer points that belonged to individual employees were given to the YB and this had their employees complaining. Cost cutting measures were in full force and lower paid less skilled people were replacing the good old boys and girls. Hence ex YB employees joined the family business. The company also added another YB only sewing facility to its buildings at 304 Carlingview Drive. This was a cut and sew only location that was needed to keep up with the furniture orders.

Communication was a bit difficult and a network of cordless phones and paging systems was introduced so people could be reached at the different locations. The company was safe because it could shut down buildings as needed if the business dwindled, but it was a logistical challenge to keep things organized. Due to the different leases ending on the different locations, each had to be negotiated so one close endpoint could be established.

Along with a new state of the art Gerber fabric and leather cutting machine, a leather sewing facility was added for one of the styles that the YB added to their line-up. The 80,000 square foot location at 30 Fasken Drive was filled and was full of goods at all times. The addition of fiber filling machines and feather filling machines were also added to the 30 Fasken Drive location and another frame manufacturer was brought on board that did nothing but supply the custom and production frames that were now being eaten up at an alarming rate. The number of employees increased, the paperwork demand also increased, the YB came out with their own internal health and safety standards. Some were understandable and some not. All these buildings were quite old, the landlord was not willing to upgrade so washrooms and exits from the building now had to meet the YB standards. These were all coming at a cost and at the same time, the term "price development" came to be a thing that the YB relied on. It was YB speak for 'reduce your prices as Mexico is coming on stronger'. Fortunately, the quality coming from Mexico was always questionable and not a threat in the short term.

D.V.I. in the meantime had completely outgrown the 44 Fasken Drive location and took on 80,000 Square feet at 3939 Nashau drive.

The company acquired (PET Business) and also took on big customers such as Sears, Walmart and various other customers for hospital mattresses and more medical and health related products. With products on the home shopping network keeping the family business production going, D.V.I. also became a big supplier for Toys "R" Us. Supplying them with beanbags, pet beds, flip flop beds and then another very big customer came on board. Spin Master who licensed Dora the Explorer, Bob the Builder and some NHL merchandise also became a driving force behind the growth for D.V.I. This rounded out a very diverse business model that also required the space, people and no longer producing just furniture related products.

D.V.I. also placed plenty of orders for cut and sew products to the family business. There was no shortage of sewing and upholstery business at the moment. All the companies were humming along at full capacity and everyone was getting its full share of the business. At this point in time things were changing. The winds of change were blowing through the industry. The dollar exchange was not completely favorable. The YB was clear with its intentions and with their move to the States came another big change. The Toronto office closed, and the switch to New Jersey and Philadelphia meant another change was on its way.

The office was to move to Houston Texas, a man named Mark came into the picture as a business developer. He was not the C.S. type, Mark seemed untrustworthy. Garth Willson and Sebastien Swenson, Hanna, Bridget and the President David Svenson, were all playing a new role as the YB retired the senior employees for fresh people with little knowledge of the products being produced.

This was the beginning of the small problems that added up to big ones later. This is when the changes began and unbeknownst to the family and most likely the YB and the YB MS as well.

An interesting fact that was not known to many, was that the family had moved once more to an even bigger property. They started up what was supposed to be an interesting business of raising ostriches. There is a saying that goes something like this, "Never invest in anything that eats". It's a fun fact that led to the purchase of a 60-acre property in a very beautiful area of Caledon. The property also had two houses on it and a few barns where the ostriches would live. This business was started on the Gore Road. At this point B.H. and

C.S. were still family friends and visited the property at times but they were on the way out from the YB.
As the saying goes, keep your friends close and your enemies closer. B.H. always misbehaved after a few drinks and he was a wealth of information. So, after a drink or two and a good meal at the farm he always gave up some useful information. In reality there was a friendship after years and years of working together. These boys were on the way out so there was no harm in having them over.
The farm was fun but the ostrich business never made money so it was quickly abandoned.
The family business kept going and going. The business profit margins were shrinking slowly and there had to be several cost cutting measures put in place. In many places the piecework prices were cut but the volumes were going higher and higher so the profits had not yet diminished. These were still good times. There were tightening regulations from the administrative side and the YB standards but never any quality control problems or significant problems.
This was a time of change and change it did, the YB was to take over all designs from the MS because there were significant differences between designs that were made and approved by the MS and North American standards. This one change came when Garth and several European designers came to Canada to introduce new designs. These new designs were to add to the already large line that the companies were producing.
There was one crucial problem. These designs featured soft wood (Pine) clip rails. Clip rails are rails that the springs attach to. These rails were always spec'd as hardwood. Anyone in the North American and European furniture trade knows that hardwood rails are by far stronger than the softwood lumber that is used to make houses in the North American housing trade.
This lumber grows quickly and is nowhere near the nice clean look of European white pine or the clean hardwood lumber used in the North American furniture industry. It required 2.5 inch staples and was weak by comparison. Nevertheless, the switch was made, a decision of the MS.
This is a small technical issue that was changed and also metal stretchers were added to the Pine taking away the previous solid wood stretchers. These stretchers keep the springs from pulling the two spring rails together when the springs are stretched.

In other words, the changes made were not conducive to the North American lumber that was available and the Spruce rails did not meet European White Pine for look and strength.
To meet the quality standards of the YB there were several key factors. One, the product or products had to meet spec. This was the key in every single product that was ever produced by any or all of the companies.

1. Follow the spec
2. Make a sample according to spec
3. Make the product
4. Check the product to make sure it meets spec
5. Check packaging and all labels and supplier codes
6. If it meets the above make a zero-series run
7. Approve Zero series and product is ready for manufacturing

A zero-series run meant a run of 10 units of each had to be made and presented. There were finished products and all the packaging for the entire family of products needed to be correct. Units were randomly selected and measured for size, labels, packaging specs and multipacks if it was called for.
Once all this was met, a random unit from the sofa run was sent to testing in Michigan. Because the units met the specs they were ready to go and another sofa was unit was selected from the run and checked, signed by the technician and put away in storage. This signed sample was to stay until or if there was a change in the product. At that point, this unit would be replaced with the same steps as the zero run of the product was previously approved.
These were the important steps in order to be able to send any goods out to the YB. If by chance a label didn't scan it was checked and corrected, if something was the wrong size by chance it would not pass and would not be approved for production. This system was well known to all the companies supplying the YB. The Pine change was made in the year2006/2007.
All the products were to be remade and new samples had to pass all tests and meet all Zero series checks before production. This was a drastic change across the entire range of good being manufactured and once again the lumber specs came into play. The size of a proper North American 2x4 didn't meet the exact measurements and was given the go ahead because lumber sizes differed. The thickness of

the ⅝ particle board was 15.88mm and not 15. These minor tolerances were all forgiven because the sizes were not perfect conversions. The perfect thing to do would have been to have a North American spec but that was never going to happen. All conversions were ever so slightly off and while the external measurements were dead on the internals were always slightly off.

"This problem in conversion and sizes was to crop up later. For now, everything passed and from this time on hundreds and thousands of pieces were made."

During these changes a serious and life changing event happened. JD's wife was diagnosed with cancer. She had a persistent cough and upon diagnosis she was told she had lung cancer. The cancer was diagnosed in the right lung and an operation was inevitable. Such news was detrimental to any family. The employees and the suppliers and everyone of course hoped and wished for nothing but the best and a quick recovery. As with any illness, especially with cancer, the outcome and the complications with the surgery are always unknown.
To the credit of the staff and the employees as well as the other family members this battle was won and all production, all orders and further demands by the suppliers were carried out to a T. As one can imagine at this time, hospital and doctor's visits were normal but life wasn't. There is an added stress that is not normal in everyday life. Up to now, no serious health issue had ever reared its ugly head, but this was one that needed to be taken care of. As the day of the surgery got closer and closer the more worried everyone became. Although there were several locations everyone was always updated and the family communicated all news to the employees. This was a tight knit group of people. Everyone knew everyone's names and even though they may have been in different locations they were close. This was not a company where you were left out. At Halloween people were given candy, at Christmas there was a Christmas party and on Valentine's day everyone had some sort of chocolate treat. If someone had a baby they would bring gifts or if someone went back to their home country they would bring something back for the family. This place thrived on the good nature of the people and everyone knew and understood this.

Having JD and his wife back after the operation was a small celebration for an amazing outcome. This good news let the family focus on the business again. With the relief of the operation being successful it was time for several more changes to come. The business was now self-sustaining and being run by the supervisors. Taking the time off was not the problem, the problem was the cancer. With a clear head and new revived energy, it was time for the big change.

Mark, the new business developer offered a business deal for doubling the current production of furniture from 300 to 600 pieces a day but there was a catch. The new YB request was to have 3000 pieces of furniture in stock at all times. This was roughly a million dollars in finished inventory and 600 pieces of furniture off the line each day as well as 600 frames, foam and other raw materials needed in waiting for the next days and weeks production and so on.

At any given time, there would be over 2 million dollars' worth of finished goods and raw material being rotated. There would be roughly ten to fourteen truckloads of goods going out and seven truckloads of goods coming in.

The biggest problem was that the YB health and safety protocol deemed the current buildings were old and not up to standard. This is where some of the disagreements started. The buildings were rented and it would have been very expensive to bring the buildings up to the newly adopted and soon to be implemented YB standards. The decision was made to bring all the buildings including D.V.I. under one roof. D.V.I. was not ready and didn't approve of this move but it made the most sense. The logistics were there, the current 50,000 plus 80,000 plus 30,000 and the D.V.I building of 80,000 square feet added up to 240,000 square feet. So, a 300,000 location was sourced. The decision was made to run the frame shop out of an 80,000 square foot location totaling 380,000 square feet of space and bring everything under one large roof.

This cut down on the heating and electrical costs, the logistics and the back and forth of employees between buildings and loading and unloading of trucks between the locations. It also cut down on the possibility of damaged goods as well. While this move was admittedly forced on D.V.I. the pressure to cut costs was a concern. This move was not taken lightly and by now there was a line of credit that was being used by the company; the growth and size of the business was not going to be funded with only private money.

The amount of inventory that was needed and the cash flow to fund the raw materials was a concern. Once the building was chosen the planning began.

The size of the move was no small undertaking. Taking the 4 buildings and placing them all under one roof with a proper production flow and an efficient layout on paper and translating all that to electrical drop within inches of accuracy. CNC machines that needed to be moved and hoses, air and different electrical requirements needed by the machines was a move that was big even for this company that by now was not a small company by any means. In the process V.P.T. Designs was taken over and swallowed up by the family business because a cut was no longer feasible to take, everything had to be all under one roof to save costs. This was still not reducing profits but far more manageable.

At this point, there were 250 people working, including the frame shop in 380,000 square feet and not including the move with D.V.I. Unfortunately, problems were to arise. Despite having picked out the building with the YB regulations in mind, there were always silly things being bought up by the person in charge of the new YB regulations. Once again, this building was not bought but rented. Doors opening the wrong way and not to the YB needs had to be addressed. The landlord built the building in accordance with the building regulations and they were not going to change it to meet the YB regulations.

Additional washrooms needed to be added, but to add a toilet and go through permits and designs made the final cost to add one toilet come to the grand total of $30,000. The toilet was a few hundred but the design, the permit and the work to break up the concrete, run the pipes all in accordance with regulations was the costly part.

Things like this were adding up. New electric forklifts were needed because the current propane powered ones were deemed unsafe to use in areas where people were working. These were not regulations enforced by the Ontario Health and Safety Board, these were the YB regulations.

Reflections:

You ever wonder how stupid ideas make it through a big company? Who does the approval and how things pass a point of no return? Yes, we often wondered that too, especially when it came to a certain company making certain decisions that were wrong, but they didn't listen. It's like learning to drive a car from a book and never having sat behind the wheel. Sending in young, inexperienced people who were learning on the job and creating problems that only that could only be solved by consulting the higher ups. Sending people to an upholstery company that didn't have a clue on the process of making frames, furniture, no cutting or sewing experience of any kind. They didn't need to know how to upholster a sofa, but they at least needed to understand the process.

These new people were causing chaos and upheaval, yet no one on the other side saw this. If they did, they chose to ignore it and ignore what the great furniture company was known for. Losing sight of the goal of good products at reasonable prices. Now they were making...

Cheap products at cheap prices.

There is a very big difference between the two and somehow, they lost sight of their goals in the race for profits and bonuses. When things broke, they fixed it. They became reactive even though they prided themselves on being proactive.

Eventually there is only so much you can cut from something before it no longer functions. Requests for 20 percent price reductions were not unheard of and when you are already cutting deep you hit bone and there is nowhere to go. That's how the rest of the problems began.

Chapter 17. Problems and more…

In general, the business was running smoothly. Nothing but the usual day to day things of people calling in sick or delayed goods from the frame shop or the hardware not coming in on time.
At this point, fiber for the back cushions of the sofas was imported from Korea, the hardware was imported mostly from Poland, the leather was imported from Italy and certain goods came from China, the USA, Portugal and Romania. All these components needed to arrive on time and by the thousands. Goods were constantly being shipped and goods were always in transit. This coordination fell on Donna who was always on top of things and it was very rare that something was not on time. By now there were a few people that made up the core team and added to the immediate family. Sarah was in charge of ordering local goods and keeping on top of production. Jessie, Lakshmi and Uncle who was an older man took care of things on the floor in upholstery. Alex handled all the substantial amounts of testing and quality requirements. John took care of shipping and receiving. While several other key people all chipped in to make sure things happened and ran smoothly it is not possible to list everyone. Testing of each and every component was required. Each and every chemical on each and every component had to be backed up by full documentation and filed so it could be called up at a moment's

notice. This task alone was very time consuming. Before the regulations only the supplier had to sign off on the documentation but the new regulation called for each supplier to agree that they are for example not using child labor. This was always interesting because some of the regulations were strictly for developing countries. This was not a developing country yet the company and the suppliers had to sign off on documents that people are allowed to use the washroom when they needed to. That people were given time to eat and take breaks.

All this was understandable and things like this were never an issue. The headaches came when drastic cuts had to be made. With the YB Houston office established and the head people in place, about a year after the move to the new location the requests for drastic price slashing began.

At this point the relationship with the YB was over 20 years old and the company was over 30 years old. The two companies had weathered recessions together and been through personnel changes and have grown in many ways over the years. There was tension now with price cutting and testing requirements where the costs were being passed down to the suppliers and further and further tightening of the belts had to be made.

When a redesign of one of the styles was made there was a competition of sorts. Canada, Poland and England had suppliers entrusted with the redesign and the criteria was to make the sofa as flat as possible and easy to assemble. This required several trips to Europe and eventually the design was awarded to this Canadian family owned company. Once the new designs were implemented it meant an 18 million Euro a year savings in shipping and storage costs for the YB a year. This was a big win. Most design decisions came from Europe. However even though the JD's company won they didn't have any credit for the design. That went to Jens, the person in charge of the project. This was hurtful but then again, it was normal for the YB. The company was awarded this and a quality award won nearly at the same time.

For a North American company to have the lowest returns and the least quality issues was a big pat on the back as European companies always seemed to have the upper hand. These were small but important accolades for this company. This gave a little boost to the now large company that was producing 600 pieces of furniture a day.

When JD thought back to the days when the first contract was signed by V.P.T. Designs for 1100 pieces a year, 600 pieces a day would have been unimaginable. When JD thought back to Bauhaus making 1000 pieces a day and Sealy was not even near to 600 pieces a day, it is almost laughable that this was even possible. This was achieved by two people with absolutely no knowledge of how to run a business, neither he or his wife had never had any business education. In this country anything was indeed possible. So far, the business ran for over 30 years. 30 years is a long time for anything. It cannot be thought of as pure dumb luck or a lucky break. This was serious, and having dealt with serious companies, it was not simply an accident that this company got as far as it did.

Now it seemed that the new YB office with the new people had an agenda. They demanded cost cutting across the board immediately. Cost cutting was and is always possible. However, to maintain specs and continue cost cutting was difficult. These were extremely important when cost cutting options came in and packaging was approved for a change or cover designs were changed, they were all with the approval and under the supervision of the technician. Not a single change was ever made without YB approval. Each change required a signed off sample to be made and put in stock for future reference. The before mentioned Zero series run had to show the changes.
These were all changes that were requested for cost cutting. Some frame changes saved a dollar of two and admittedly and knowingly the Houston office approved the changes. It was unknown if the changes were communicated to the MS. The production continued and hundreds of chairs, sofas and other items were made with changes to the spec.
Interestingly enough, the visit report reflected the work done on any given day. Random inspections were also part of each visit and recorded on the reports. The technician always came with someone else from the office as per the YB rules. It would have been impossible to make changes and if the company, had it would have meant an immediate stop in all production. The risk was too great and the quality control person was always with the technicians on every single product audit. Changes were not possible without the YB knowing… period. Any and all changes were approved by the

YB. On top of that, each year, each product was randomly selected from stock and shipped out for product testing to an independent testing lab in Michigan to ensure that the staples, glue and filling stood up as they did before.

During this time the foam costs came under scrutiny and the family business was forced to cut its one supply of foam. The YB had always had an open book pricing with its suppliers. This was a well-known fact and they cross shopped one supplier to another for frame cost and foam costs. This was always the way the business operated. Open and fair costing and the business was allowed to make a certain percentage.

Now however they were digging and digging in places where there was no more savings to be had so the specs had to change. An example would be a box. Some packaging cost upwards of $60. Using a single wall box over a double wall would save up to $10. These were simple changes. Take the price sheet, punch in the new spec and new price. Voila, savings can be had and so this went on from 2007 on.

This was as far as this company would go... Reaching this height was not easy but doable and it happened over a 30-year span. Now to stay on top and keep this momentum going...

Unfortunately, disaster was not far away. Due to several mishaps price cutting and a dishonest partner, D.V.I. was forced out of business. While there were other complicating factors the younger son closed D.V.I.

While this happened, another opportunity came along and that was to buy Distinctive Designs. This opportunity was taken because this company had diversified a little but not enough. With this acquisition it was possible to grow the non YB business to 6 million dollars per year and keep the 25 million per year with the YB and run the product down the same lines as the other custom furniture. Along with this acquisition kid's chairs, headboards, mattresses and other products were being produced but slowly the orders were dwindling. The YB chose to, without notice shift all operations for mattresses and some other business away from the family. This was not part of the plan; it was done over roughly 9 months, but after that the 1.2 million-dollar machine became a paperweight, sat idle and people lost their jobs. The business was still manageable as it proved itself over the years.

As with all things, life goes on. Picking up the other business was perfect timing. However, what was not good timing was that JD's wife had found out that there will be another fight with cancer and this time on her left lung. This was another blow to the family and this fight was not a short one.

The procedure was a familiar one, the family had been through it before, tests and tests, operation and hope for the best. It sounds simple and dumbed down but that is exactly how it was and how it went. While the operation went well, things were not well. JD's wife had complications and her lung was filling up with liquid and she had trouble breathing. She was in terrible condition after the operation and her suffering went on with her not feeling well. After days on end in the hospital and little improvement she wanted to die. This was difficult for family members to hear. She was not well but managed to pull through and she fought back and managed to return home after a long hospitalization. Further bad news was to come, when they did the biopsy they found that the lump had small cell cancer in it. Small cell cancer attacks the brain and can spread very quickly. The decision had to be made. To do chemo was a given but the doctors suggested radiation to the head to kill any possible chance for the small cell cancer to spread. The chemo was familiar but the radiation was not.

Eventually the decision was made to go ahead with the radiation and looking back it was a mistake. At the time it was an unknown and after the radiation it was compared to the frying of the motherboard in a computer. Also, after she had the MRI, she was unable to go to the washroom. The gadolinium contrast medium that she drank for the MRI ate away at her intestine, it had to be removed and she had to have a stoma.

This was over several months and she hated living with a pouch stuck to her side. While she was managing, things were not good. She had stopped going to work and stayed at home. She had given up a little on life and things were not going well for her and the family.

The business hummed along and while the family members took turns it was most stressful on JD. Staying home and keeping his wife company was of course possible. But this was not normal. A helper was hired so JD could spend time at the office and keep on top of things and still spend time with his wife. The kids took extra time to be with her, since there was no way of knowing what was next.

Eventually things looked a bit more positive and at times JD was able to convince his wife to come to the office and say hello. She was bald, weak, feeling absolutely terrible and honestly, she didn't look healthy. One of the last Christmas parties she attended wore her out even though every single one of the 250 employees was rooting for her, praying for her. After that there was an infection in the stoma and the doctors suggested reversing the stoma. These are things that are beyond one's control. This family knew manufacturing and furniture, foam, frames and production. For everything else they needed to use judgement and listen to the doctors and specialists. The time dragged on, and while she didn't have "cancer" the treatment was killing her. Slowly over the months she deteriorated and the stoma that was reversed didn't do any good. She was fading before their eyes, and there was nothing anyone could do. Her body was unable to get nutrition out of the foods she ate. The worst part was she was aware that she was dying. She had given up because there was no positive news coming her way. The family knew it was a matter of time, she knew it was a matter of time.

The family was in turmoil, by now the YB was coming on strong and they were not asking for a 5 percent or 10 percent price reduction. No, they were asking for up to 20 percent on certain items. The meetings were no longer friendly. Each meeting was tough and with open book pricing, the YB could very clearly see that they were gnawing away at the well-being of this company. The only way to cut costs was to change the specs even further.

Most products at the YB use particle board, in North America, the building industry OSB (oriented strand board) is used. This material does not look as clean as particle board. All production was done with this approved material and had been used for years and years. As further cost reductions were needed, covers were redesigned, boxes and box specs with other packaging was also redesigned and even foam grades were changed.

The newly redesigned products were placed side by side with the originals to make sure all the units looked and felt the same. Since most changes were unseen by the end user, the changes were approved. The savings were recorded, and notes were made on each visit report.

The visit reports were important, anything that was a problem in quality, fulfillment, each incident, each concern was always typed up and recorded. The visit reports were always prepared and signed on the spot. On occasion they were sent after the fact if things ran late. In most cases things were calm but there were heated moments and arguments because some cost cutting could not be achieved.

Those meetings were followed by, "You will lose the business to China" This was heard too many times to mention and the business was not moved to China. Instead the grilling came relentlessly, on the same topics, on a near daily basis.

Quality issues if any, were always addressed. There was even a live tally system that allowed the supervisor to keep track of quality controllers that walked the production line. If they saw something out of the norm, they would tick a box and the supervisor would see a live quality control screen. If there was a high number of anomalies on certain criteria, it would send an alert and immediate action could be taken.

Regardless, with the new team in Houston came a new breed of people. Ruthless and very uneducated in the world of furniture. They came from the candle department or fabric, but no upholstery experience. There was a high turnover of incompetent people and each time they had to be brought up to speed. People like Rama who wanted price reduction on her first meeting without even knowing what was at stake or seeing prices. The first meeting was in Buffalo, New York because this YB employee didn't have a visa to Canada. Things were unravelling, and yet there was a big, big push for the YB 2020 expansion plans. This expansion was believed to have brought on this extreme cost cutting measure. Their plans were to release more and more orders. However, if the supplier is not making money on the product, the more orders you give the more money is lost. This was simple math. At some point, no matter how much raw material you buy and how many times the sub suppliers are beaten down, sooner or later, there are no more cost savings.

There was however a plan. The YB asked if they could bring in 20 people from all over the world to "help" in cost savings measures. This was agreed upon, and a plan was made to have a very large international meeting at 80 Royal Group the current location for the company.

By this time, the Distinctive business that had been purchased was up and running. The younger brother looked after parts of sales and developing sales with a few sales people and some other employees that had come over with the company. This business was being built up and the custom furniture was a steady stream of income.

Although it was less than a third of the current overall sales in the business.

There were also price increases from glue, foam, cardboard and thread suppliers. Gas prices were on the way up and trucking was often charging a surcharge on shipping due to gas prices. All the while the YB was asking for reductions and reductions and were not getting exactly the percentages they wanted.

At one point a leather sofa was shipped in from China as a sample on how they reduced the costs. Interestingly enough the sample that was shipped didn't meet the outlined specs either.

This meant that the China office was also cutting costs by changing specs. This was a slap in the face to the YB. it meant that other offices and technicians around the world weren't following spec. It was not possible to meet spec and meet prices, something had to give. The individual offices tried to meet the MS quest for lower prices. This was clear now and visits to the local YB stores also proved that not all raw materials from China were meeting spec. When this was brought up, the evidence was brushed under the carpet.

Now there were frequent visits from the VP of the YB North America as well as technicians. Preparations were made for the big visit that was nearly 6 months away. Between now and then further meetings in Houston were set up and presentations were made. There would be some cost savings but not without millions of dollars in investments. The frame shop could be upgraded with new CNC instead of farming out the CNC cutting. Without D.V.I. there could be a move to a slightly smaller space but the 2020 plan called for ramping up and not slowing down. Things were in upheaval and meanwhile JD's wife got worse and worse and was now in the hospital. It was clear that she would not be coming out alive.

JD's wife was the heart of the business. An entrepreneur that carried this business on her back and grew it alone then together than alone and together again until this point of over 30 years. It was her hard work that put the company here. Everyone chipped in but she was the heart and soul.

At work she had built up a great relationship with Donna and Sarah as well as the supervisors. Her and Donna were very close. She took over most of the office administration work that JD's wife did and she learned a lot and did an amazing job. Without her the business would surely have suffered.

Sarah too picked up the holes that were left behind. It was as if they were part of the family and they worked hard to help anywhere they could and this was greatly appreciated by the family.

Weighing 44 kg and not being able to keep down food, her body was starving to death. There was no possible way to kick start her body to begin working and get the nutrients out of the food she tried to eat. A long time ago she signed her will and final wishes. When she was put on life support by the doctors, the family knew it was against her final wishes to "extend life" and if she did stop breathing, she wished not to be resuscitated.

JD and the youngest son didn't want to make the call. This unfortunate task fell on the older son to call the doctor and ask him to remove her from life support. The family was shaken to the core. To make a call that will end your mother's life is very, very hard. In the end it was her wish and while selfish, the family didn't want her to pass away, her quality of life was non-existent. It was best to respect her wishes. According to the doctors she could hang on for a week or maybe two at the most.

By this time the farm had been sold and everyone was living in new houses. While everyone else was used to not being with mom all the time, JD was going home to an empty house. The times before the final hospitalization were tough. A frail and very old looking bald woman who was a former shell of herself lay in bed for weeks on end. While JD's wife was never slim, she had a round face with short hair and was always quick to smile like the rest of the family.

In the final days there was always someone at the hospital. It was a slow death... It was a time to say all the things that one didn't say or didn't know how to say. The family said goodbye.

JD knew that death could come any minute. As he looked at his wife she would breathe and he watched her and wondered if this or this or that breath could be her last. This went on for a day or two and the morning of March 20 2011 she called out to JD several times before she drew her last breath.

Reflections:

I truly wish that someone, anyone from the great Yellow and Blue Mothership reads to at least this part. Slim chance I am sure but while there is always hope, I just can't hold my breath.
The ruthlessness that came with the new mindset of the YB was revolting. Ignorance and blindness that came with the Houston office was something we often thought about. Each meeting with them ended up in a fight. The want and need for price reductions was unrelenting to the point of stupidity and at the cost of product or packaging quality.
No longer did the supplier matter… No longer did the customer matter. Make this product for this price, no matter what it takes. Someone at the Mothership was very out of touch with reality. Prior to this, the good old boys worked with the suppliers, consulted with the top suppliers and asked for opinions. Now it was a regime that said, "Do as we say or don't do at all" Did what we were told, and in the end, it bit us in the ass. If only we had that fortune teller at the local fair to tell us otherwise.
No, the passing of my mother didn't affect production or quality, nor did it divert our attention. We had well trained people on the ground and they were looking after things.
That would have been a poor excuse to use from either end. It made no difference on the product leaving our back doors. Sure, as a family we suffered and as a company we felt the missing piece of the puzzle but that was life. Another hurdle to cross and another problem to solve which we did in time.

Chapter 18. Next

This was a time of reflection...

JD sat under the flashing lights of Dundas Square and wondered if it was all worth it. Right at retirement age when they were taking trips and when they could travel and live a little, JD's wife and the mother of his children passed away.

Was it all worth it? Was the business worth it? Saving money for retirement and never giving your life a second thought. Pushing your mind and body to the limits, working all hours of the day 12, to 18 hour days were common.

Weeks on end of working two jobs for the both of them, building, growing, expanding the business, for what? In business we are used to getting things done. Work on this, get this ready and don't forget about that while you wrap up ten different things in a day as you squeeze in lunch and manage dinner somehow. Everyone is working hard and in this case; you could look out in the 300,000 square foot plant and ask if it's worth it. Look at Steve Jobs, or David Bowie, Michael Jackson or as far back as Elvis. All the money in the world but mental and physical health cannot be taken for granted.

There was no way you could pick up the phone and beg, scream or threaten the doctor to make your wife better. You can call your supplier and tell them to get things done even if they work through the night. But the doctor is doing his job and they do not want to see people die. There is no way to get your way. This was not in JD's hands, it's not in the family's hands. This was not an online order, or a purchase order for good health that you could take out of inventory. This was a life that could not be saved and one must wonder how and why we do what we do.

Slowly this family was pulled onto the hamster wheel. From a small business with a few pieces of furniture a month to a hundred per month to thousands a year. Products flew out the door and it was all coming without really trying. Few sales people and none for the YB. Those were done through hard work and team work.

The people on the floor, the people that supplied this family were all at the funeral. Busses were rented and to this day it is a very memorable experience and one that in a strange way puts a smile on the family's face.

While the loss of a wife and mother was tragic, the praise and respect for her from suppliers and competitors was overwhelming. The employees that had worked with the family for over 20 years were devastated. In the end they came to work, got a paycheck and went home but they were part of the family. They saw things and learned. They grew with the business and watched the expansion. Now they were saying goodbye to a woman in an open casket who was not herself. This wasn't the woman they knew and that was the painful part.

"A quick death would have been preferred."

The show went on, while the family members all grieved, JD's sister and her husband were in attendance. Being considerably older they thanked the powers that be that they were still in good health. An occasional scare here and there but still in good health. It is always a shock for older people when someone considerably younger passes away.

With the family looking back at what was, and reminiscing about the good old days, they also needed to look forward. These past few months had been hard. As with most things, doing things out of the normal routine is hard until you get used to it. It was hard going to the hospital each day. It was hard watching a family member slowly die before you and not being able to help.

The stress of all that was gone. The family needed to regroup and refocus. Get back into the routine and occasionally pass the office where your wife, mother or friend used to sit. Those little things hit you each day at the office. Because she had been ill for a long time her duties were already passed on to Donna with Donna's work split with Sarah and so on. Good honest people are hard to find and there were plenty of good honest hardworking people in this factory. They were the type of people that could and would pull together. They may have not been the highest paid people in the industry, they may not have had the benefits of other big companies but they had the right attitude.

"A big heart, hard work and the right attitude will always trump a talented but lazy person."

This rang true for JD, he had played soccer with many talented but lazy players. He had also seen many talented but lazy workers who could but didn't succeed because they were lazy. However, when you looked down the line and saw the many women and men that had been trained to do work they have never done before, you knew that they had the right attitude. The single mom, or the new immigrant from Afghanistan, the Haitian boys that started at this location as their first job right off the plane had the right attitude. All these people and so many other countless stories that lived this world with the family and worked hard now had to pull together and face the YB. These strong individuals made up this company and made it work.

The constant bombardment from the YB and the weekly visits for two to three days was getting very stressful. They were on a constant attack and on occasion 2-3 people would come and effectively stick their nose into every small part of the business.

Soon every operation was looked at, scrutinized and often people would ask and suggest things. At times, they were totally unqualified people who took care of logistics and had no clue about how to make a piece of furniture. The unique aspect of this place was that there were dozens of skus being manufactured. This location always, always filled in for the times it was tornado season in Mexico and shipments were delayed. Or the times China failed to deliver. That is why nearly all the furniture skus were made at this location for North America.

The major difference was this, the location in China was focused on one family of products. Same for the location in Mexico. It is easy to streamline a production line for one item or one family of products. Here the inventory was a min-max system. 300 in stock on an item and if 50 were sold, 50 needed to be replaced. There were 20 skus or more and each schedule was dictated by what was sold or what the sale item was. The production would run, 100 of this, 300 of that or 50 of something else and since it was a min-max system all packaging, hardware, foam and covers needed to be in stock. The YB watched the inventory levels on their end. Occasionally, products from one week could be lumped together with the next, but not without them screaming since the minimum level of stock was reached.

It was like pushing a rope at times. They were living in the factory 2-3 times a week flying in and out and wasting time. Instead of finding ways to help with longer production runs as switchovers were costly and time consuming.

While the price reduction or "price development" meeting was still on, there was a very large presentation in Houston. This was the make it and break it plan and it didn't go over well. The company was asking for a price increase of 20 percent and the YB was asking for 20 percent lower prices. The term butting heads was an understatement. The difference was the sticking point and with the 20 person visit coming it was let go until the meeting was over and the team would "HELP" this company reduce costs and help with the production flow.

Everyone knew this was now some sort of witch hunt. If they didn't want this supplier around they should have sat down and said, "We need a divorce, we have found a new partner" instead after 25 years they played games. This new group of people led by the wicked witch of the south was going to trample over this tiny company. Using the word tiny is hilarious but considering the YB does billions and billions of dollars of business in a year it was. Compared to COM-40 in Poland or some of the other very big players in the USA where they pump out 1500 to 3000 pieces of furniture a day, this was still considered small. Even though it was indeed a large company, it was a drop in the bucket for the YB in terms of dollars and cents. The way things were going, nothing made sense and when everything is a problem you know it's heading towards a divorce.

The goofiest example of this was the fire suppression system. The new YB requirement was that all suppliers must have a fire suppression system on top of the YB regulated spacing of fire extinguishers. This building was a new building, only 5 years old give and take a year. It was so well insulated that the heating bill was less than the 21 Fasken drive location that was 50,000 square feet. Yet they mandated that the company put in a $500,000 sprinkler system.

The landlord was not going to pay for this, and the company was not going to pay. The building met the City of Vaughan regulations and with the fire escape routes and drills being adhered to this was a safe working environment. Unfortunately, without passing the YB-WAY, the company would automatically not pass the YB-WAY assessment and production must come to a halt.

This was not bullying to a point where if you don't want to do business with this company simply say so. But they were making it an issue. The local fire chief had to be called in and write a letter to the YB that local regulations do not call for such a system. The YB suggested a free-standing fire suppression system that was being used in Mexico and the fire chief's exact words were, "If you install that, I will shut you down".

This came to blows one day when the president and vice president of the YB were in a shouting match with JD and the older son to the point where there was no backing down. Shut us down, fine shut us down but we are not paying, you want it you pay. Suddenly after months of back and forth the case was closed and the company kept producing.

The cuts were coming, daily threats to reduce costs but there was no way to reduce costs further, the company was just breaking even.

The company had not been profitable for 2 years. The family drew a salary and that was it. The YB was now in nearly every day, and it was nothing but fighting. The company had received the best quality award, it had saved the YB millions a year in paper pallet design and reduced costs across the board. Yet after 25 years, it seemed that this company couldn't do anything right. The company was now being run by the YB. Make this not that, we need this and more of that. On top of this, the plan for the 20 person team was still a go and it was going to be very stressful. To top it all off they are here to "help" was the constant repeated speech from all YB employees. To help with production, to help with price reduction and to help with the development of business that is expected to be ramped up.

What the YB employees had in common was the mindset. They were all shipped off to a retreat and brainwashed into thinking that the YB way is the right way. There is no other way than the YB way and the YB must act like the Borg in Star Trek, "We are the YB and you will be assimilated. Resistance is futile, your life as it had been is over. From this time forward you will service us. You will be assimilated. Resistance is futile."

This was a common theme, no one takes responsibility for a single thing. Not one person says, "I did that" no, every single thing comes from a committee of people and the YB committee decides. There is not one person that has your back. Not a single person takes action and not a single person will say they did or didn't do something. One person would say something and the other would pretend it didn't happen. The visit reports became one thing and what was said became another.

Crucial things were not written down and when it was added by the company before signing they were taken out. This was not fun anymore. Several visit reports were in the "Refused to sign" file because they were missing crucial information being discussed during their visit. As the big meeting was nearing the partnership was turning into a dictatorship. They were even mandating that to reduce cost the company should be renting out parts of the building for storage. This was to make sure the company could be ready for the 2020 ramp up.

These were hard times. The company was privately owned but corporation run. The YB employees were threatening, rude and disruptive and they scared lower level production people. Things were being said on the floor that the owners were not aware of. These were scary bullying tactics that were as the Romans said "Divide and conquer". The employees were terrified of having the YB people on the floor. Every time they came they were asked to stop. The people were on piecework, upholstery and packaging were halted while they check things and the people were ok with this but not a day to day stoppage

Shouting matches erupted in the main office as demands could not be met. The YB would circumvent certain people and check production schedules and want to make changes as they communicated with their head office. There was something brewing in the office and it was not favorable to the company or the Houston office. The MS must have been onto something because in all the years all 25 of them, this company had always seen a calm professional workforce and respectable people talking and dealing with suppliers in a very professional manner.

Why was all this now the suppliers fault? Why was it all on the head of the supplier? If they wished not to continue the business there was a 6 month out clause in all contracts. At any given time either company could have stopped, giving 6 month notice. That was not the case and didn't end up being the case.

Instead, there was a waste of resources by stopping and restarting production and switching up orders. Order amounts causing the previously smooth-running production to drop from 600 pieces a day to 450 or even lower on days when the needs changed. Throwing a wrench in the spoke wasn't enough, they had to slash the tires and cause as much damage as possible. By now after months and months of torment, the company had to dig into lines of credit much deeper to pay suppliers and payroll at times. There was trouble and disruption but all the while staying positive that all this can and will be worked out and maybe positive things will happen when the team comes to visit.

Things were put on hold and they were left pending. It was better to take a breather and the YB was kindly asked to refrain from coming each and every week, let the company be and let them operate so they may recoup some of the losses that have taken place.

With every single product now modified, the modifications recorded, and prices reduced or the term that was used was "giving back' as much as possible, every price and spec was updated in order to have all things up to date for the 20 person visit.

Reflections:

If anyone on this planet can explain how under such strict procedures and tight quality standards and SOP's someone could pull the wool over the eyes of the Yellow and Blue, I would be happy to listen.

As I went through the points earlier… Every single screw that went into a product was known. Even the rough number of staples were known because they too had to be costed out and although I cannot recall at this moment what that was, but it was about 3 per every 4cm.

When you are aware of such detail in the products, and you see these products daily being produced by the hundreds and thousands please tell me what went wrong. There was never an answer from anyone at the Houston office. The busses kept running over every single one of us as the buck was passed.

If and when we made mistakes, we owned up to them. Even if it cost us money, we owned up to it. Never having a product recall as you often hear on the radio about shelves or cribs by the same company. Never having to pay back anything for massive returns and if we did it would be in the public as something was deemed unsafe.

All the changes and all the product descriptions were always made with the authorization for exactly those reasons. We didn't want to have a bad name, nor did we want anything to be recalled. This was so simple and yet no one would stand up at the Houston office.

Hanna was the leader in this and to this day I hate her for it. Garth was the biggest snake in the grass and the only person I can truly say I hate, and I don't hate many.

Chapter 19. The shit hits the fan

This process of adjustment and the working conditions from 2011 on was hard on JD and his family. It's been a long two-year struggle with the YB. The company was holding on and gaining some traction in the custom furniture market so while it wasn't all doom and gloom it was not very positive either. The company never lost any skus as promised so it seemed the YB was bluffing. With all its threats, things were far from smooth as the threats were not getting any less but the wait for the big gathering was there and it was a stalemate until that event was held.
April, in Canada can be a wonderful time, the smell of spring is in the air and the daytime temperatures can fluctuate drastically but with the sunshine it sure feels nice after a long winter.
After the passing of his wife, JD moved to a different house. Understandably the old house that was decorated by his wife and where she was so ill had many good memories and many not so pleasant ones. To sleep in the same bed and the same bedroom was a difficult thing to do. Each morning and night, each weekend, the house was difficult to stay in. Her death was a long drawn out process and JD decided it was best to move. Leaving things behind and trying to adjust to the process of living alone was not an easy one

but overall two years had passed and while it didn't heal all wounds it was enough time to adjust and get on with life.

JD kept in shape and played soccer every week, ran, worked out and rode his bicycle regularly on trails and on the country roads. On this day, the night before the very big and important meeting, JD went out for a ride in hopes of getting a good night's rest. Being in the country he rode a bike that was suited for the terrain and enjoyed being out.

That night, the oldest son was at home, the home phone rang. It rang several times, but the home phone was rarely answered. It was usually telemarketers and anyone that needed to speak to him would call his cell phone.

However, because the phone kept ringing, he answered it.

Shockingly, it was the OPP. the Ontario Provincial Police, JD was in the hospital. The family loved the Caledon area, and they had stayed in the area, the very area that he first visited in 1976 and 1978 upon the family's arrival. JD was in the Orangeville hospital.

The two boys rushed off to the hospital where they were greeted by the doctors and police. They were told that JD is in stable condition but… he fractured his skull in 3 places, punctured the lung on his right side and broken ribs. He also broke his left shoulder as he flew over the handlebars. His face was very badly scraped up and honestly looked like he should have been cast as a zombie for a movie. He had quite a bit of memory loss and numerous scrapes and open wounds all over his hands and face.

JD had gone out for a ride that evening and rode down a hill. He must have pulled the front brakes, and according to the police, he had to be going about 35-40km/h at the time of the impact. He landed and stayed in one spot long enough 10 meters away to create a large puddle of blood on the gravel and dirt road.

Living in the country means that you rarely see or meet your neighbors. By a stroke of luck, a neighbor came and found him lying in a pool of blood and called for help. If not, darkness would have set in and he could have passed away from hypothermia. The disorientation could have led to him being hit by a car or succumbing to his terrible injuries. JD was so disorientated that when the neighbor found him, he tried to get into the persons pickup truck and drive away, all the while clutching the bell off the bicycle.

It was a terrible sight to see. As most emergency cases go, these things take time. They had to keep an eye on the bleeding in his head, they were ready to drill a hole to relieve the pressure and so there was nothing to do but wait until he was stabilized. A helicopter was going to take him immediately to Sunnybrook Trauma Centre, but due to terrible fog the helicopter was unable to make the trip. The oldest son went with the ambulance, the youngest son went to lock up the house and check on things. JD's dogs would have been out, and it was most likely unlocked, such was life in the town of Caledon.

The ambulance ride was long and they monitored JD all the way. His memory loss was worse than expected. He couldn't remember his own name; he couldn't remember his dog's names and mixed up people's names. After he was stabilized it was very clear that he would not be an overnight patient and he would have to be hospitalized for a long time.

The two boys had to decide what to do about the meeting. Looking back, would it have been better to cancel? No one will ever know, but there was absolutely nothing to hide and the proper people were in place to handle the visitors so the next morning the meetings went on. Having been up until 4 am, the kids went home, showered and went to the office.

Immediately the tone, despite the news about the owner not being well was questionable. The team was stacked with two "senior" staff who when they spoke made the regular staff jump and the technicians known to the family acted like they didn't know anything during the introductions.

This was a side of the YB staff that had yet to be seen.

With people from Scandinavia, Brazil, China, Poland, and the Houston office everything was being scrutinized. The owners and staff from the family business also had previously visited other manufacturing plants but were never there to "help" the supplier achieve lower prices. These people were not all in the upholstery division or from production backgrounds. They were team members that were broken into groups of 4 and given tasks to analyze different aspects of the family business and they had the run of the production floor.

By the time the afternoon break rolled around, there was plenty to discuss and the quality control supervisor was frazzled beyond belief. Materials like the OSB had been questioned, the pine had been questioned and technicians like Garth were acting as if they had never seen this before in their life when these materials had been used for nearly 15 years.

The Spruce that was being used was a sticking point and that too had been in use for over 5 years. As the day went on things were turning sour and the senior people were acting like God, the YB God that is. Every question sent people scrambling. Rather than question the technicians about simple things that had been approved on items that had been produced for a long time, they chose to question the supplier. "Why did you do this? Why was this changed?" and so on. This was not only shocking but very bothersome. At the time the focus was on JD at the hospital, so the only time that the two other owners, the oldest and the youngest son got involved was when the shit hit the fan. Actually, this was beyond shit hitting the fan. This was complete diarrhea on an unprecedented level that shocked and scared everyone in the plant. After their two-day inspection and so called "help," they shut down production and brought this locomotive to a halt.

Grinding production to a halt in this company meant immediate losses. 600 pieces of furniture a day at even a low average of $350 per piece was a $210,000 per day loss. This was a low average across the board. The loss and slow bleed had begun. This was a shock and the people sent into "help" called for a recap of their findings.

This was the equivalent somebody coming to your house and questioning what you do in your kitchen, your bathroom. Telling you to rearrange your house and all your routines. All this makes sense to you and you may listen to one or two suggestions. You are not stupid, you have a great education and you built your house the way you think it should function. There may be some very logical things in the suggestions but not all of them.

Once they begin to tell you what to eat, what time to wake up and that you should exercise more because they don't like the way you look. Then they tell you that they will bring in more experts to "help" you achieve these goals, you may not like them anymore. Oh, and they will be in your kitchen and you will be tripping over them every morning, every night. Problems may arise.

When the YB recap began they took their most popular Ektorp model and began their dissection.

The first group looked at shipping and receiving, where 3000 pieces of furniture were lined up model by model and row by row. While some of their suggestions were good and would help improve the flow of goods, they also realized that their paper pallets didn't like being moved around much. They were damaged easily and the fact that there were many different sizes of multipack items made standardizing a skid very expensive. But they said if you add this and that you can save $5 off the cost of the product. Taking $5 off an item right off the top is usually not possible but they continued.

The production team was the best… This company ran nearly all the YB upholstery skus. When they suggested long runs and each line doing a special item it was countering their own min max system and filling orders to a maximum level. If the sales were 100 sofas of a certain style there can only be 100 made. Making 1000 is what every company would like to do, making 10,000 is what all production lines would hope to achieve so there is no change over and no downtime. By running long runs and a week of each product on each line would be considerable saving.

Having had their say, another $5 was shaved off the selling price. They knew full well that this is impossible, unless the YB could also take that product or store it off site. When they were countered by the supervisors and production people they replied with "these are the suggestions" Suggestions that they wanted to implement to save money on the finished goods for the profit margins of the YB.

Next up was cushion filling, packaging and the buying of packing machines, gluing systems and once again the concept of better purchasing power and better prices. All automation runs well when one product is being built. Henry Ford built one model in one color, perfect. Apple would love to sell one phone in one color. The window manufacturers would love to manufacture one size only. Imagine if clothing manufacturers adopted a one size fits all manufacturing method. The YB is not stupid, they knew that their production methods worked in a company that made one sofa, one style and made that all year round. The training of employees, the production process and increase in production would be considerable but that could not be done with 30 skus. Models being switched in and out, packaging, frames, springs, hardware, pallets, foam and covers all had to be swapped out. Lines reloaded several times a day to meet their own system requirements as they checked the system daily.

They needed to change the way they ordered, the way they needed to arrange with purchasing and the inventory system that they had created. It was a useless meeting for 20 people to gather and have a teaching seminar from non-upholstery production people. But it was a perfect meeting to achieve what they wanted to. They wanted others to see how things were made in this factory. That in itself was not a problem but stopping production was.

The local technicians began to question the changes. The senior technician was not backing down on checking every spec on every item. As previously stated, every item had some sort of deviation from spec. This was a huge task to take on, and the visiting team didn't have the time to stay and check. The senior technician was asked to change his schedule from China and Brazil to be back at this location in a week.

In the meantime, people on the floor were at a standstill. Three large issues came up: the OSB, the Pine and things not meeting spec. All of these were clear items that were being used with permission for years and years. They met and exceeded the specs from the YB. Test results for chemical levels of formaldehyde the list goes on. The YB had test results and acceptable levels of chemicals on all the items used in every single piece of furniture.

The small technical issues were not the concern here. The two big one were. There were no reasonably price alternatives for Pine; and going back to particle board would be very costly. Both changes were very costly. Going back to spec was by far the biggest issue. Trying to explain that going away from spec was the idea of the North American trading offices was nearly incomprehensible to the senior technician who lives and breathes the specs. So, the trading office took the heat as well as the manufacturer. The signed samples with all the current adopted materials were in the show room.

As puzzled as the technician was, he had no choice but to live the YB bible and stop production. As simple as that sounds he had to work with the Houston technician on a plan and the plan was not pretty. Check each of the items in stock for the Pine and the knots in the pine were given criteria that was very puzzling. The plan was set in place and the unpacking and checking of 3000 pieces in stock began.

JD lay in the hospital completely disoriented and unaware what was going on. If this ever happens to you, shut the company down and walk away. Lessons like these at the time were not available and JD didn't even know his last name. He was unavailable for consultation with a punctured lung that could collapse at any minute. He had massive head trauma. JD was trying to put the pieces together and when he couldn't even recognize people and couldn't do simple 2 plus 2 math, he was in no way able to be brought up to speed on anything that was happening back at the plant.

The doctors kept on about how lucky he was to be alive. Knowing how bad things were and if only he knew how bad things were going to get, he may have chosen the alternative.

Over the days ahead it was very ironic that JD's head and the company were in the same shape.

While JD was stable and lucky to be alive, the company began bleeding money. 3000 pieces had to be reworked and checked. The knot on the Pine and the sizes of the knots that were passable were a rundown moving target. The goalpost was here, then there and finally over there.

As organized as this plant was to push out such numbers it became a disaster, it looked like a tornado ripped through the place. Products were disassembled and hundreds of pieces were to be trashed. The "NEW" standard that had been approved for years was now being implemented because the North American Trading office was now also under the microscope. It was now clear that this office made changes to save costs but the MS was never informed.

Unfortunately, someone had to take the fall and this company was the one. Hundreds of frames that were finished goods had to be opened, loss of expensive boxes, materials and the sheer amount of manual labor and hours and hours of rework had to be paid while production was at a standstill.

Much like JD's time in the hospital, the days were tiring. He couldn't comprehend what happened and once stabilized he tried to put things back together in his head. Many things had to be repeated and while it was funny in many ways the whole thing became a disaster. The kids and the staff running the show were running into walls at each turn. Behind in shipping, late orders and yet not able to ship. Not being allowed to ship until the senior technician returned 2 weeks later. Reworking, re-packing and putting things back in stock was a tremendously daunting task.

Every single aspect of life was very hard. There was confusion to such a level that there was no one plan that could work. Pay people, but don't ship, you are not allowed. The YB took care of organizing trucks according to shipping levels and destination. There was no way to ship goods.

"Two weeks turned into a month. Over a million dollars of production in a week added up to 4 million dollars lost per month."

All the while, fifty percent of the employees were home and the other were reworking products and doing their best to have goods ready for shipping. The Pine wood had a solution but instead of $3 or so per rail it was now $10 per rail. This was the only local lumber that met the YB criteria but this increased the cost of the product drastically. After a month of incredible hard work and arguments with the YB, the production slowly ramped up and the company was resuscitated and kick started back to life. A significant loss had already occurred, the company should have been closed immediately. Unfortunately, JD was told that for 3 months or until he passed his tests absolutely no work or stress of any kind.

This was easier said than done. Looking back, the question was asked numerous times. Would things have been different if JD were there that day? The answer is a simple "no." No they wouldn't have been because the finding and the conclusion of the meeting would have ended up in a shut down.

While JD managed to settle back home, he was lucky to have someone to take care of him, the kids and the employees had an amazingly difficult task of picking this company back up off the ground. While none of this could be shared with JD, the lying was the worst part. JD remembered the company but could not be told anything, doctor's orders.

His recovery was a hard one. The similarities between JD's recovery and the company booting back up was mind blowing. JD struggled with flashcards, he struggled to remember names and places. His broken bones and fractured skull began to heal but still under doctor's orders he was not allowed to talk, visit or do any kind of work. As he healed he began to get the itch to get to work and while he was brought in the office eventually, everyone had to lie to his face and smile that life and business was completely normal. Donna had to lie and say that the financials were ok, the supervisors had to smile and also lie that production was normal.

At this time, it looked normal but it wasn't. JD was not around long enough to see that each rail and each 90-degree edge of the wood and wooden materials had to be sanded. These were all done by hand but JD saw the overview. He was guided and led only to things he needed to see; all the while being lied to about the company that he loved with all his heart. The company at this point should have been taken to the back fields and shot dead right there and then.

"To lie to your father was easy, to live with telling the lie was very difficult."

There was no easy way around it. Doctor's orders were doctor's orders. When JD went for his check-up, he failed several times because he couldn't remember the name of the large grey animal with the massive horn on his nose.
This was a hilarious state for JD to be in. He failed several times because no matter how hard he studied and practiced the damn rhino failed him every time. In many aspects JD was a big kid, his head and brain had such a shock that it messed up everything in there. They grey matter was scrambled and waiting for all the neural connections to be reconnected one by one took much, much longer than anticipated. While the wounds on JD's body healed the brain was another matter. It was a very slow process that took weeks and months to heal. Simple things like, "this is a thousand dollars" was actually ten thousand dollars. These simple connections between what was seen and what was said were missing the connection. JD thought he said ten thousand dollars but he said one thousand dollars. It is very hard to correct a person who thinks they are correct and yet they are not.
The recovery was slow. JD couldn't drive, nope not allowed and rightfully so. There was no doubt in anyone's mind, except JD's. He felt he was fine and not remembering that stupid little grey rhino on a flashcard didn't mean he was not fit to drive. He was however lucky to have his sister Livia and a good friend Olga to take care of him. The doctor stressed that this will take a long time and even afterwards there is a very big chance that onset of dementia was highly likely.
Playing soccer well into his 60's helped. JD was fit in both mind and body. No complications with the heart, blood pressure or other diseases meant that his recovery would most likely be complete. These things were unknowns but health wise JD was recovering quickly. The mental health and the connections in the brain were a little slower. A fractured skull in three places was a serious matter. At this point there was no way for JD to know that he was being lied to. It was all an illusion of well-being at the company that he loved

so much. The struggle went on, just as JD's struggle to be independent and pass all his tests. He studied hard and walked as much as he could to get his body back into shape after a long hospital stay and a lengthy home stay. JD was lucky that it was summer and he was able to enjoy the property he lived on and get some sunshine. Sunshine gives everyone a sense of happiness just as the song goes. Sunshine on JD's shoulders also helped him improve and he wondered if he would be brave enough to get back on the bike that he wiped out on so badly. To everyone's surprise the bicycle survived with only minor scratches.

All the wounds healed on JD's body and his recovery was well on its way. The thought of having to tell JD what had happened and how the company was in a financial mess was not a fun one. The months of lying and smiling to someone's face as if the world was a perfect happy place was hard on the kids.

These were lies on a grand scale. Millions of lies with the loss of millions of dollars. JD was itching to get back to work, he wanted to come back and while things were progressing the doctor still didn't give the OK and the kids were delaying it as much as possible, hoping to get the company back on track first.

The deal made with the YB was to get back to spec but the costs were where the rift lay between the YB and the company that was drowning. Reworking, reapproving all the models and making the Zero series approval runs and recertifying everything was an insanely daunting task. All hands-on deck, from sample makers to the suppliers.

Explaining this disaster to the suppliers was also very complicated. Why, why, why? There were a million why's and a million fights and arguments as they wanted more money for the new specs.

One of the biggest blows came when production was slowly ramping up. The YB with the "help" of their senior technicians implemented a ZERO tolerance rule. This meant that each piece of furniture had to be perfect.

Furniture is not a television set. Which is the example the YB used often. No customer would accept a television with a scratch on it. That is true, despite this very good analogy the television is not cut from natural materials such as wood and fabrics. The covers are not held on by staples and the outside of the television was not cut and sewn by hand. The frames were all cut by CNC machines, they are within a 1/16th of an inch as far as tolerance but the foam covering is just that it's foam and it expands and contracts. The wood used is material grown by Mother Nature.

The YB imposed themselves on the sub suppliers as well, ZERO tolerance on everyone. This choked production to a point where it was impossible to sand every single edge and have as many quality controllers as employees. Hundreds of frames were rejected by the YB, hundreds of products were thrown away because it was less expensive to make new ones than to rework. This was the last of the moving targets that they knew would cripple this company.

Random visits as if hoping to catch them doing something wrong. While JD now knows the shit that went down, he thankfully never lived the day the shit hit the fan. If he was there the only thing that may have changed is that he may have punched out the entire visiting team for tearing his beloved company apart.

Reflections:

This was a trying time that we never ever expected to deal with. Watching your father lying between life and death from one hour to the next was not normal. Saying bye at the office and rushing to his aid hours later was not normal business practice. It was not in any of our standard operating procedures. This was not written in any of our protocols, nor did we get the memo.
This simply happened and it happened at the worst time in our company history. Often, I wonder if it had to happen like this for some reason? Was it written somewhere? Was it something that could have been avoided?
No matter, but the true evil came out in the men and women that attended that meeting during those few days. Lies, absolute lies and deceit is what my brother and I felt and what my dad felt upon his return.
Every single thing we did was under the YB supervision. Heck we couldn't take a breath without asking them if it concerned their products. We felt we were run over by every single bus that was available...

Chapter 20. The witch hunt

Sadly after 35 years in business and having worked with large companies such as Sleep Country, Sears, The Bay, Walmart, Toys "R" Us and many more, this company was being treated as if they couldn't do anything right. This company had been the supplier for the YB for 25 years. One of the oldest furniture suppliers in the YB supply chain. The company was presented with a quality award for having the lowest returns, and that was only a year before the shit hit the fan.
The overall returns for this company was 3.85 percent. Not a small amount but the lowest of all the other suppliers in this category.
What needs to be understood that this was not only the quality that may or may not have been a manufacturing fault. No this included damaged goods that may have been damaged after delivery, during delivery or damaged while being delivered. It also included customer changes of mind. It also included any damages that may have happened in the store.
When this was all dissected and graphed only 1.85 percent came down to a manufacturing fault. That could be covers ripping or very rarely if a spring popped out and so on.

"But Pine rails breaking was not even on the high end of the list."

Most damage was due to transportation and customer change of mind. Keep in mind that if the customer didn't like the cover color and they sent the frame back as well as the cover, that too was a strike against the company quality record. Suddenly, nothing this company did was good enough. The design award that the company got earlier and the quality award meant nothing.

"A YB person practically lived at the factory and the situation became a very aggravating standoff between the YB and this quiet family facility."

The people on the floor feared the YB. They were scared when Garth and other YB people showed up. They feared being shut down and yet everyone from Jessie to Lakshmi and Alex were doing nothing but their best on the floor. Unfortunately, the moving goalposts and the targets moved from one day to another. The YB technicians would agree to something upstairs with management and go down to inform the supervisors of something else. Phone calls would go wild and they would say, "that's not what we meant, we meant this" Arguments, screaming and yelling were now constant in this quiet company. The fights were not with the employees but the YB staff. Randomly, readied goods would be stopped, more and more random checks implemented and change of mind from one technician to another was now common.

"This once amazing partnership had turned into a witch hunt."

All frame suppliers were now held to a cabinet grade level. Russian Plywood, often called Boat Plywood had to be implemented and like all new materials had to be certified. Paperwork took a lot of time and finding the right acceptable materials was time consuming. Implementing particle board meant more damaged goods because it is far weaker than OSB. All the packaging material had to be back to spec and tested, approved one by one. Life was a mess and the stress level reached new heights. Wherever there was a spark, explosions would erupt. The YB people were hated by all. From employees to owners and suppliers. Nothing anyone did or dared to think was good enough. If they didn't approve it, the goods were dead stock until they nodded their Borg like head in agreement.

The purchaser at this time was fired. Rama was let go and the VP of YB North America became the direct contact for the family business. Why was she let go? No one knows and no one ever will.

The senior technician was practically steamrolling over the North American technicians. The North American technicians were trying to fix their mistakes but at the cost of the supplier. Something went wrong and unfortunately this supplier was paying the price. Early payments of 10 days were arranged with the MS to keep the cash flow going so the suppliers could be paid. At times it was so bad that the now line of credit was maxed out and unless the YB paid, salaries couldn't be paid. Supplier payments were stretched further and further to the point when raw materials were on COD. Of course, they were scared, this machine needed to be fed. The 600 pieces a day was cut to half so that they can "help" secure quality goods. The prices were negotiated on 600 pieces a day, when the orders dropped the prices from the suppliers went up.

Boxes are a great example, one box may be $10, order 500 its now $8 and order 1000 and now its $5 order 10,000 and you could see the cost drop drastically to $4. Unfortunately, the low orders meant higher costs. Explaining this to the YB was easy but they refused to take the cost increase. They controlled the orders and yet they wanted lower costs. It was a constant fight, argument and yelling and screaming to the point where communication was cut off. This partnership was no longer a manageable one. The trust and communication in this partnership had eroded to the point that a marriage counselor would surely have given up mitigating the damage. The implementation of the ZERO defects policy was a killer as this was after all a sofa, not a television. Knowingly sabotaging a company is shameful, it's wrong and goes very much against the YB code of conduct. But it was happening.

During the middle of this upheaval JD was able to remember the silly mind stopping rhino and passed his test. To this day it is believed he had cheated the test somehow. But in all honesty, he studied hard and was able to pass.

This was fantastic news and one to be happy and thankful for. But not for the oldest son who took him to the doctor on this particular day. Having passed, JD was very happy. It was a happy day for him but for the oldest son it meant that he had to come clean about everything.

The happiness that JD felt would be drastically reduced. The doctor cleared JD for work but for driving he needed to be accompanied for another month or two just in case.

Leaving Sunnybrook hospital that day was very memorable and was a mixed bag of happiness, shock and bad news. Coming out of the long winding road at Sunnybrook was a slow one. JD's oldest son had to break the very bad news of what had happened, how it happened and why things happened. He knew JD would have a thousand questions. By now JD's mind was clear and he was fully aware of things and other than a small block here and there all seemed to be in good order in JD's head.

This was a time for celebration in many ways. The business was important but JD having been cleared was worth more than anything. Knowing how much JD loved ice cream they headed to Baskin Robbins. JD loved ice cream, so this was a great way to break the bad news. Bayview Avenue and York Mills Road was the closest Baskin Robbins location.

It was a wonderful sunny day that particular day and while the Baskin Robbins didn't have a complete patio area they did have chairs outside and the two men sat down with ice cream cones in hand. JD was celebrating being cleared by the doctor but his son was not celebrating. How do you break such bad news to anyone and how do you explain the lies?

There was no easy way to put this…

"I have some bad news, please let me finish as quickly as I can and you can ask as many questions you need to afterwards."

Explaining the story of the Titanic is easy, hits an iceberg and it sinks. Explaining the sinking of this company was by no means an easy story. This ship had several holes punched into it and the crew had their hands tied and the lifeboats were removed by the YB. The delicious ice cream taste filled JD's mouth but his mind was filled with the terrible news of what had happened and how the truth was kept from him. He understood that at the time he could not have borne the truth and the family was following doctor's orders. This was all clear but trying to comprehend all this was not easy. He was just cleared, to have all this thrown at him was a staggering amount to take in. That car ride to the office was memorable as the questions coming from JD were questions that were asked over and over by all the employees, the supervisors and managers. There was no clear answer and no matter how hard JD tried he had little understanding of how this could have happened.

Every question was answered with, yes, we said that. Did you bring this up? Yes, we did. Why didn't they look at this report or that sample? All the questions running through his head had been asked and for some there were no answers and all this was mind blowing to JD. Yes, he was cleared for business but he was not quite ready for the business at hand. Like the people that were surrounding him who were perfectly healthy were in a tailspin, JD was even more so.

When it came to the financials, the company was in deep trouble. It needed a cash injection to keep it afloat. Consulting with the Accountant it was clear that without the injection this company would not make it. JD's immediate reaction was to save the ship and not go down with it. This was a knee-jerk reaction but having just been cleared and being the majority shareholder he had the last say. JD was desperate to save his life's work and the blood, sweat and tears that every member of his family poured into this little business that could.

The little business that could was now a giant monster, who had its knees bashed in by the YB for no known reason. The question was why? If they didn't want to continue, let's go our separate ways. There was no reason to string this supplier alone and beat it to a pulp. If the numbers, meaning the returns and the complaints were so bad, which they weren't, but if they were, then go our separate ways. Why the jumping through of fiery hoops and the barrage of people beating up the individuals and the company to make such a point. Looking back, it was a matter of pride for the YB North American office to blame the supplier at all costs. If they didn't, their heads would roll and the supplier would not be blamed. Instead the blame was placed on the supplier…

"But why?"

The multi-million-dollar question of the day was "why". That day when the factory employees left, JD and his sons went down to see the production floor. One had to fully comprehend the extent of the new implementations and the new rules that have been placed on all production and the people by the YB. When you have passed every test and every quality check, in this case 25 years and never had a product recall and never had a stoppage in production for any reason in the 25-year history with the YB what went wrong? To this day the question remains and there were no answers that make sense.

"This was a witch hunt that was orchestrated by the YB Huston office who in search of cheaper prices cut and cut to achieve profit margins."

"A desperate attempt at achieving cost cutting so the office would get their bonuses at the cost of fucking over and pillaging a supplier."

Hanna, the VP at the Houston office was and is a ruthless person who drank the Kool-Aid along with the other YB workers. They would stop at nothing to achieve a goal set out by the MS. The MS is a multibillion dollar beast with hunger to destroy anything it sees fit to destroy and gobble up. Instead of sanely looking at a particular case it is clear that they may as well be cold blooded killers, following a leader with no values.
To the public, the cost or lack thereof, of cheaper prices are not relayed. They do not know which company was taken advantage of. The public has little understanding of the cheap prices that are being presented. It's all the wonderful YB that is bringing the sales and the new low prices.
This is not strictly the YB, but others will simply say the price is too high and we won't buy from you. That is the main question here. Why was it useful for the YB to pillage this supplier? If the price or the quality of the merchandise is not up to standard, don't buy it. Simply tell the supplier that "we are no longer doing business with you" instead of taking the supplier to hell and back. All other companies in the normal world would do the same. That's business and business is not a game to play with and bully your suppliers into submission.
Maybe the YB thought that this company made too much money? Maybe the YB had a new regime at the Houston office that was incompetent and didn't know what they were doing? Maybe the technician was the mastermind behind this and set this supplier up to fail? The question remains…why?

At that moment JD tried to understand why his head hurt. He needed to inject cash in this company and save 250 people, save jobs, save his pride and save the company from going bankrupt.

Facing the possibility of closing was not an option. It was too late to pull the Distinctive Designs custom furniture line out because all of the income was needed to keep the company afloat. The bank saw the state that this business was in. They were asking for a solution and wanted to know what was happening. There were few answers except that the company was working with the YB for a solution. The YB didn't want a solution, it didn't want to close this company either, so they claimed. The goal from them was now clear. After all this, they came back wanting new lower prices, even though the company couldn't make ends meet as it was.

The company was not allowed to produce to the 600 piece per day capacity; each month it operated it lost another 2 million dollars. Not allowed to produce, limiting orders and despite all this, asking to go back to spec and lower the prices by 20%. No, the YB was now making itself and its intentions very clear. They were going to take this company to cleaners, dangling the carrot just enough that there may be a slight possibility that they could work this out. Hanna was the clear ringleader in this regard. Being a tough negotiator and a tough businessperson in any business is fine. We have all been there. When there is no budging, the final straw is added and the deal does not go through. The deal is either over or one side gives in.

In this particular case the company was not only taken to the cleaners but destroyed by being pulled into a web of lies and deceit by a ruthless YB. VP Hanna was cold and ruthless. That's fine, no need to butter up people in business, it is what it is.

The custom line in this same factory was doing great work, very few complaints and no bad online reviews. This quality problem that the YB was supposedly now finding was not there, no product recalls, no viral issues found online.

When JD tried to make sense of it after his newly passed medical exam, he still thought that an amicable solution could be reached between the YB and his beloved company. Against the advice of the Accountant, he put his personal money in the company to pay the employees, pay the rent and avoid the inevitable. At the time, he wholeheartedly believed it was the correct and upstanding thing to do.

This was a shock to his system and something he would never have thought was even possible. Yet here it was, the reality was the cash injection helped him and his sons hold on a little longer.
Unfortunately, the return of JD to the business did not help. The promises kept coming. The YB even offered a loan. But with the loan came stipulations. All the YB approved companies had to be paid first. All payments would have to be approved by the YB. All and they meant all invoices and bills would need to be okayed by the YB before payment, and they would need to be submitted to the MS. Essentially, they were running the 35-year-old business that JD and his family built. This was not going to happen.
The Houston office refused to cut the company loose. They knowingly took even further advantage of this company that was now a beached whale and looking into the sunset before it closed its eyes and took its last breath forever.
Promises of temporary price hikes came but never materialized. The push for back to spec took precedence over everything and when that was done the push for lower prices came even harder and harder.
The final straw came when the YB took a cut from one of the payments and paid a leather supplier in Italy instead of paying this ailing company. They had no right to do this, and they were stealing money from one company, to protect the other from a possible loss of payment. They knew full well that this company was going down and they took money from the company that it could use to pay immediate bills and employee wages.
At this point, after months and months of struggling and JD running out money. He decided the company could not operate anymore and decided to close the company.
The decision was a devastating one. His name, his family and good name of this well-respected company was to close its doors forever. When the YB was informed of this they were angry and upset. Asking how they are supposed to fill the void left in the supply chain? They also asked to complete whatever products the company could so they would not be left hanging.
That was the plan, since that was money that would go towards the bankrupt company's settlement with the other suppliers. Going bankrupt was not a choice, it was not done at the hands of the owners. This company operated efficiently with great workers, such as Donna, Jessi, Randy, Rubby, Gus, Johnny, Brian, Vikarm, Alex,

Leo to name a few. These people were all disposable to the great YB.

To the world, the YB is a God of sorts. A company that is seen by billions through rose colored glasses. To most, this company is environmentally responsible, caring deeply about the world and their employees. It is presented as a world leader in many aspects and to their credit yes, they have managed to do good in their industry as a leader.

But the dark truth of the way they conduct business and ignore the well-being and health of their suppliers and to a certain point many of their own mandates. Writing their own version of the ten commandments and then systematically choosing to ignore the things that may not be convenient to them. Where there is smoke there is fire. Where there are illegal logging questions and illegal logging paperwork there are products made with old growth trees rather than the YB mandated ones. These are all evidence to the fact that the YB is a serpent that crushes the people, companies and even forests that do not give up its raw materials as the YB wishes.

Reflections:

These were sad days. Watching the company you built sink, was dreadful. I felt sorry for every single person who worked for us. Trying to keep up a positive front and telling everyone that we are working on it was the truth. Not letting everyone know and not being able to tell them that the outlook is very negative at the moment was hard. Often people say. "Oh, it's great having your own business" It often is great; you get to do everything you need to do before you do what you want to do. You come second to the business, the employees, the payroll, the taxes and the orders coming in and going out. Somewhere in there you try and carve out some time for you and have a coffee in peace.

Alright it's not always like that; but ask a startup or a company that is going through some rough times and you will understand and maybe you, you understand from personal experience. Sure, having your own business has its perks. Gas, phone, insurance, and many other things can be written off and so can some business trips and so on. But… the responsibility that goes with employing 250 people is also on your shoulders.

When they clock out and go home for the weekend you need to make sure that those people have a job on the Monday and that all will be good for them when they return. The washrooms are clean, the lunchroom is in good shape and that yes, we have money to pay them on the next week's payroll.

This was the problem… At this point we ran out of money. The line of credit was used up, extended and used up. Begging for money and quick payment from the YB, who instead comes and kicks you in the ass once more instead of helping you. Instead of helping, they cry to you for disrupting their distribution and how they need to bring things in from Mexico or China and how it's costing them money. They turned it around and made their incompetence our fault. To this day I feel let down, I feel angry and disappointed in myself, in the YB and the organization that the YB stands for. It is hard to deal with liars, cheats and kiss ass employees that could stand by and watch hundreds lose their jobs and not stand up to tell the truth.

The people at the YB are ruthless assholes and jerks, who live like robots and care about no one else but the collective. They have been well trained and should have been an army rather than a company.

Chapter 21 The dirty truth

The YB-way is the Bible for the YB and its suppliers to live by. The one this section refers to is a 2016 Version as it seems to be right in the Introduction Guiding principles and a direct copy paste:

"At YB we recognize that our business has an impact on people and the planet, in particular people's working conditions, as well as the environment, both locally and globally. We also strongly believe that we can do good business while being a good business. This is a precondition to our future growth that will be achieved along with Suppliers that share our vision and ambition."

So, they claim to do good business while being good. It says so right there in the YB way. In their "People and Communities" webpage they have, "Putting people first", and "Building good relationships" on the same page. The wonderful all-encompassing company that clearly, very clearly is people first and at every turn is about human rights, caring and being green. The YB puts out an amazing amount of propaganda to look good to the public. Yet behind closed doors it's all about profits regardless who they trample over.
The following are but a few companies that have been left in the path of destruction by the YB. There are many articles of illegal logging and FSC certified wood and people being allegedly paid off or

accepting gifts. To the people believing that the all mighty YB is all good you need to wake up and smell the coffee, because it is as evil as it gets. Profits and larger profits rule, and this is the motto this company lives by. Its ruthless business practices are covered up by its so-called charity work. Yes, anyone can give away a few hundred million when they are raking in billions of dollars in profits by raping and pillaging the manufacturers.

DARTMOUTH, NOVA SCOTIA - The Royal Bank of Canada (RBC) will receive more than $530,000, the final proceeds that bankrupt Scanwood received from IKEA for its final batch of wood dressers.

IKEA is closing a wood furniture plant in Danville, Virginia, and moving the equivalent operations to plants in Europe, reported *Furniture Today*. The plant opened in 2008 and produced bookshelves and living room storage furniture for domestic IKEA stores; it will cease operations in December, causing 300 people to lose their jobs. The Swedish mega-retailer cited production costs, particularly for raw materials, as part of the reason for the move.

According to him, Estonian manufacturers like to complain about IKEA's cost and price structure, but the fact is that cooperation with IKEA would have required huge investments also from the suppliers. "IKEA is not planning to drive its subcontractors bankrupt once in every two years. It is paying by due date," he adds.

The company blamed the shutdown on a dispute with one of its suppliers. Mastercraft in August sued a vender, Michigan-based SABA North America, saying the glue it supplied didn't meet the IKEA's standards. The lawsuit is still pending.
IKEA, Mastercraft said in a court filing, rejected a shipment of furniture and canceled future orders when glue in the products tested positive for a banned chemical. IKEA is now one of Mastercraft's

largest creditors, with a claim of $2.95 million. The company expanded to great fanfare in 2012, when it secured the IKEA contract. It relocated from Wilsonville to Stayton, southeast of Salem, and quadrupled its payroll to 158 employees.

IKEA is investigating allegations it has used illegally harvested timber in its furniture.
In a *report* NGO Earthsight claimed timber company VGSM had supplied timber to the YB that had been cut illegally from forests in the Ukraine.
In response IKEA said it had asked Assurance Services International, the Forest Stewardship Council's (FSC) independent auditor, to investigate the findings.
https://www.cips.org/supply-management/news/2020/june/ikea-investigates-claims-of-illegal-timber-in-its-furniture/

SWC Management, who own Paz Stone, the company that supplies and installs stone benchtops and glass and stone splash backs for Bunnings and Ikea have gone into administration.

https://www.afr.com/property/residential/national-building-supplier-swc-collapses-20191217-p53krm

I feel very sorry for the 400 employees losing their jobs a week before Xmas and also pissed that I was due to have a benchtop installed the day they went into administration. That makes 4 weeks (from order) so far unable to use the kitchen to prep food....or do any normal kitchen stuff.

IKEA's 'customer care' claim to be looking for other stone companies, but it remains to be seen whether mine will ever be installed.....or I get gouged another 'installation fee'. It was ~$1500 for Paz Stone to measure, cut and install. All up >$7500 for the benchtop.....

It's especially irritating that Bunnings and IKEA probably paid them peanuts for supply, which possibly contributed to this.

(Jun 19, 2009)
Royal Mattress, a former manufacturer and retailer of mattresses in the Hamilton area for 42 years, is bankrupt.
Phil Kriszenfeld, 44, who took over the business from his dad Joe 16 years ago, said the decision was "devastating" for him, mostly because of what it means for the 18 employees who were still with him to the bitter end.
"They are the best people you could ever have," he said. "When times were tough the last few months, no one (complained), they all just dug in and worked harder.
"If anyone who has worked for Royal Mattress is applying for jobs out there, I have advice: hire them."
At its height a few years ago, Royal Mattress had nearly 70 employees who worked either in the manufacturing branch or among the six retail locations in Hamilton and Burlington.
However, it lost a major account with IKEA North America to a cheaper supplier overseas.
Then the company stopped all of its manufacturing of mattresses and futons about a year ago. However, Kriszenfeld said he didn't think that contributed to its demise.
He said it was a simple matter of spiraling costs and a drop in sales.
https://www.thespec.com/business/2009/06/19/plummeting-sales-bankrupt-royal-mattress.html
https://www.baltictimes.com/news/articles/27443/
https://www.oregonbusiness.com/article/item/12303-oregon-furniture-manufacturer-files-for-bankruptcy

As all this is the tip of the iceberg. Just a few examples of the many companies that have been taken for a ride. Some were in business for only a few years and some for much longer.
None of the companies were ravaged as much as this one. A long-term family business that was given the runaround, essentially whipped and beaten to a pulp by the YB Houston Trading Office. Hiding the fact that they themselves made changes to products to lead the way for product development, the YB speak for price reduction. The fact that the technicians, both senior and junior levels chose to ignore the evidence and see the facts before them and admit

the mistakes made. The Borg mentality was evident and the fact that they and all of the YB was in on the dirty little secret is disturbing. All this was evident to JD as he tried hard to understand what had happened to his lifetime of hard work. It was beyond depressing to see the company that he founded and built to be a shell of its former self.

No employees, no production and no more business. It was now a warehouse of equipment that would be sold for pennies on the dollar. This was not going to sink in quickly, this will be quicksand pulling you down until you can no longer breathe. This is a substantial loss. This is not losing a few dollars; this loss is in the millions. Many people do not have to deal with millions of dollars in sales or paying suppliers in the hundreds of thousands of dollars and most will never deal with this.

The term "the sky is falling" comes to mind when all the dominos tumble one after another. JD felt sick by what had happened. How did this once healthy thriving company find itself in this mess? With his health slowly getting back to near normal, it was time to meet and see people he never wanted to meet.

Lawyers, trustees and liquidators were not words he was used to hearing, let alone using in a sentence. People often say and hear the words bankruptcy. It means you can't pay the bank and they take your things to liquidate and pay the suppliers as much as they can. It's a simple process in many ways. However, there is no one you can trust.

"You are down and out and yet there are vultures at the door, smiling and picking at the flesh on your bones."

All of these people are scum. They are there to take advantage of the injured and take all they can when they have nearly bled to death. It is a process that is painful, usually there are limited options and even fewer good solutions. You no longer own the company; you cannot make decisions anymore and the ones you can make are all painful. It is very hard to think at times like this. Everything is a blur and JD was certainly not thinking clearly. No one can think clearly when your life is laid out before you in shambles and no matter what you think may be a good idea it most likely isn't. Even finding a good lawyer was hard. Are there any "good" lawyers or are they all money sucking leeches?

A retainer of how much? JD nearly had a heart attack and then anger built up. More and more anger to the point that it made his head explode. The terms angry, mad, furious simply did not cut it. There was a rage that was building against the YB. A company that came with an agenda to bring this company down to its knees and then instead of chopping the head right off, they stabbed, poked and ever so slowly sucked it dry like a hungry vampire.

For a company the size of the YB there is corporate and social responsibilities that they must adhere to. God knows they preach it enough in their propaganda laden articles. They give you the warm fuzzy "we love you, we are here for you". That is why the world must know that it is mostly bullshit. Give away a few million here and there, rake in billions while you suck your suppliers dry. It's not only the YB, but it's the way they conducted themselves in this particular case that makes everyone need to know how they behave behind closed doors. They are not and do not practice what they preach. That is what needs to be understood.

The YB is a big corporation. It was supposed to be a business with ethics and responsibility to the suppliers and to the workers because they are YB workers. The YB pays their salaries and unfortunately in this case, the YB failed and the people that were involved in this massacre should be ashamed of themselves.

Was there error on part of this supplier? Possibly, as the relationship deteriorated, both sides should have assessed the situation. Unfortunately, being caught in the middle of the tornado made it very hard to see the sunny beaches and the wonderful coastline. After the 20 YB employees visited this company it was forced into a situation where it was beaten to death. There was no way out and JD often wonders what would have happened if the meeting would have been cancelled due to his accident.

As the examples above show, it always comes down to price and supply and shifting business. That is completely normal but when you build up a company to a certain size and a certain volume there is a certain amount of codependency. A supplier meets all of your standards and helps you make money as well. This supplier had many innovative solutions and manufacturing methods that were shared with the YB. After a 25-year relationship there should have been a plan to cycle down and pull out slowly if the relationship had soured.

There were numerous questions that will never be answered in this story unless someone can speak up and explain the internal reason behind this story and the events that led this company to destruction. There was so much anger in JD that it made it hard to think. The decisions that were to be made were not business related, not production related or making a new line of products. These were hard legal and financial questions that had to be dealt with and this was very unfamiliar territory. This was terrifying… Bring in people that will submit a bill and not a small bill for their services while your company spirals down the toilet.

It was a difficult time and not knowing who to trust or whose advice the company should take was the hardest thing to sift through. A barrage of emails and questions and to complicate matters the idea of suing the YB came up.

The bankruptcy was what it was. A dismantling of the assets of this company. From the frame shop at 30 Fasken Drive to all the sewing machines and office equipment to the forklifts and down to the last pair of scissors and spools of thread, everything was all auctioned off and collected.

This was the saddest time. The trustee had the key to your factory. They opened and closed and checked up on you to make sure you are not stealing from the company that you once owned. They are doing their job but they treat you as a criminal, suspicious at all times. You feel as if you did something wrong, you are guilty and yet there was no trial.

Reflections:

While all this was going on, we had several calls from other people all over the world

We are in the same boat; can we sue them together?

That was not possible but hearing other people and knowing that in the States and in Thailand the same kind of behavior was happening made you wonder.
Why, oh, why can't we all use our clause in our contracts? Why all the promises and the carrot and stick games only to end up with the same result.

Chapter 22. The lawsuit

Article in The Star, Toronto, by Ashante Infantry

A defunct Canadian company which purported to be "the largest manufacturer of IKEA upholstered furniture in North America" has launched a $25 million lawsuit against the Swedish-born retail giant for breach of contract.
Vaughan's Zsemba Apron and Upholstery Ltd. (ZAU) was one of the many independent suppliers The Netherlands-based-IKEA Supply AG relied on globally to produce its retail divisions' popular ready-to-assemble furnishings, from reference samples and drawings and sometimes through their own innovation.
But that once mutually rewarding relationship, which accounted for 75 per cent of family-run ZAU's business, ended badly.
The Vaughan company filed for bankruptcy in May, two months after terminating its commitment to the furniture behemoth as a result of "wrongful acts and conduct" which the lawsuit asserts cost ZAU $5.5 million in lost profits from 2010-2013.
In allegations that have not been proven in court, ZAU said the companies enjoyed a strong relationship until 2010 when IKEA "unilaterally and substantially reduced the prices that it paid for products purchased from its manufacturing suppliers, including

ZAU" and should have known that this would "cause them to operate at a loss."

The statement of claim seeks to negate the original purchase agreements, citing a "power imbalance and the dependent relationship between IKEA and ZAU which was fostered and encouraged by IKEA when it required ZAU to dedicate the majority of its production efforts and resources to IKEA…

"In essence, the bargaining process was a "take it or leave it" process with ZAU now completely dependent upon IKEA and forced to sign whatever contract IKEA would require….

"By acquiring finished goods at unreasonably low prices, and by refusing to pay reasonable prices to reflect the actual costs with a built in reasonable profit, IKEA profited from those transactions to the detriment of ZAU."

Houston-based Maria Carolina Perez, a spokeswoman for the IKEA Trading Services, Inc., which is also named in the lawsuit, said in an email that the privately held, multibillion-dollar brand was not aware of the ZAU claim and "we do not comment on potential litigation."

IKEA Supply AG is a wholesale company, purchasing goods from various suppliers on a global basis, and supplying them to IKEA retail companies throughout the world. IKEA Trading Services, Inc. is a service company performing trade solicitation services in North America under a contract with IKEA Supply AG.

Perez added: "IKEA does not comment on specific and individual information regarding supplier relationships, however, I can tell you that Zsemba ended their business relationship with IKEA. In March 2014 they communicated to IKEA that they were not going to continue production. Throughout the business relationship IKEA fulfilled its contractual obligations….

"IKEA can confirm that we had ongoing discussions about several aspects of Zsemba's performance, compared to our global requirements. IKEA will act as necessary to ensure that our products are produced according to the agreed quality, sustainability and working conditions. If the product does not meet these agreements, IKEA reserves its contractual right to stop deliveries to its stores, having the best interest of our customers in mind."

Zsemba principles — father George, sons Gabor and Zsolt — told The Star a once collaborative relationship with the largest flat-pack furniture retailer in the world, which peaked with $34 million in sales in 2004, deteriorated as IKEA pushed them to deliver goods cheaper while raising quality standards.

In an interview the men said it was tough to compete for the IKEA business against jurisdictions with lower minimum wages and government subsidized plants. In 2009, ZAU lost a $9 million spring mattress contract to Mexico. The $4 million wooden bed bases order wasn't renewed either the following year, going instead to North Carolina.

Now, the massive Highway 427 and Highway 7-area factory is a graveyard of sewing machines and contemporary seating. The lunch buzzer echoed through the plant as receivers audited the goods and equipment for auction, hoping to relieve a $2 million debt.

"I feel like crying," a visibly emotional George Zsemba said as he took a reporter through the complex and detailed the demise of his 35-year-old company.

The family, including wife Ann, who died of cancer in 2011, emigrated from Hungary in 1978. Employed at cutting and sewing jobs in small factories, George, with the help of Ann and the boys, began making industrial aprons in their basement. They kept moving house to accommodate the growing operation which expanded to include cushions for wicker furniture.

In 1988, they got their first IKEA contract to make leather cushions for the comfy Poang chair. Six years later, the operation finally left the basement for a 12,000 square foot Brampton facility. By the late '90s, they'd moved out near the airport, eventually commanding four buildings on Fasken Dr. to accommodate the IKEA work which included slipcovers and mattresses.

ZAU settled into its final location seven years ago to meet IKEA's safety and technological requirements, undertaking a 30 to 40 per cent increase in overhead costs, the family told the Star.

Longtime IKEA shoppers would recognize many of the loveseats and sofas that sat arm-to-arm inside the sample showroom, especially one low slung black leather classic.

"That's the Klippan; it's the one you see in clubs; and it's the couch that Penny sleeps on in Big Bang Theory ," said Gabor.

Although the company, which shipped directly to 14 different IKEA stores, was bestowed with a quality award by IKEA in 2012, the Zsembas told The Star the relationship worsened in early 2013 when they were asked to reduce costs by 15 per cent.

According to the statement of claim, previously approved raw material and products were rejected; IKEA implemented a zero-tolerance policy allowing them to "reject any product no matter how minor its defect in quality;" and after IKEA said it would not accept merchandise otherwise, ZAU was forced to close the factory for two months last summer to address changes "IKEA unreasonably demanded."

Additionally, the lawsuit alleges, IKEA executives "took steps to delay the approval" of a loan ZAU sought to defray some of the increased expenses. And the multibillion dollar furniture brand, sold in 52 countries, announced plans to reduce its commitment to ZAU purchases from $25 to $17 million.

George, 68, told The Star he used more than $1million of his retirement fund to keep ZAU afloat, but the company lost $6 million over 12 months ending this February.

The lawsuit says "the relationship with IKEA became untenable. ZAU's losses continued to mount and by March 2014, ZAU had no choice but to end its relationship with IKEA or face bankruptcy."

The company wound up in receivership anyway when RBC called its $1.8 million loan last month, the family says, putting the last of the manufacturer's 250 employees out of work.

The demise of one of Canada's few remaining furniture manufacturers affected sub-suppliers, as well as, retailers like The Chesterfield Shop.

"It was kind of a shock," said owner Steve Freedman who'd bought from ZAU for more than a decade. "I had quite a number of orders that I'm trying to make good on to customers, so it's been a bit of a scramble.

"There's really not a huge selection of choice of people that will make a good quality product and particularly customizable that you can change colours and sizes and configuration. Overall, they were nice people to do business with and I'm sad to see them go. It's a loss for the Canadian furniture industry."

Gabor is going into consulting and Zsolt is launching a small startup making beds. But George is turning his attention to gardening, soccer and foundation in his wife's name.

"That was my life and that time is over," he said.

Correction- July 2, 2014: This article was edited from a previous version that mistakenly said Ikea is now Swiss-based.

The Toronto Star article and what has been written in the previous chapter is the gist of this family's hard work. It puts things together well in a nutshell but of course it misses the rage and anger felt at the time of printing.
Many words could not be put into print for legal reasons and this was simply an overview of how things went down. The real emotion, the true opinion and the words that the family wished to say would never make the papers. The reason for the lawsuit was simple...

"What they did was wrong."

The tears glitter on JD's cheek, they roll down into his unshaven beard and he makes no attempt to wipe them away. His blue eyes stare at the street light and there is a blank look on his face. This cuts very deep, understanding at that point that things will never be the same was agonizing. Not knowing what to do next was aggravating and in his head the anger built even now. There is no way to put out the small spark that erupts into a blazing fire that cannot be put out when JD thinks of the past.
No, you cannot change the past, make amends, forgive and move on is possible but JD cannot get himself to do that.
The hurt of *what they did was wrong* rings in his head and he cannot let go. There is simply no way for him to get past the torment he and his kids had been put through. JD is angry, because not only did the YB wreck his life's work but also the future of his kids. This was a family business. It was supposed to be one of those businesses that displays "In business for over 50 years" Not the current "business goes out of business after 35 years of hard work." This was supposed to be a long-term business. His kids would retire from the business and hopefully it would live on and on. The business had its products in millions of homes. The diverse range of products made that possible and now those products would outlive the business.
This was the reason for the lawsuit. JD felt that there had to be payback. The YB had to pay for what it did and how it conducted itself. How the YB didn't live up to its own rules. How it neglected the codes they preach. Be good to people, treat the planet with respect and do good with your charitable contributions all over the world, but fuck one of your oldest suppliers and hope it goes away?

No, no, no. The world needed to know that the all mighty YB is as dirty and cheap as they come. Twisting the arms of the suppliers at will because you are so much bigger and stronger than they are? Is that good business practice? Corporate governance at it best...
After JD and the family picked the lawyers to sue the YB it was evident that JD had the last say and while the kids were unsure, JD wanted revenge. This was his life and his company that they have wrecked. The good family name now lays tarnished and bloody on the ground. This is what hurt JD's pride the most and sometimes one's pride can get in the way of good judgement.
Suing someone sounds easy and to make the declaration of suing someone is easy. But the amount of work behind the lawsuit was something that was simply unimaginable.
The trustee had the documents, they were no longer JD's. Permission needed to be given by the trustee to sign out the documents needed. The 25 or so boxes of visit reports, furniture specs and the computers were needed to begin with. All this had to be signed out.
As the lawsuit was in progress, the kids went on and tried to create something, anything that was in their line of work. It was hard to switch and create something new. It was also hard to try and approach old customers that were hurt by this.
Surprisingly the family had a lot of support and not surprisingly there were some very, very angry people. However, most were understanding for one simple reason....

"They all went through it with the family."

The suppliers that were also brought under the Zero defects policy saw and understood that this was not the family's doing. People such as Berny Holland from National Wood Products, Johnny Povigliano from Frametech, Joe from Modern Frames, Rob from VIP and even our most upset supplier Richard from Verick Adhesives.
Richard was one upset supplier who later apologized. He too was going through a rough time with his business. While he insulted JD's wife in anger because he was not getting paid there was nothing personal behind it. It was simply an example of anger brought out in times of trouble for both him and JD.
The lawsuit was about anger, pain and the hurt that was felt across the board. This was about the loss of future. It was about what could have been, while no one can predict the future, the family's

livelihood was taken away. While the kids had other small jobs here and there, they lived and breathed this business as much as JD and his wife did. They were the ones hurt the most in a sense because they were far from retirement and still had decades ahead of them. Each member of the family broke down in tears. They and their families were directly impacted by this closure. The big YB didn't give a shit about the people that had made their products for 25 years, brought them profits, cost savings and innovative ideas. Their true colors showed in the way they treated not only JD and the family but the 250 workers, the suppliers and their families.
All in all, this one closure had the trickledown effect on thousands. This is where the YB failed to get a grip on their ruthless decisions and acts of terror towards this one tiny furniture maker. Tiny because in the grand scheme of things it's a spoon full of water out the vast ocean the YB swims in all around the world.
While the Star states a lawsuit, it wasn't a lawsuit that ended up in court. While there is a gag order on this, the lawsuit would have to have taken place in Switzerland under Swiss laws and a whole lot of expense incurred so the process went like this:

"The president of the YB, David Svenson plea bargained that the YB be pulled out of the lawsuit and therefore they agreed to mediation in Toronto with a Swiss mediator. Regardless the whole thing was referred to as a lawsuit and prepared by a lawyer in Toronto, Harvin Pitch who is a partner at Teplitsky, Colson LLP. Harvin is a fun fellow who reminded the family of Colombo in the TV series of the same name from the 70's."

The lawsuit required a tremendous amount of information. It was unbelievable to see the amount of correspondence back and forth. This task of working with the lawyers was up to the oldest son, while the youngest son and JD were available at all times. The information flowed from the lawyers to the oldest son for research on topics for quality and inspections. Financial and sales information flowed through JD and the youngest son.
Digging up reports from years ago. Following emails and tracing back documents that were years old. Reading and understanding each thread of topics that were now evidence. Simple replies of "yes or no" were not tremendously important.

The lawyers didn't know anything. This business was new to them. Each week, days were spent in the lawyer's office downtown to teach the lawyers that were getting paid by the hour how to understand the difference between hard wood such maple and soft wood such as pine. All this information was understood by the family but new to the lawyers.

Wood tracing was a huge part of the YB mandate. Each lot of wood had to be traceable. There are plenty of accusations online of the YB paying off people and getting false documentation that the wood was certified. This is where the technicians had their claim of not knowing what kind of wood was used and why the Spruce was approved blew up in their face. The quality controller had all the documents submitted to the appropriate person at the Houston office who took care of this very important step. All chemical testing for the boards and wood tracing was there. For the YB to say that certain wood was not approved was an all-out lie.

Every bundle of particle board or OSB was traced and traceable along with the pine. Therefore, they knew and if they didn't approve it, they wouldn't have the documents. But they did and it was all uploaded into the system. The way the system worked was simple. It was a shopping list of documents signed off by the YB person in charge and scanned. From there the documents were uploaded so the YB can log in and check from the MS. This was understood and cleared by everyone at the YB. Without those documents things could not move forward.

But you are thinking… the documents could be fake and the wood could be bought here and there and therefore it could be the manufacturers fault. The thought behind it is valid. The execution is not because they knew how much board feet of wood was bought and that had to match the amount of goods shipped. Same thing applied to the foam and sheet stock such as plywood, OSB and particle board. There was a second check in place that could be traced very accurately and if the documentation and the numbers didn't add up there could be cheating, but there was never any cheating.

Explaining technical things such as testing and processes in production to a lawyer and their interns was a tedious process that the family did each week. Understanding an ordering and shipping system was not simple when the lawyers are thrown in the deep end and are expected to grasp how a sofa frame is made and how its cut, sewn and glued etcetera. This all needed to be proven and each argument the family had, had to be dissected from the other point of view.

Things didn't make sense at times; emails had to be explained and understood and interpreted in a dumbed down language that could be then translated into legal jargon by the lawyers. This was painstaking and a timely process that was frustrating and very aggravating. All the while hundreds of thousands of dollars were being sucked up by the lawyers in preparation.

Harvin and his team had to be brought up to speed on every aspect of the business and this was very hard. This was a small team and for sure the YB had a bigger and possibly more educated team. They had lawyers that were familiar with the way they operate and had possibly participated in previous cases.

Reflections:

I hate lawyers… Please if you happen to be a lawyer it's nothing personal. I am sure that becoming a lawyer was years of hard work but explaining to a lawyer and teaching them the ins and outs of your business is a headache.

Poring through years of emails and trying to see what is relevant and what is not is a difficult task. Explaining every email and the details that follow is not their job, it's your job and in this case, it was my job. This process was frustrating enough to pull out what little hair I had. This was not nor is not against anyone in particular. Harvin was and is a hell of a character and I loved working with him but making people understand something that is second nature to you is very frustrating.

Often, we yelled and screamed at each other and looking back it was a hell of a learning experience. Going through the details of the case was something I never want to go through again. Many times, we had 6 people in a room, and everyone understood things 6 different ways.

Following up with emails and sometimes riding on a single word in one email and trying to figure out how it can be used against us or in our favor was a difficult process.

Both the lawyer and the client learn a lot about each other and the business they are in. Having faith in your team and trusting their point of view is crucial. It's the law and not what was said but how that email pertains to the case and the argument.

This process was extremely frustrating and the time it took makes me understand why so many cases take such a long time to come to trial.

Chapter 23. The cookie crumbles

Weeks and weeks of preparation went into the lawsuit. Detailed emails unearthed from the many hard drives that contained production, technical and personal emails between quality, production, finance, ordering, shipping and testing and the technicians. One thing that made things very complicated was the switching out of technicians. Now this may or may not have been done on purpose but traces of emails were lost and often not concluded when Garth, Atul, Sebastian and Kevin were often rotated. There were claims of not knowing or they switched this and that because they believed things were wrong or brought new specs for old products and so on.
Looking back, it was a great way of not passing on information. On the other hand, it was also 100% proof that several technicians from the YB Houston office saw, felt, touched, inspected and sat on the many different production models made for the YB by the family. This was further proof that if there was a product that was out of spec, how could it be further and further passed by the rotating technicians if it was not meeting the requirements of the YB.
Why was there no red flag waved until the very end? Until the European technician came to "help" with cost cutting. Only then this was made an issue. Every angle had to be explored by the lawyers and each point scrutinized to the point where it was painful to listen.

Oftentimes a break was needed because arguing back and forth was not like seen on television. Being in the same room with your team that is scrutinizing you for your own good was hard. Having to defend your comments and actions before your team was practicing for the real deal.

This lawsuit would not be in a courtroom setting. It would not be seen by jurors, but the family sure wished it would be. This would be before a single mediator and he needed to be convinced one way or another. The arguments were validated and the stress levels were high in preparation. Because the information of the evidence (Discovery) was exchanged by the teams, the YB knew the family's argument and the family knew the YB counters. These were all very long and very time consuming processes. There were many, many sleepless nights. Trying hard to recall information from years and years ago seemed to break your mind because it is not information you tend to store long term.

The process would be taking place much like a court proceeding but in an office setting, with two desks and two sides and an Arbitrator (NOT Mediator) sitting at the front as a judge would. The proceedings would be similar as testimonies would be held over a 5-day period and the results; well they would take months.

Many days and nights went by with the family often getting together to discuss one point or another and while many arguments and shouting matches took place it was not personal, it was frustration. Why can't we say this? Could this topic be brought up as it is important and relevant?

Much information was important but useless to the case. It works well in a story but not as a presentation of facts. As much as the lawyers were learning about making furniture the family was learning about law. Many things are important, not all are truly important when the points are made. The story behind an email is hearsay, the email is the fact and this is where the case lay.

Facts and the training of your team on each point was going to be the make it or break it in this case. While things were broken down to quality, technical, financial and other sub segments they needed to make sense as a whole. The order of events leading up to the upcoming arbitration seemed so far away but with the amount of information that needed to be exchanged it didn't seem far enough. In between the arbitration, a meeting was arranged by the lawyers and the family. It was supposed to be for an out of court settlement.

If the two sides agreed the arbitration would not be called for. The YB reluctantly agreed to this and a meeting was set up in a conference room. There were statements to be read by the family, and the YB members were supposed to listen and hopefully come to some sort of an out of court agreement so both sides could save some time and money and move on.

Looking back this was a waste of time. The YB people in their Borg like state were emotionless as each family member read out a statement for which the YB could or could not comment. By the time the statements were read it was clear that the group was as cold blooded as sharks. Not a single remark, smile or even an ounce of compassion. No questions, concerns or an ounce of humanity. Like soldiers, they sat emotionless and cold, not taking one word to heart from the family they have destroyed.

Quite the sight to see really, they must have been to many meetings such as this in their lifetime. For a company that shows so much love and concern for their customers they sure showed very little care and lots of disregard for the suppliers that make the YB the big company it is.

By the end of the short presentation and short plea of sorts to settle this case outside of the arbitrator the slap in the face came. An offer of $120,000 dollars was put on the table by the YB. This goes to show that the people in the room had little understanding of what has happened here.

These men and yes, they were all men. All four of them were disconnected from the events that took place. There was not a single person on their side that had known or ever been in contact with this business they destroyed. That detail was likely done on purpose, anyone that knew the family could possibly have an ounce of kindness in them and well that of course was forbidden in the YB. No instead they flew in from their Scandinavian home all the way across the ocean to attend this meeting that to them was an obvious waste of time. This $120,000 was not hush money or go away and stop bothering us money. This was an instigation to attack more because we think you are worthless and we'll see you in court type of money.

For all intents and purposes $120,000 is a lot of money and by no means is it nothing. But it is very small for a company and the family that lost their livelihood and a family business built over the span of 35 years. There was no negotiation, their legal representative didn't come back and say we can negotiate or talk about this. That's it, that's all, move on and off they went.

This was a long shot but it was something that was attempted. As always, the family was very low key and very down to earth and respectful but once again simply swept under the rug by the YB.

Since this failed it was back to work on the arbitration case. By now both sides of the team learned to communicate. The minutiae of it all was understood and facts were facts despite how one person would think it's important it may not be. With all the information now exchanged and understood to the best of everyone's ability the case was put together and all points of attack and discussion had to be reviewed.

The months of preparation, hundreds of thousands spent on lawyers, separate finance auditors had to be brought in at a separate cost. With the arbitration date closing in, tensions rose. No one in the family had ever appeared in court, so while this wasn't court it was nearly the same process and the arbitrator was the judge.

Being taken through a dry run of the proceedings made it easier but this was nerve racking, because unlike the lawyers that do this every day the family didn't. Each person had their roles to play in this. Each person would and could defend their points on their topics.

When JD remembers the days of arbitration he winces at the thought of going through it again even if it is only in his head. 220 Bay Street was the location of the Arbitration. Standing at the foot of two tall, dark intimidating towers made anyone seem small and insignificant. JD looks at himself in the reflection of the glass and imagines himself the day he came here for the very first time.

It was a busy time because the Blue Jays, Toronto's baseball team, was making a run for the playoffs. The city was buzzing with excitement and people would randomly stop at convenience stores to catch the game. They would hug perfect strangers who were also cheering on the Toronto team. It was a good time to be downtown unless the game was held in Toronto since at that time the traffic would be a mess. It was a time that is clear in JD's head.

This was not a long time after the accident and a 99% recovery was made, not going to say 100% because there are still days when physical pain rears its ugly head. On cold days JD feels pain in his right hand that was slightly mangled by the tumbling bicycle. Or the pain he feels in his shoulders on occasion. The memories of standing before the large glass building is clear. Dressed in dress pants, dress shirt with a sports jacket and nice shoes was something JD no longer enjoyed, but that day and in those days he was ready.

The reflection of himself today disappoints even JD. His life is no longer the man he once saw at the entrance to the glass building on Bay Street.

That day the family was ready. Meeting the YB lawyers and Garth the technician would not be pleasant. It would not have taken much for the family to jump the bastard and beat the daylights out of him. Despite the event taking place many years ago JD would surely attack the asshole if he were to see him. The low life two faced asshole who can be blamed for single handedly destroying a business still deserves an ass kicking.

Remembering the meeting this day makes JD cry. The layout of the arbitration room is clear in his head. Very nicely appointed office space with a small kitchen and a center island that was surrounded by break out rooms on the side. At the end of the large space was the room the arbitration would take place.

This room was set up as a courtroom would be. The lawyers brought the boxes and boxes of documents that would be needed over the 5 days of testimony and question periods. JD remembers being nervous and unsettled. Actually, everyone was unsettled. Everyone who otherwise would have nerves of steel for all other meetings but not this one. Everyone was dressed nicely and waiting quietly for the Arbitrator who was a little late. The YB team was also late so when the Arbitrator came in it broke the ice a little and after a round of handshaking and introductions the family and the Arbitrator took their places.

The YB team was late, not by a minute or two but several. Once again showing the same disrespect they showed all along. The cocky attitude of the lawyer as he showed up with his tie hanging around his neck and not yet tied, he asked for a minute to gather himself. After the formal introductions and presentation of the case the arbitration began.

This was not the same as a math test in high school, this was closer to an interrogation. The one lawyer could and would grill each person on the particular topic but the Arbitrator was also very much involved in the questioning. Much more so than a judge would be. This Arbitrator would need to know the details of each topic.

Every detail would need to be spoon fed to the Arbitrator to make sure he understood the topics and the discussions. Something like the sizes of wood knots or the construction of a furniture frame needed to be explained by drawings and photographs.

There were several interesting topics, one of them was the discrepancy in the wood used. The products the family made were all on display often at the YB stores. Interestingly enough they were still on display at the time of the arbitration. The units the YB deemed unsuitable for sale and had to be reworked were on display. If there were issues all the samples should have been recalled.

The knots on the wood were present from other suppliers and little things like this were compared between the YB and the family's lawyers. On these topics so called experts were questioned. The first day was an overall presentation of things that led up to this and despite having breaks and lunch the day passed very quickly and it seemed like very little was covered.

Seeing the enemy and having to mingle with them and controlling one's temper was not easy. That group right there pillaged your company and tore it to pieces, how do you keep your cool? It took a lot of deep breathing and self-control for JD not to punch the assholes in the face. Knowing nothing good could have come out of it JD and the family kept their cool. This was a paperwork fight, a show of evidence had to do the work, the physical fight was not necessary but would have been very pleasurable at the moment. To wipe off the smirk off the YB's faces would have been lovely but it never happened.

Day two began with more technical things such as other people not meeting or not following the YB spec. These details and photos were taken from the floor models available in some stores from the USA and some from the local stores. Things like CNC cut frames could be identified by the circular toolpaths the CNC must take. In every 90-degree corner cut by the CNC there must be a rounded corner that would equal the size of the tool or a notch would need to be cut by the tool to create a 90-degree fit. A round tool bit couldn't cut a square corner.

Immediately the specs were thrown out because the YB required all suppliers to have the accuracy of a CNC cutter. Knots that were deemed unusable were also readily used by suppliers from Mexico and Europe. Weights of foam for example, two cubes of foam being the same size can weigh much less or much more by depending on the density of the foam used. Therefore, the denser the foam the more it weighs. This was highly technical and when the evidence was shown that the specs on said items were correct but the competition was cheating, creating a sticking point on the specs. The element of doubt was being raised and that was what was important. With each new piece of evidence being brought forward, the confusion was setting on all parties. The spec was not clear, none of the specs were clear. The YB was not able to explain why each supplier had different specs.

No expert could explain why or how these things happened when specs are done for the whole world by the MS and distributed accordingly. The only explanation is that nothing is actually done to the latest spec. In which case no one can or no one should be singled out for the products they make as each trading office is operating by its own specs and rules.

These discrepancies can only be explained by Garth, the MS and its various team members who are in charge of documentation. Like all specs they were not clear and seemingly not carved in stone.

Day two ended and while it seemed productive no one knew how the Arbitrator saw things. This was in his hands and how he viewed the presentation of facts. The family felt confident as the evidence was overwhelming, there was a double or even a triple standard among the YB group. Nothing added up no matter how one tried. Nothing could be put together; it was like a puzzle that the pieces didn't fit. Everything was random and misaligned, nothing was making sense or lining up in any one direction at this point.

Next day it was Hanna's turn, the little bitch didn't bother showing up. She had to hide and attend arbitration via video from Czechoslovakia. No respect and not an ounce of compassion from the woman. She was two faced and sneaky as a fox. How such people can sleep at night knowing they are fucking people over. They were living and breathing the MS.

These people were not thinkers, they were not even doers, they were pre-programmed, brainwashed robots that served their God the almighty Yellow and Blue. Nothing else mattered to these people. To speak up for the supplier was not allowed. So, when Hanna came on, she sat emotionless before the camera and lied through her teeth. She was in charge of placing the orders and talked about how the quality had to be brought up in order for the company to go back to 600 pieces a day. How the ZERO defects policy was indeed there to "help" the company and once they achieved ZERO defects they could get back on track.

Even car companies that are very successful cannot achieve absolute ZERO defects. This is how unreasonable the YB and the MS were. During her examination, it was clear that the Yellow and Blue Mother Ship made it a mandate to close this supplier at whatever means necessary. But the reasons behind it were a mystery.

Day three quickly came to a close. The atmosphere in the room was somber. No one was up or down, no one was winning except the Blue Jays as they roared into the city for their playoff games and stirred up the excitement downtown on their home turf this time. The streets of Toronto were nearly empty and the bars and restaurants full with people cheering on the home team.

When day 4 began it was all about accounting. Amazing how a company's worth and losses can be counted in various ways. How numbers can be twisted and manipulated in so many ways. A company making money can be sent into a loss and a company losing money can be manipulated into making money. This day had everyone's head spinning and between the differing ways of calculating from YB and company accountants there was no way of telling who would have won or lost that round. What was clear was that the YB was not in bankruptcy and the family business was. What was also clear was that the family was not a cold calculating monster out to trample anyone. No, the YB was that monster out to rip apart anyone and anything that stood in its path. No wonder the internet has several articles on the YB taking money, giving money and mankind deals and illegal logging. They don't want to lose, they want their way all the time and unfortunately for the people in the way, they get trampled or paid off.

At the start of day five no one knew what to expect. The Arbitrator had 7 days to conduct his business but he announced that this would be the last day and it would be a wrapping up of some key things and answering some of his questions. This was a relief in many ways but was also going to mean that this day needs to count. It was the bottom of the 9th and bases loaded. With the Blue Jays actually playing and being in the playoffs this was indeed the case. A home run was needed but there was no one on base and the family could only count the evidence they had.

The umpire in this case was the Arbitrator. Safe or out was his call, but that call would not come for months. Right now, every bit of energy was focused on the last day of this proceeding.

The months of digging and following email threads from several computers set up in the living room. The thousands of emails and various correspondence between numerous people along with the 25 Bankers boxes of documents that were read. The documents highlighted, photocopied, scanned and emailed were all for this day. The hundreds of photographs that were taken and poured over were no longer needed. The boxes of evidence that would be useless after this day were stacked up and ready to eventually gather dust and disposed of.

How can a family's entire life can come down to be the decision of one man and a 5 day argument? How is that fair? This was not a complicated murder trial but it was the case of one business killing another. In many ways it was a murder trial as the YB did suffocate this family company. In conclusion maybe the YB can stand trial for murder.

In the end Harvin and his team did their best. Could they have done better? Possibly, but there is no one particular item or topic that would stand out as such. The team left the room and the large office building feeling satisfied and upbeat. There was nothing left to do now but wait.

What was amazing was that after this day, the very intense searching and preparation was gone. It was still stressful and the time of waiting would be a test of nerves and a test of patience. As time passed it was time to move on, no one wanted to ever go through such a thing ever again in their life, that was for sure.

Once again JD had moved houses, selling the property he had was inevitable. His health was not bad but with sore hands and shoulders it was hard taking care of the property he purchased especially in the winter. He of all people needed to spend time and reflect on the past and the present.

The kids too moved on and had to earn money outside the family business for the first time. Things were changing and time crawled while waiting for the decision to be handed down.

Working for others at the moment had its advantages. It meant that the family didn't need to think of payroll taxes, opening and closing the company and dealing with employees. This was a time of patience and waiting.

"There were days of mass anxiety and worry, there were days of calm, patience and confidence."

The time to reflect was good. It was a test of willpower and longevity. Getting together for family gatherings was tough. No matter what the discussion always came to the business and there were and still are differing opinions as to how it was to be handled. Even though it was over and done with and nothing could be changed, the family was split on how the money was spent and why the arbitration had to go forward. These were things that will not be solved because they are all in the past.

Moving forward from such a disaster is not easy. JD was not himself and with the change of scenery once more and his health not 100% it made him focus on trying to get healthier. Eating healthy and being healthy is important. Regardless of what happened he wanted to be healthy and live his life. The YB may have ruined his business but they didn't take away his life and spirit to live. He had known that from the day he and his family set out on this journey to Canada in 1978.

From the moment he and his family escaped, he knew that if nothing else he would have his freedom. Not only did JD get his freedom; he lived, built and enjoyed the hard work he and his family poured into this business and the life they built in Canada. He was proud of the fact that he made it, very few people do.

One day the phone rang, when JD looked at the number, he knew who this was… He took a deep breath and answered the phone… In the arbitration only one thing was stipulated and that was that the results of the arbitration must not be disclosed.

The only thing JD recalled immediately was what the Toronto Star newspaper quoted him saying.

"Things will never be the same… That was my life and that time is over," he said.

Months later the news came, the YB Houston trading office was dismantled completely. Some employees like Hanna were relocated and some were fired. It seemed like the Mother Ship realized that it too had made mistakes. But their family business wasn't destroyed in the process.

JD may not be in the best of health; the kids know where to find him and quite often he says hello. He chose to live his life in a different way. Clutching his backpack, he gets on a bus each month and visits the kids. At each visit he gets cleaned up and before he leaves, he takes out a wad of cash and splits his earnings with his children.

"Life is no longer about making money, life is about survival."

Reflections:

When it came right down to it, as the weeks, months and years pass, no one cares. We are stuck with the memories of a once thriving business and the many employees that we have had the pleasure of working with. But when it came down to it, they were mostly just that. Like many throughout our history, they showed up for a paycheck and went home.
There is nothing wrong with that. It's what makes the world go around and drives the economy, that's business. Many employers may ask...

Why are my employees not as passionate about my business as I am?

The answer is simple, they are not you. Don't expect them to be you because they are who they are. If you are not happy with them keep searching for better employees.

I would like to mention to Donna Mercer and Sarah Thompson. While I am back tracking a little, these two amazing ladies took over for my mom while she was sick and after her passing, they took on all her roles in the company.
Both ladies are 100 percent trustworthy devoted people who stuck around not only until the end but went on to help me after the closing of the family business. These two ladies always went above and beyond to make things happen.

"A very special mention to Tony Toto of QTK Quality Tops and Kitchens, Tony, you know why."

To all the employees that worked with us over the 35 years in business we would like to thank you from the bottom of our hearts. All the hard work you put in alongside us to make things happen and grow this little business into a big business would never have been possible without your hard work and dedication. Many of you who worked closely with us, such as Jessie, Lakshmi, Alex and of course Donna and Sarah, you know what we went through.

You all know how things went down, sideways and finally fell to pieces and you all know who was at fault because you lived these trying times with us.

Many times, we couldn't say what was going on, oftentimes we didn't want to share what was going on and tried hard to protect you and make things right. It unfortunately didn't playout in our favor and the company had to close.

If someone or anyone is missed in the list, please forgive me as it was hard getting an employee list so many years later. Please pass on the message and feel free to get in touch with me if you care to. We hope everyone is doing well and always remember, you too could be one wrong turn away from being JD. Try not to get lost...

The Last Word

While this story is true and some parts have been added to stress the fact that this can happen to anyone and we are all one wrong turn away from disaster. I stress that the homeless factor is for perspective only. The feelings of JD are real and so are the things that happened to him while he contemplated the decisions he made.
A series of unfortunate events can land your ass in deep trouble and you never know when you too could be looking up from the curbside. It does not need to be business related, your issue could be personal such as a divorce, cheating or a death in the family. It could be related to a mental breakdown or mental illness. No one knows what the future holds, look at the COVID19 mess the world has landed in, many people could end up in similar situations as JD.
This book, this story is wrapped in reality with a touch of drama, but the story is very real. Looking back, this event in our lives was terrible. To revisit the past and try and get these facts straight was hard. It was very difficult to remember something that we as a family are trying hard to put behind us. There were tears shed in certain parts of this story. In many areas I wished to write more details but they are painful.
The suppliers that joined us and partnered with us on the journey of incredible stupid changes and requests that were handed down to us from the YB were too numerous to mention. While I have forgotten a few such as Flavio from Grip Clinch and Peter Wiesz from Leggett & Platt who spent weeks with us, getting us the correct equipment so we could move things along and know the truth as we do. They lived the mess with us.
There are no words of wisdom to keep anyone out of trouble. There are no rules or regulations on what to do and what not to do. We all have different ways of running a business and we all learn things as we go.
The only word of advice I can give is to leave your ego and pride out of any and all business decisions.
DO NOT THINK OF WHAT OTHERS WILL THINK OF YOU BECAUSE OF THE DECISIONS YOU MAKE. IN THE END, IT WILL ALL BE FORGOTTEN, AND YOU WILL HAVE TO LIVE WITH THE DECISIONS YOU MAKE OR REFUSE TO MAKE.

www.ingramcontent.com/pod-product-compliance
Lightning Source LLC
Chambersburg PA
CBHW052311220526
45472CB00001B/68